IMAGES
of America

TALLULAH FALLS

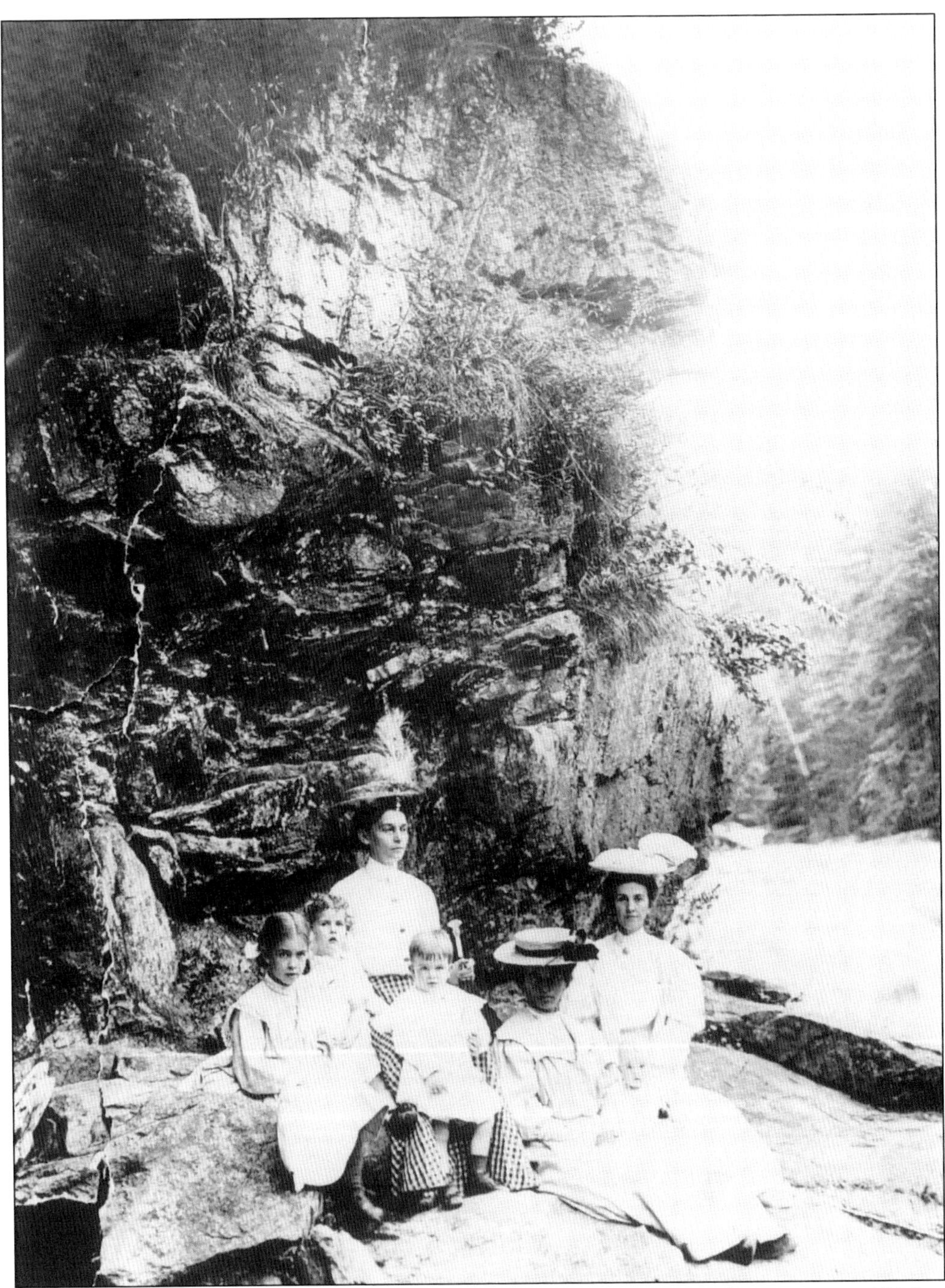

In front of a massive rock cliff the ladies of the Glover family enjoy the scenery in 1906 at Tallulah Gorge. One result of the Industrial Revolution was that the late Victorian period became an era of travel. Ladies' recreational attire at the time included long dresses, buttonhook shoes, and elaborate hats. (Courtesy of Georgia Department of Archives and History.)

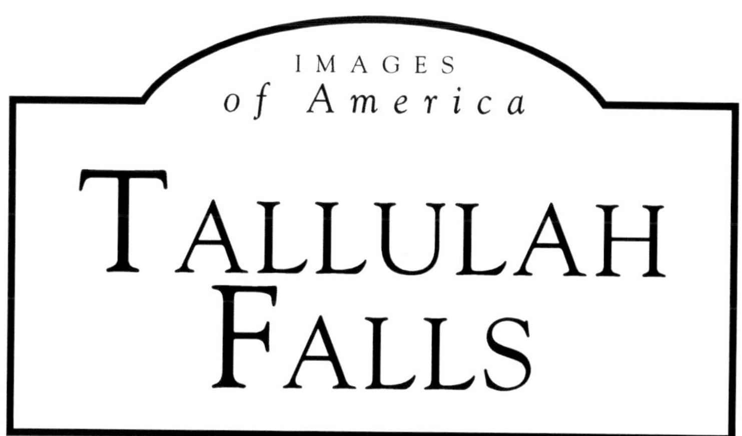

Margaret Calhoon and Lynn Speno

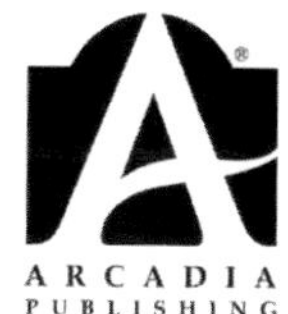

ISBN 978-0-7385-5449-5

Published by Arcadia Publishing
Charleston, South Carolina

Printed in the United States of America

Library of Congress Catalog Card Number: 98-87319

For all general information contact Arcadia Publishing at:
Telephone 843-853-2070
Fax 843-853-0044
E-mail sales@arcadiapublishing.com
For customer service and orders:
Toll-Free 1-888-313-2665

Visit us on the Internet at www.arcadiapublishing.com

Dedicated to our families,

George Calhoon, William Calhoon, Laura Jane Calhoon Lyttle,

and Dave and John Speno,

for their encouragement and patience.

Contents

ACKNOWLEDGMENTS

We wish to thank the following archives, institutions, and individuals who have made this work a reality. Georgia Power Land Department Photo Archives permitted the use of their excellent images from collections that were donated by Katherine Bravakis, Mrs. H.J. Calloway, B.F. Colmer Jr., Gail Geary, Charles Hardman, Bill Hix, J.D. Huddleston III, Barry Inman, Fred Pitts, Charles Rattarree, and Fred Stuart. A special thanks goes to Caroline Abbey, Robert Ramey, and James Wilson of the Georgia Power Land Department. Images from the varied and unusual Vanishing Georgia Collection as well as the Mines, Mining, and Geology Collection came from the Georgia Department of Archives and History. It is always a pleasure to work with Gail DeLoach, photo archivist there. We appreciate the assistance of Mary Ellen Brooks and Nelson Morgan at the Hargrett Rare Book and Manuscript Library of the University of Georgia for allowing the use of the Tallulah Falls Industrial School Collection images. Special thanks to Miriam Drake and Ruth Hale at the Georgia Institute of Technology Library and Information Center for their help. Ruth Hale, Head of Archives/Records at Georgia Tech, was very helpful in our request to reproduce images from the Magid Collection, an interesting source of attempted industrial development in Georgia. Foxfire graciously permitted us to use images from their publication *Memories of a Mountain Shortline* by Kaye Carver and Myra Queen. The images from the Tallulah Falls School are unmatched in telling the story of the mountain settlers and Tallulah Falls School. Thanks to Dr. Charles Green and Sharon Roller from the Tallulah Falls School for allowing us to use these images. Gae Stovall of the Georgia Department of Natural Resources deserves many accolades for her help on this project. She has an unequaled knowledge of the history of Tallulah Falls, which was invaluable.

Individual photographic collectors who contributed their images are: Jorene Lavender, who allowed the use of photographs taken by her great-grandfather, noted Tallulah Falls photographer Walter Hunnicutt; Edwards Studio; Luck Flanders Gambrell; Mrs. M.M. Fincher; Rope Roberts; Ronald Vandiver; and Gary Doster, avid postcard and Georgiana collector.

We are very grateful to Dr. Laura Jane Lyttle and Larry A. Whitfield for suggestions and corrections in manuscript preparation and for their exceptional command of the English language. An extra-special thanks goes to J.D. Huddleston III, Georgia Power retired, for his advice and expertise in the history of Georgia Power Company and historic engineering in general, as well as in encouraging our efforts.

INTRODUCTION

Tallulah Falls, located within Rabun and Habersham Counties, was virtually unknown to the world except to nearby residents until 1819. Situated on the eastern edge of the southern Appalachian Mountain chain in northeast Georgia, it did not even appear in gazetteers until the year 1843. The town of Tallulah Falls, always small and insignificant in regard to business and commercial activity, received fame only by the fact that it developed adjacent to a spectacular manifestation of nature.

A great gorge was etched out of the rugged land by the gradual boring path of the Tallulah River, producing magnificent falls. The earliest written account of Tallulah, published in 1819 in the *Georgia Journal*, stated that "The cataract of Niagara and its great whirlpool and banks, is the only superior natural curiosity to the Rapids of Tallulah, that I have ever seen."

Native Americans lived in the Tallulah Falls area for thousands of years. The present day Creeks and Cherokees evolved from these earlier cultures. The name "Tallulah" is believed to have originated in the now extinct language of these early inhabitants. Legends relate that the Cherokees shunned the gorge itself because they believed that a menacing race of small people lived in the cracks and crevices of the rocks of the gorge overlooking the falls. Considering them enemies, the Native Americans stayed away.

The earliest Europeans to see Tallulah Falls were probably traders from South Carolina who did not leave a record of their travels. A visitor to the falls in 1821 reported seeing initials carved on an elm tree beside the date "1718." In 1817 and 1819, after the Cherokee land cessions, Scots-Irish, German, French Huguenot, and English immigrants settled in north Georgia. These settlers received land lots of 202 1/2 acres in Georgia's land lottery to reside in this wilderness. Only a few tried, as the 1820 census showed only 3,600 people living in Rabun and Habersham Counties. Here they lived and raised their families in the coves and river bottoms surrounded by the mountains. Trails and a few rough-hewn roads along the ridges of the mountains opened up, but early settlers lived in relative isolation and were generally self-sufficient.

The Appalachian culture was interrupted only by a few early visitors to the area. In the 1830s and 1840s, some wealthy coastal planters and businessmen built summer residences in the mountains for their families to escape the heat and disease, mainly malaria and yellow fever, that were dangers of the low country. These seasonal settlers located about 12 miles away from the falls and visited the gorge frequently. Soon tourists were making their way to the area and by the 1840s, groups of visitors were common. Poor roads and rough accommodations did not deter those anxious for adventure.

Noted early visitors included John C. Calhoun, statesman from South Carolina. John Howard Payne, author of the song "Home Sweet Home," came in 1835 to see the natural wonder. William Gilmore Simms, famous antebellum southern author, traveled there in 1847. A geologist and one of the founders of the Sierra Club, Joseph LeConte, made numerous trips to study the unusual geology of the gorge. Often contingents from various towns in Georgia devised their own home-grown "grand tour," which included Tallulah Falls and other sites in north Georgia, traveling on horseback or wagons, caravan-style.

The gorge also provided a place of refuge. A number of "hermits" from time to time chose to live there in seclusion. At the close of the Civil War, General Robert Toombs, an officer and cabinet member of the Confederate States of America, took refuge in Tallulah Gorge to evade capture and arrest by Union soldiers.

With the arrival of the railroad in 1882, hotels and businesses sprang up. "Tallulah is destined to be the resort of the South," proclaimed the *Athens Banner-Watchman* on August 17, 1884. Indeed by the turn of the century almost 20 hotels and boarding houses welcomed visitors to Tallulah Falls. Visitors flocked to the mountain retreat, creating a grand Victorian summer resort. The natural features of the gorge and the falls provided inspiration and high adventure for those seeking its pleasures. Dramatic names were given to the natural features which were pointed out on the guided tours conducted daily.

By the second decade of the 20th century, tourism was declining in Tallulah Falls as the railway expanded, the automobile gained popularity, and the river was developed for hydroelectric power. With the extension of the railroad into North Carolina, many passengers continued on farther north, deeper into the mountains. New rail lines into South Florida took tourists farther south, and the widespread use of the automobile made possible excursions to more distant sites of national interest. With the increasing need for electric power in Atlanta and around the state, the Tallulah River was developed for hydropower by a predecessor of Georgia Power Company. Ultimately six power plants were built on the Tallulah and Tugaloo Rivers between 1913 and 1927: Tallulah, Burton, Nacoochee, Terrora, Tugalo, and Yonah. As the demise of most of the Victorian resorts came about around the nation, so it was with Tallulah Falls. Then in 1921, during the Christmas season, a fire spread rapidly through the town of Tallulah Falls, destroying most of the hotels as well as residences and businesses. There was no fire department in town to battle the blaze, and little that was destroyed was ever rebuilt.

Today, Georgia Power Company is in partnership with the Department of Natural Resources of the State of Georgia to preserve the natural environment and cultural resources by operating the gorge as a state park. A campground, trails, interpretative center, lake, and recreation facilities are available to the thousands of visitors who come to Tallulah Falls each year.

Although the grandeur of the great tourist hotels is gone, the remaining buildings of the town, the fascinating history of the area, and the marvelous scenery make what was the Niagara of the South a very special place.

One

The Niagara of the South

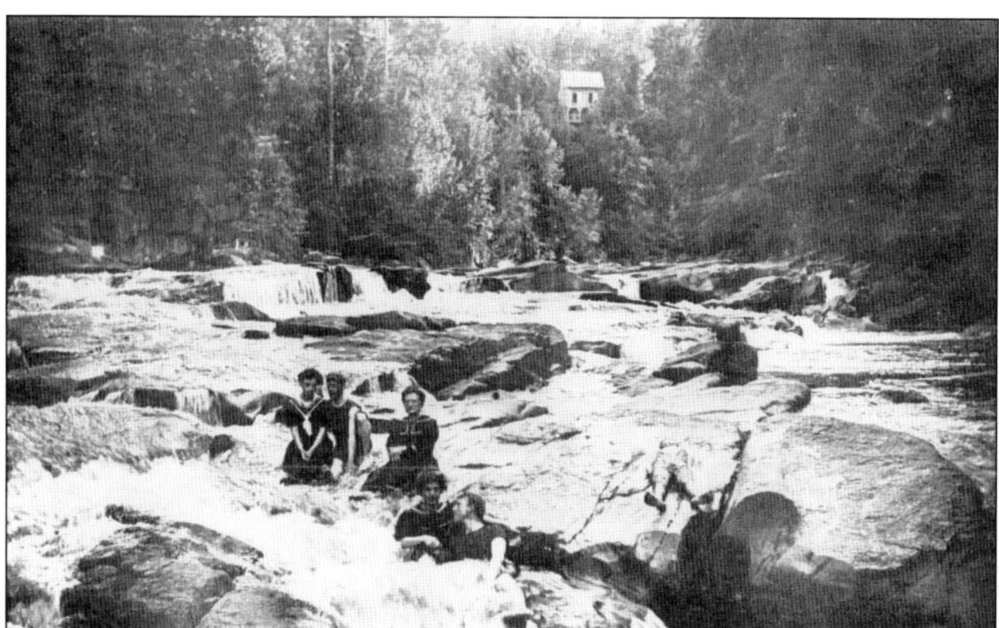

Here, a group is bathing in Indian Arrow Rapids which was near the Cliff House Hotel. The Tallulah River developed a rapid current at the beginning of Tallulah Gorge, forming rapids known as Indian Arrow Rapids because of the arrow-like swiftness of the water flying over the rocks. From this point, continuing for the next 2 miles, the river journeyed through a series of falls, pools, and rapids. There were five major falls and many minor cascades which together constituted Tallulah Falls. (Courtesy of Gary Doster.)

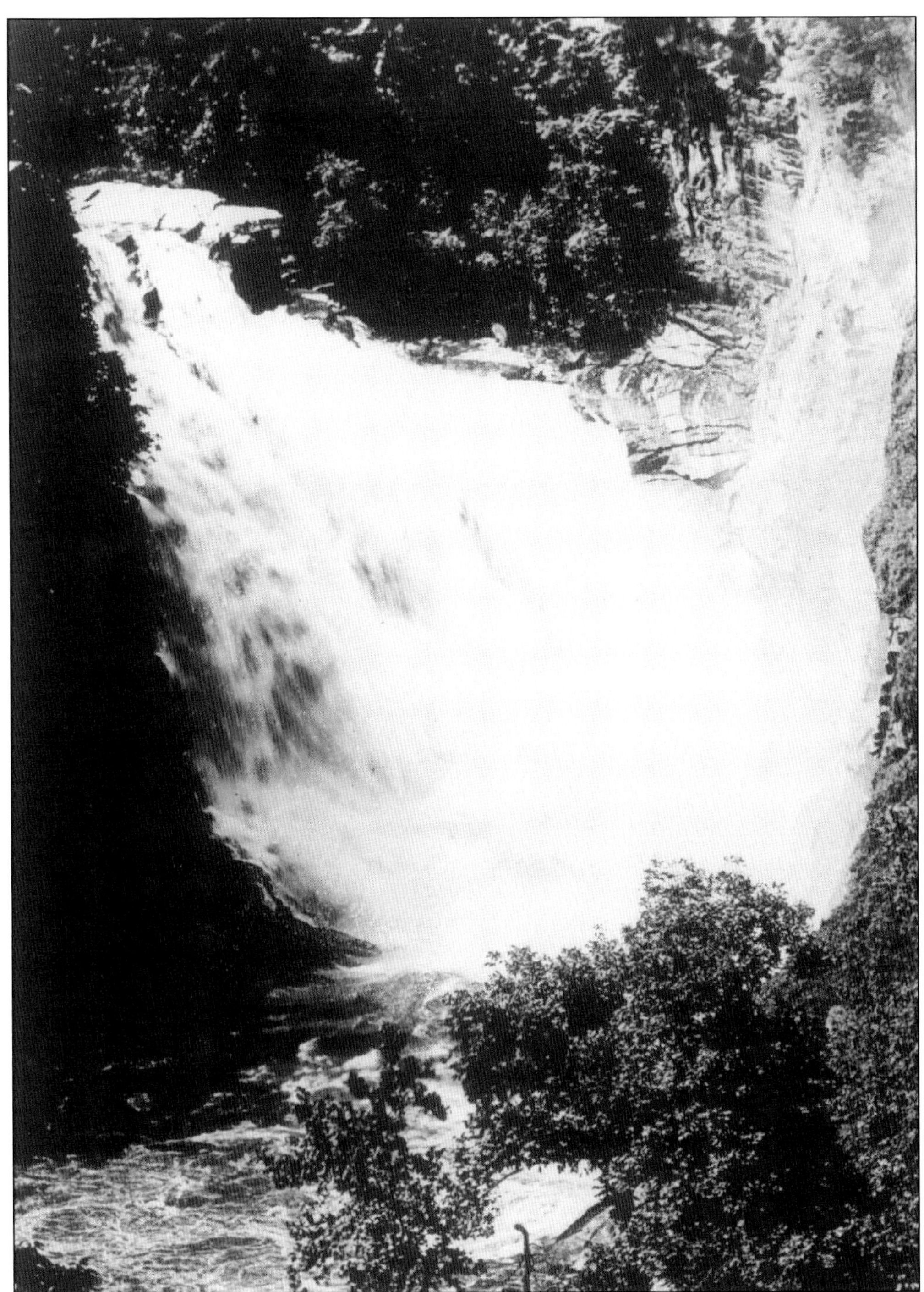

The highest of the major cataracts or falls is Hurricane Falls. A visitor to the falls in 1891 described the wonder: "Through a very narrow channel, defined by high perpendicular cliffs, the foaming torrent rushes with frightful velocity, and, plunging wildly over the rugged precipice with the roar of an approaching hurricane, falls a distance of ninety-six feet." (Courtesy of Georgia Power Land Department Photo Archives.)

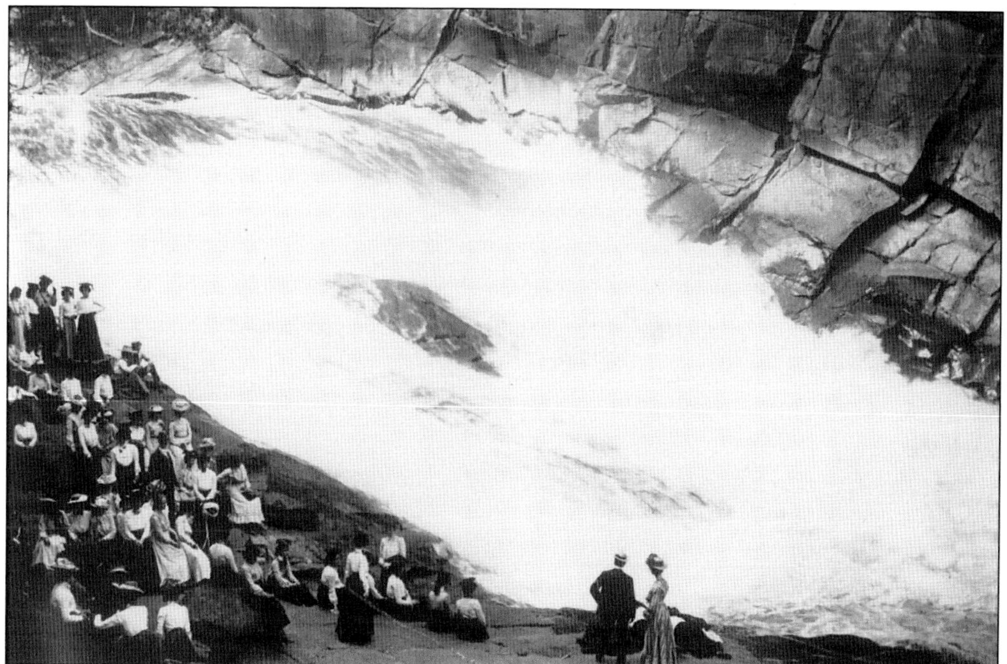

Ladore Falls, originally named L'Eau d'Or Falls, is depicted here with the sparkling waters glistening in the sun like gold. Not a perpendicular drop, the waters sped over an incline of about 25 degrees, descending a total of 46 feet. Here a group, probably a high school graduation class, is on a trip to the falls in 1900. (Courtesy of Georgia Department of Archives and History.)

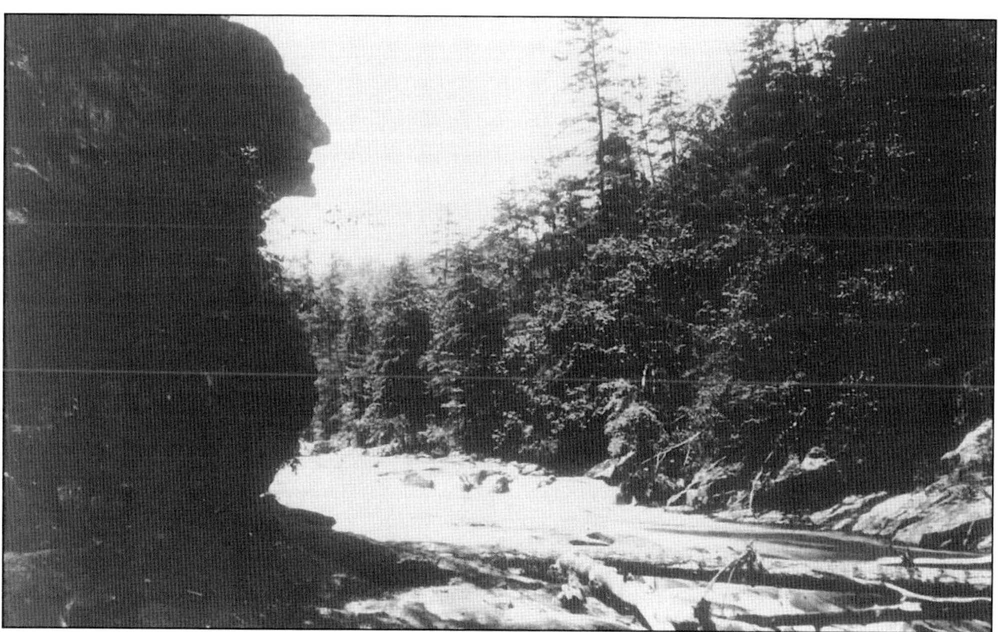

Witches Head is a distinctive overhanging rock formation above Indian Arrow Rapids. The pronounced facial features, evident in the rock, give it its name, Witches Head. (Courtesy of Georgia Power Land Department Photo Archives.)

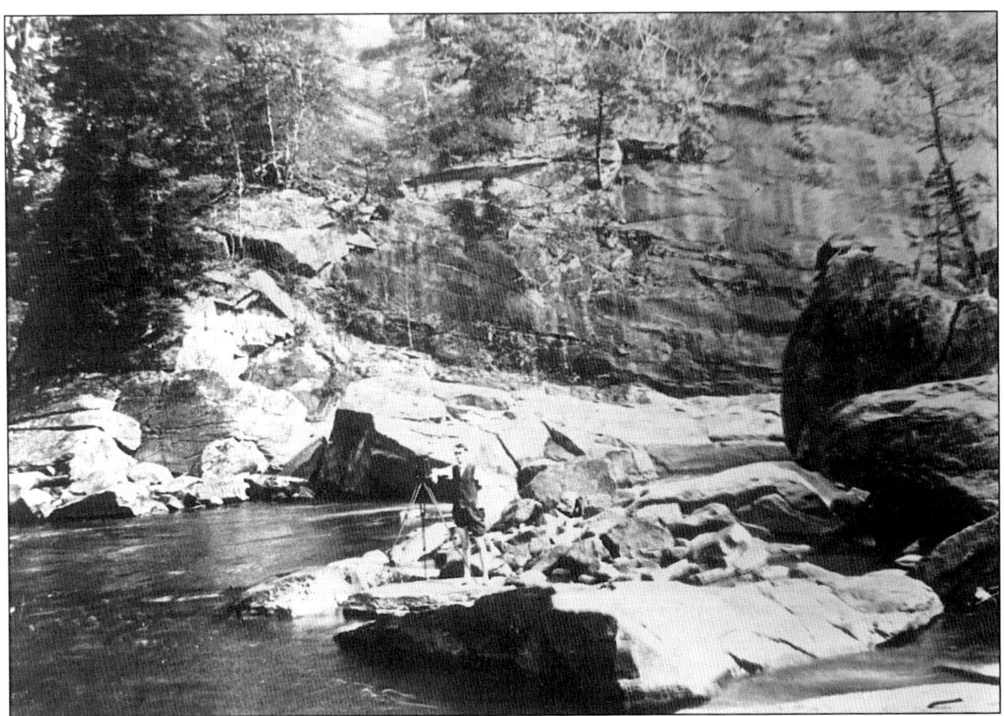

Deep within Tallulah Gorge a photographer, in the center of this image, sets up to capture on film the breathtaking natural wonder. (Courtesy of Georgia Power Land Department Photo Archives.)

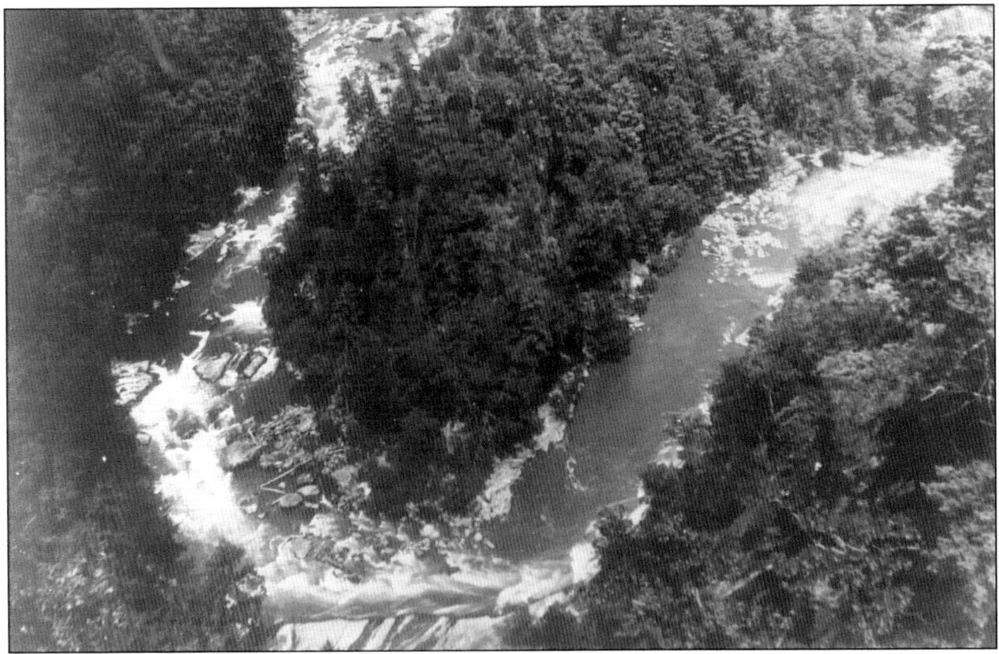

Far down the gorge is a great bend in the Tallulah River. Because of its shape it is appropriately named Horseshoe Bend. This photo was taken c. 1911. (Courtesy of Georgia Power Land Department Photo Archives.)

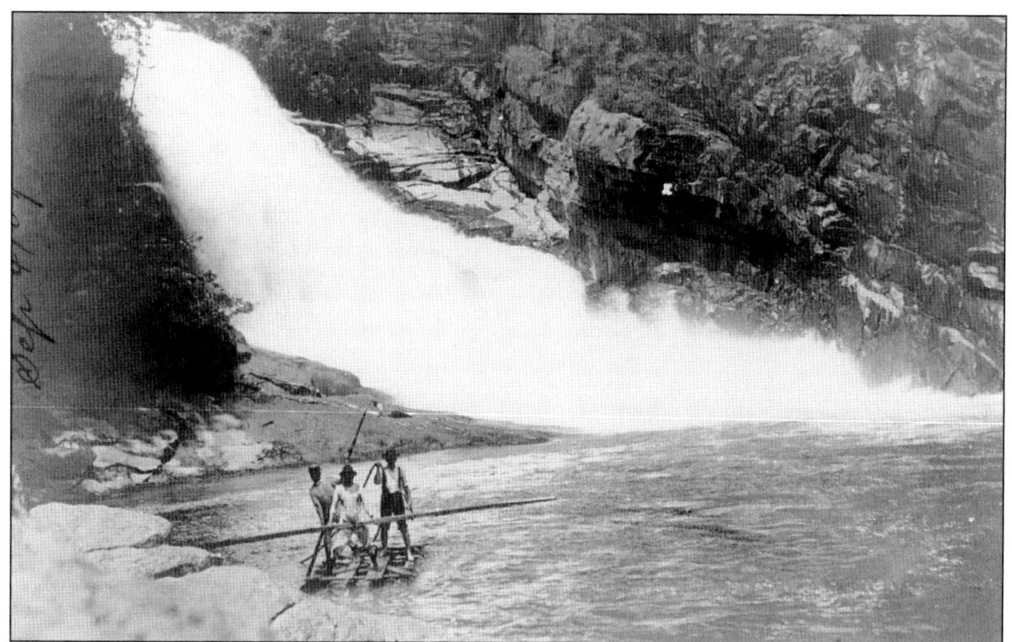

Along with the grandeur and beauty of the gorge and falls of the Tallulah River, danger lurks. The "boiling, seething and raging waters . . . suggest the horrors of the bottomless pit," noted Georgia history professor Merton Coulter. On September 4, 1909 a rescue party at the foot of Hurricane Falls dredged for the body of an unfortunate visitor who got too close to the edge of the cliff. (Courtesy of Gary Doster.)

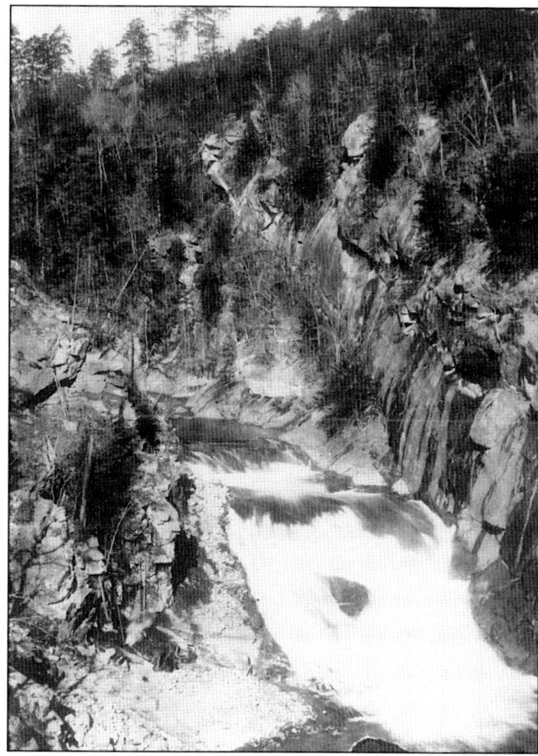

"I was dumb with admiration and awe, for I felt like an atom compared to that wonderful natural curiosity," commented a visitor in 1886 about Ladore Falls. (Courtesy of Georgia Power Land Department Photo Archives.)

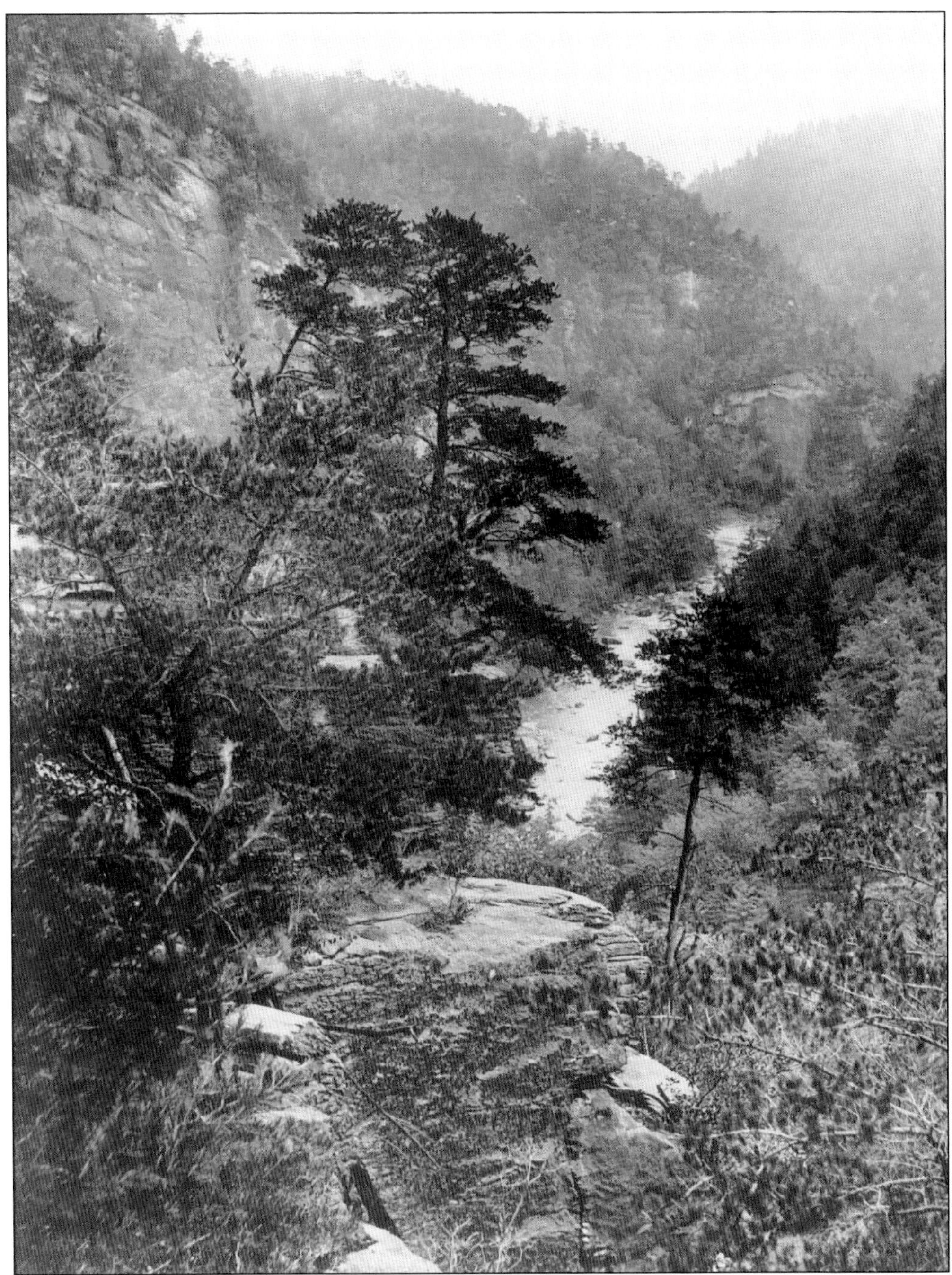

The Grand Chasm, shown here *c.* 1911, extends about 1 mile in length and ranges from 300 feet to a quarter of a mile wide. The walls of the canyon farther down from here are 1,000 feet high in places. (Courtesy of Rope Roberts.)

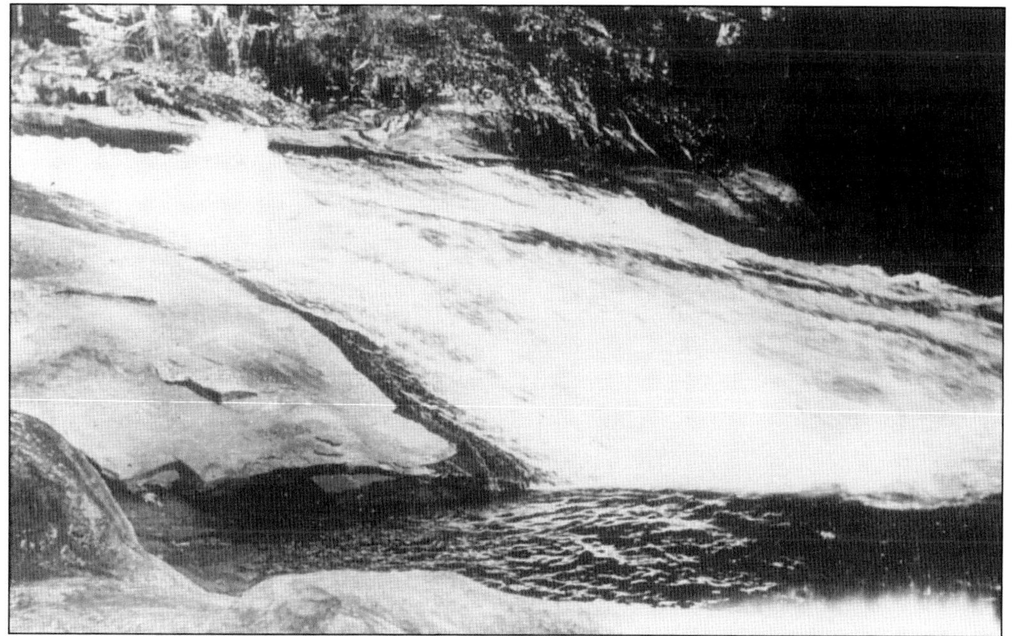

The last of the primary falls is Bridal Veil, at the lower end of the Grand Chasm. From the beginning of Indian Arrow Rapids to beyond Bridal Veil, the river falls 450 feet. The current is gentler here, and the misty spray of water reminds the observer of the lacy beauty of a bridal veil. This image was taken *c.* 1911. (Courtesy of Georgia Power Land Department Photo Archives.)

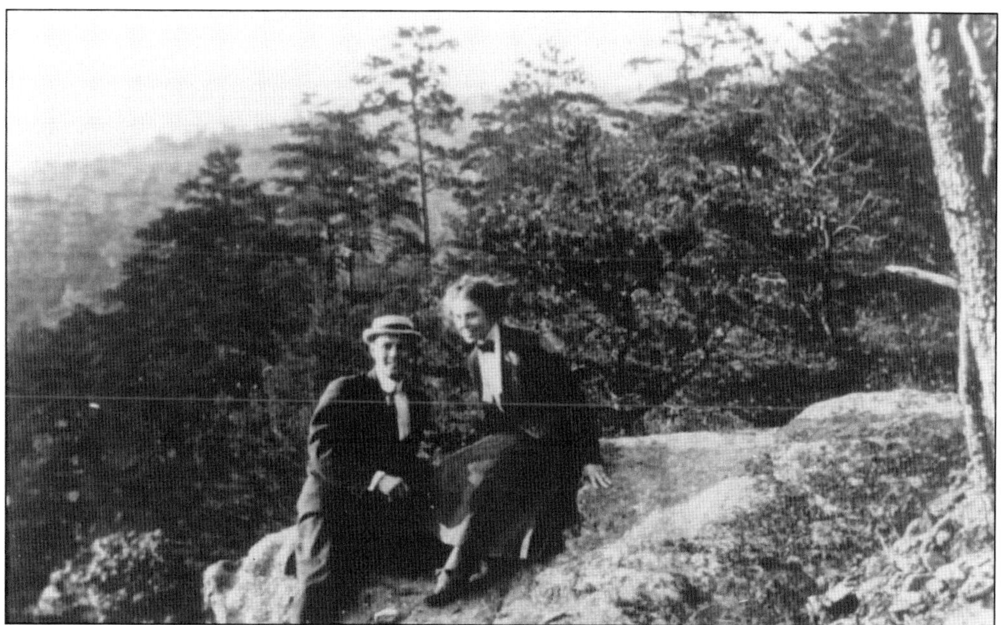

Clare Hancock, shown here with an engineer from the hydroelectric construction project, perches on a precipice called Point Inspiration, which is the highest point near the falls. It is located on the north side of the gorge with a 1,200-foot drop to the river. The photograph was self-taken *c.* 1912. (Courtesy of Georgia Power Land Department Photo Archives.)

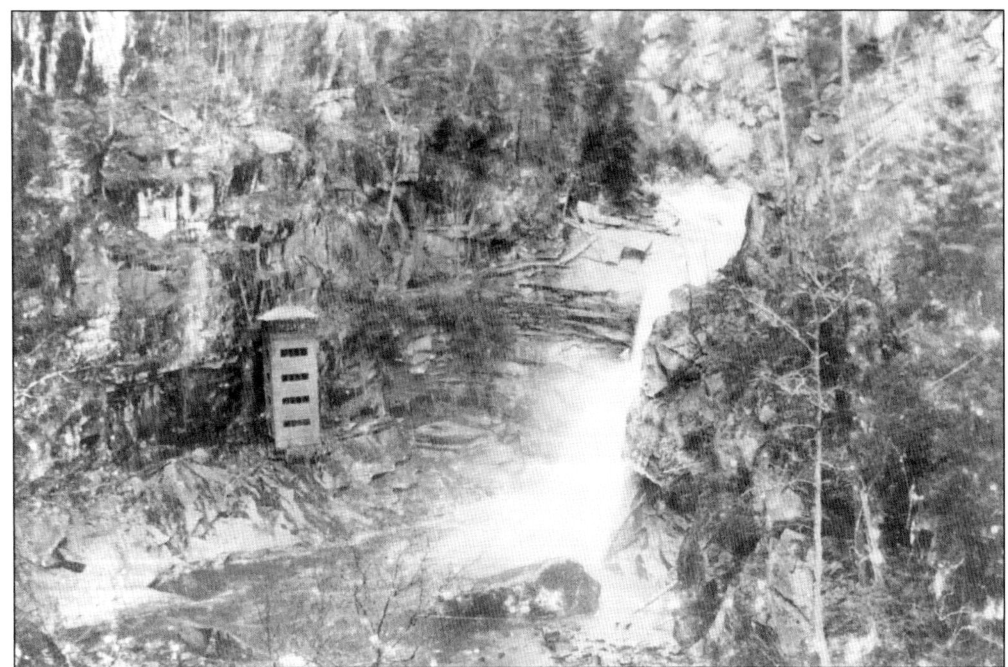

Tempesta Falls makes a perpendicular drop of 76 feet. The Cliff House Hotel observation tower and catwalks are at left. At the very top of Tempesta is Hawthorne's Pool, named for the Reverend Hawthorne, who accompanied a party from Athens in 1837. While swimming alone in the pool, he was swept over Tempesta Falls, and his body was recovered several days later. (Courtesy of Rope Roberts.)

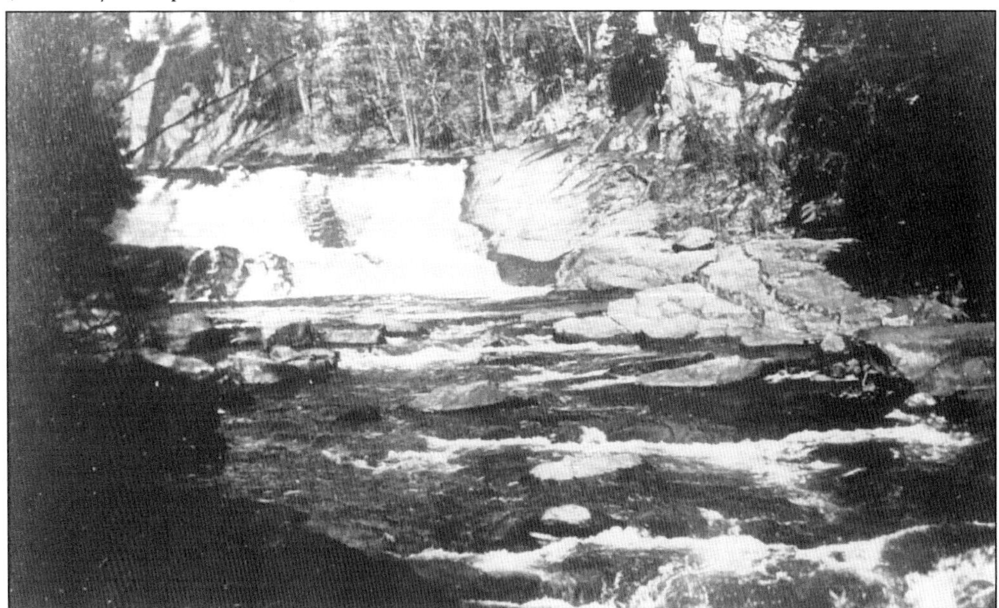

Oceana Falls, one of the major cataracts, is seen here from a distance. A visitor in 1891 stated that Oceana "tosses and tumbles, like the foam-capped waves of the ocean, over the ribbed and rugged surface of an immense inclined ledge of rock for some fifty feet." (Courtesy of Georgia Power Land Department Photo Archives.)

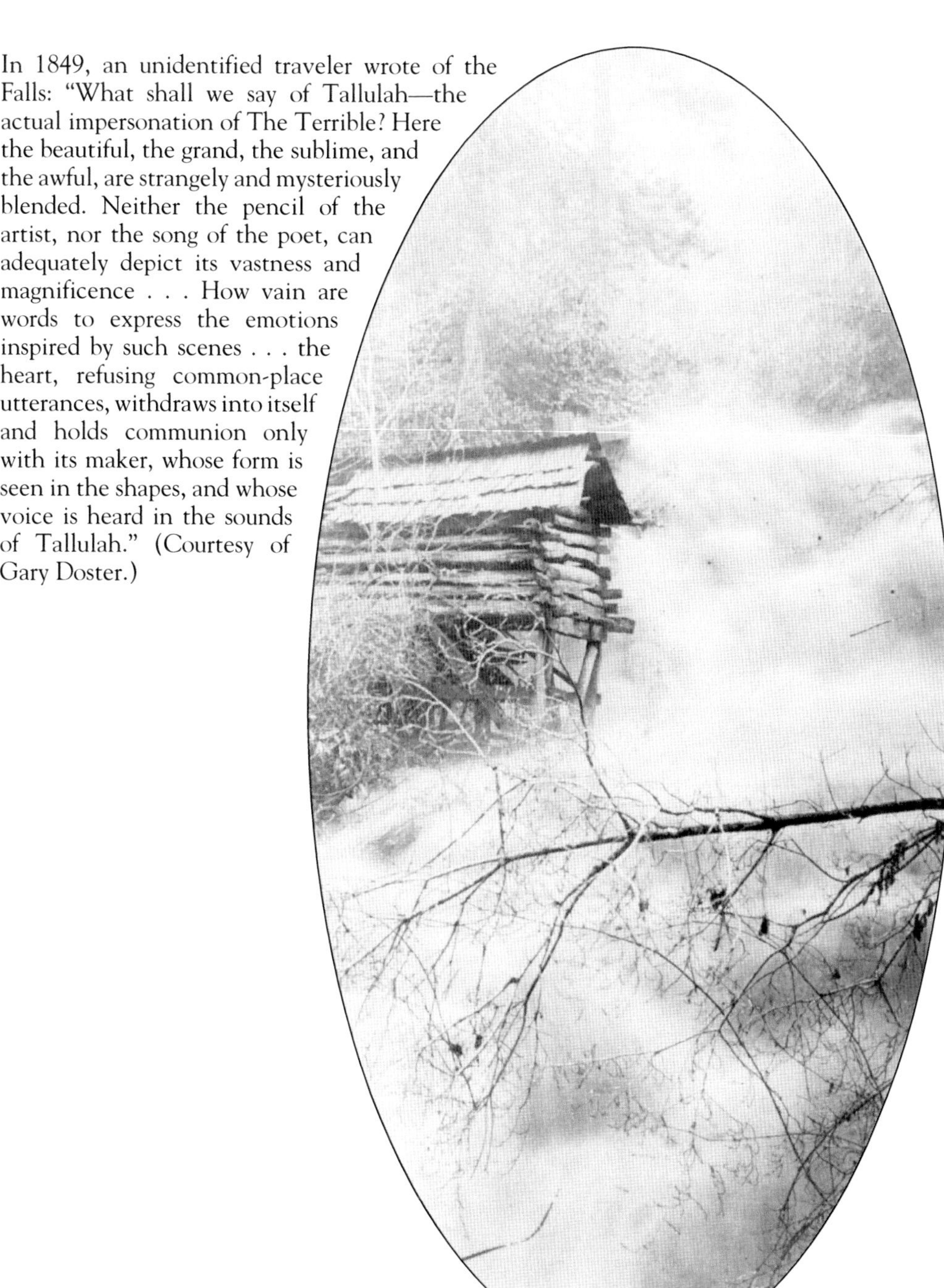

In 1849, an unidentified traveler wrote of the Falls: "What shall we say of Tallulah—the actual impersonation of The Terrible? Here the beautiful, the grand, the sublime, and the awful, are strangely and mysteriously blended. Neither the pencil of the artist, nor the song of the poet, can adequately depict its vastness and magnificence . . . How vain are words to express the emotions inspired by such scenes . . . the heart, refusing common-place utterances, withdraws into itself and holds communion only with its maker, whose form is seen in the shapes, and whose voice is heard in the sounds of Tallulah." (Courtesy of Gary Doster.)

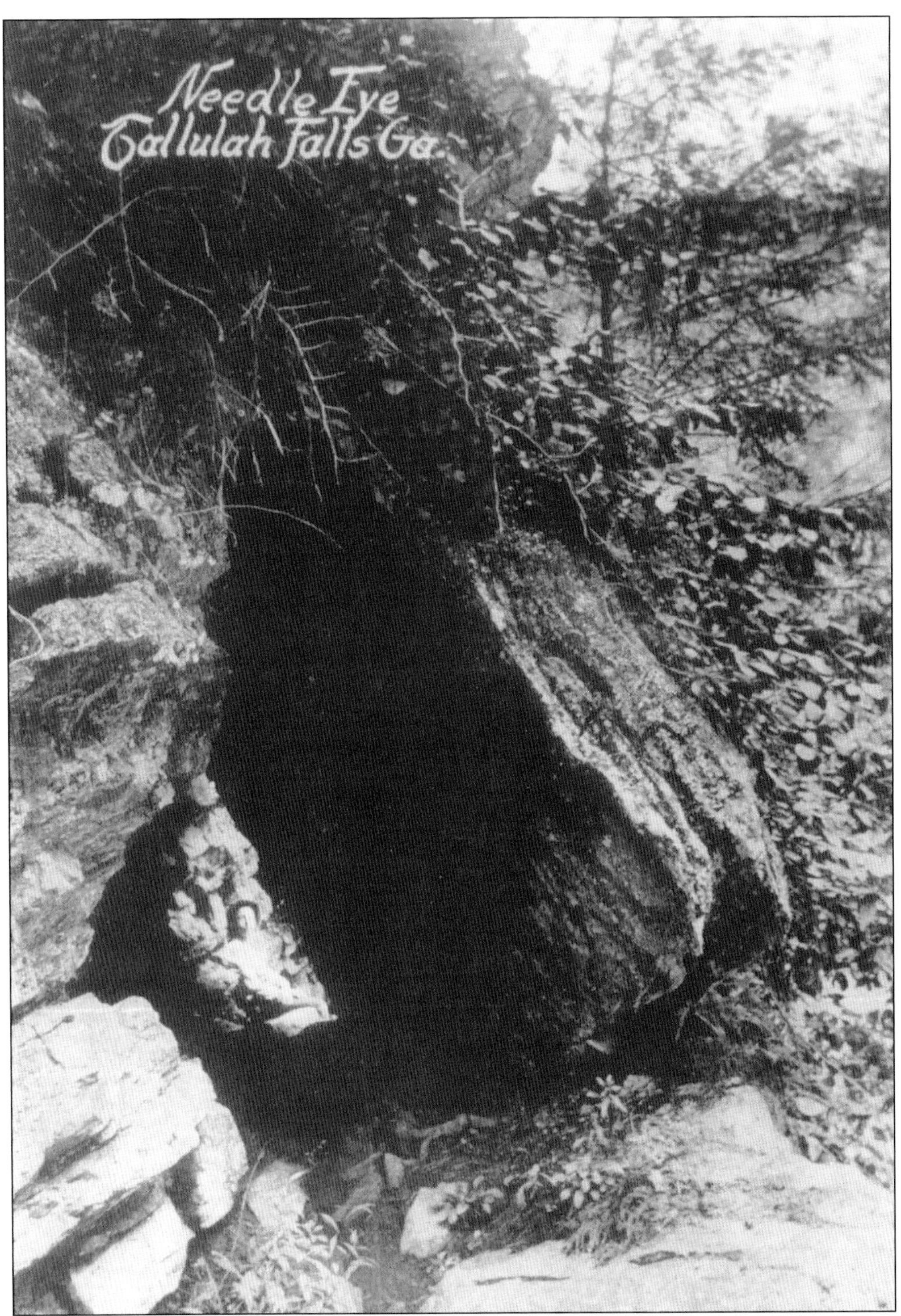

A large rock shelter called Lover's Retreat is entirely secluded. The exit on the left, called Needle Eye, is so narrow that it is almost necessary to crawl through. A face peers out through Needle Eye. (Photograph by Walter Hunnicutt, courtesy of Gary Doster.)

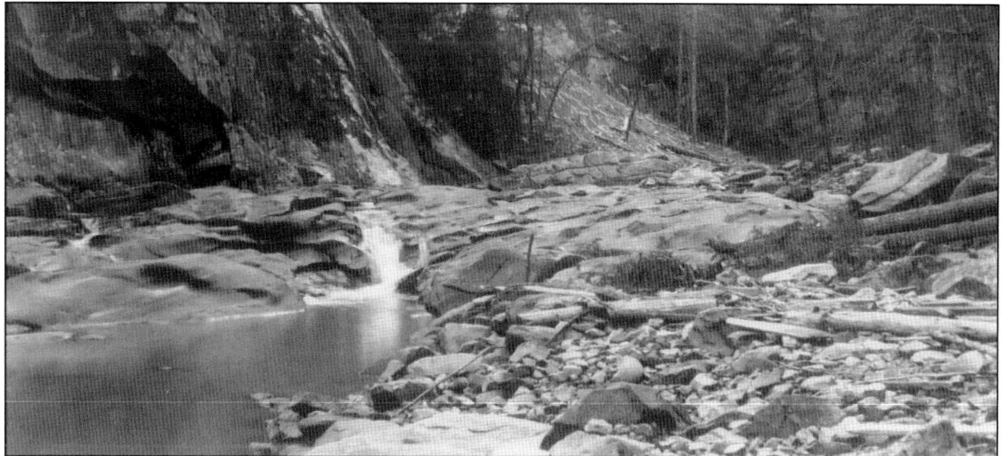

This was "a wild, uncultivated and barren country, [where] no art [had] been introduced to deface this grand exhibition of nature," said David Hillhouse in 1819. Prior to that time, Tallulah Falls was a well-kept secret. Hillhouse was the first to record a description of the gorge, declaring it to be "one of the greatest curiosities in the United States." (Courtesy of Georgia Power Land Department Photo Archives.)

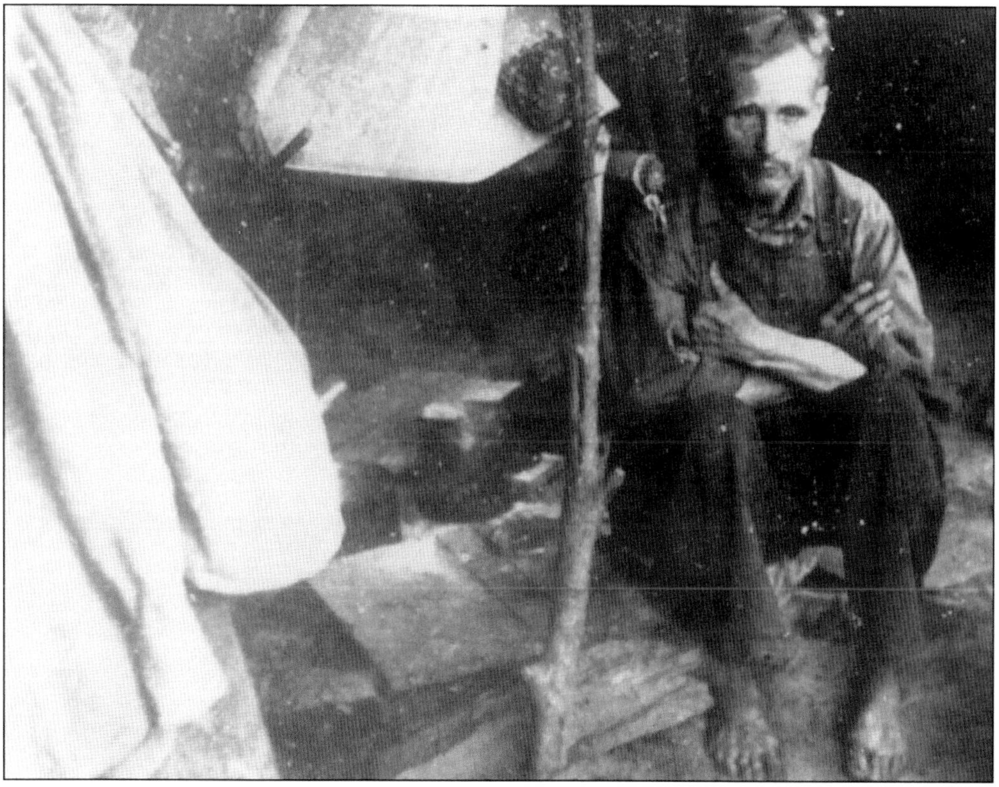

Several hermits have inhabited the gorge from time to time. Adam Vandever, probably the first white settler, had a son, John Cole Vandever, who was the first to reside as a hermit in the gorge. In the 1930s a Mr. Ledford (above) was found by a newspaper man and friends there. Legend has it that he had been involved in a family dispute and was ostracized from his kin. (Courtesy of Georgia Power Land Department Photo Archives.)

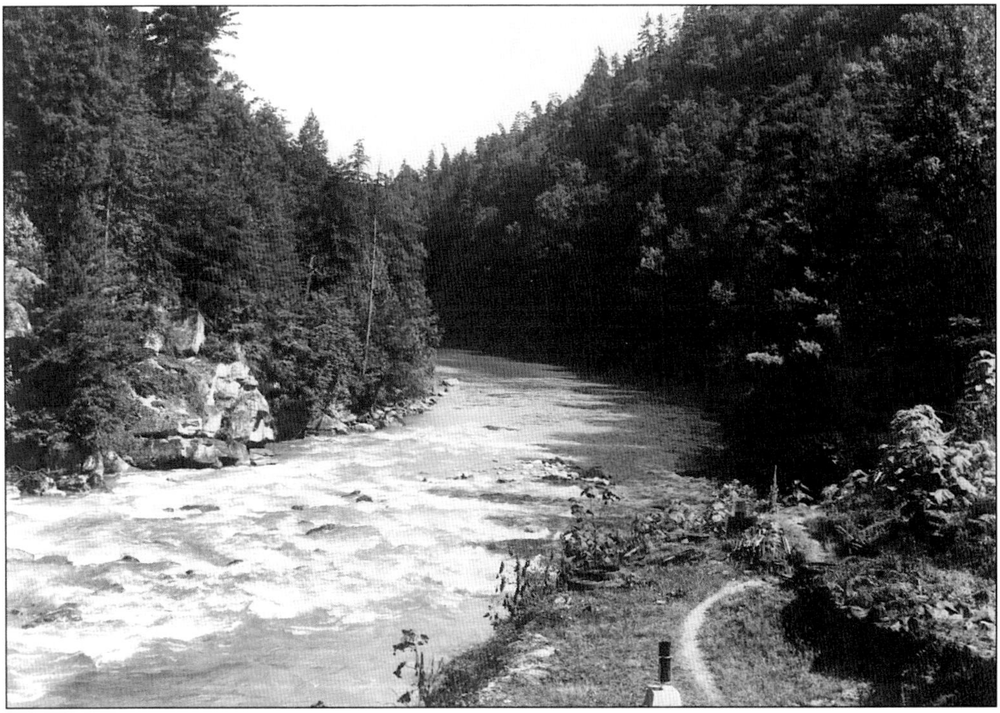

In this spot, the raging Tallulah River proceeds at a slower pace and meanders downstream below Lake Rabun, *c.* 1926. (Courtesy of Georgia Power Land Department Photo Archives.)

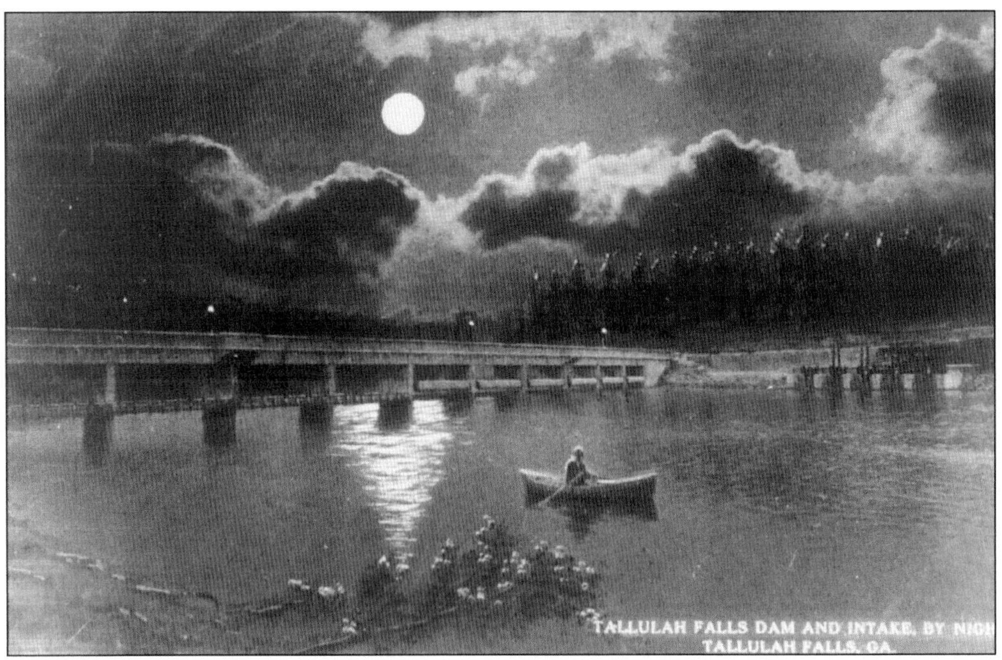

Lovely Tallulah Falls Lake, formed by the dam in 1913 at left, is enjoyed by a boater at night. (Courtesy of Gary Doster.)

Two

A Rugged, Independent People

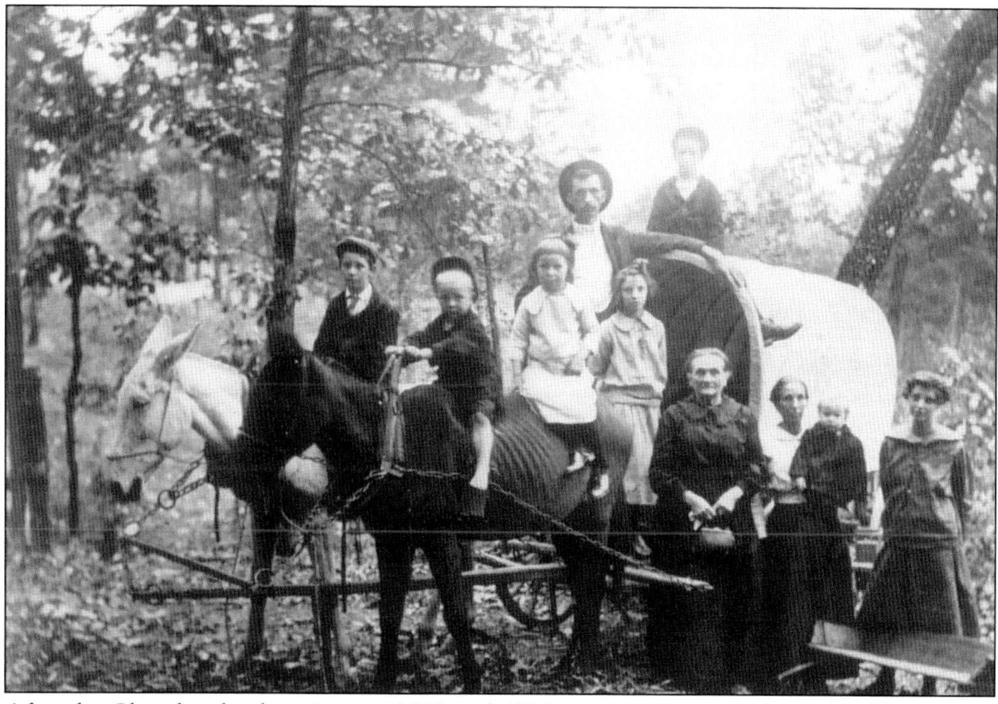

After the Cherokee land cessions in 1817 and 1819, immigrants came down the Shenandoah and Tennessee River valleys to Tallulah Falls and the neighboring mountain areas. They were of Scots-Irish, German, French Huguenot, and English ancestry. Several generations of one family, such as this one, usually migrated and resided together. Due to their geographical isolation, parts of their culture remained intact for many generations. (Courtesy of Tallulah Falls School.)

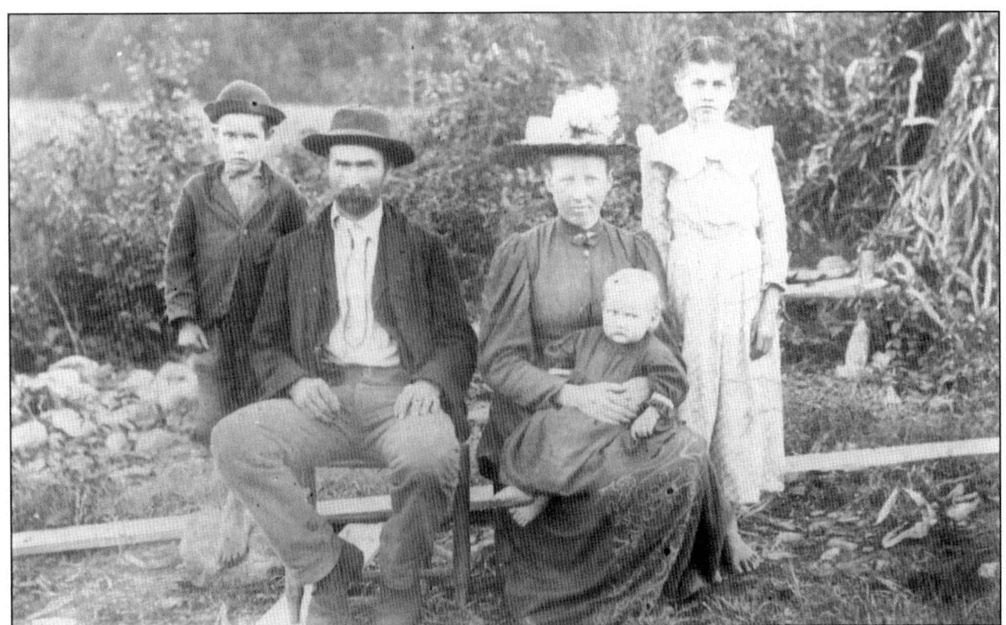

The David Nations family assembled for a portrait on their family's farm c. 1899. Land lots of 202 1/2 acres were distributed by the state land lottery to families who then settled the area. Farms consisted of log buildings, fences, and cleared fields, which were scattered in coves and along creek and river bottoms. (Courtesy of Georgia Department of Archives and History.)

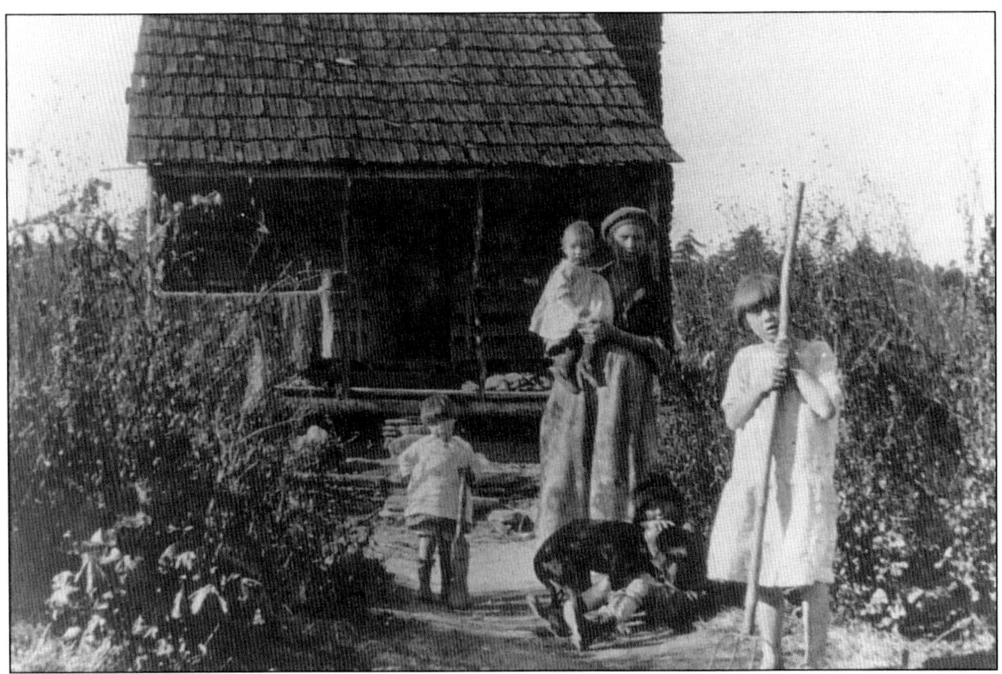

Houses generally consisted of one-room cabins shingled with oak or cedar splits. In order to survive in this rugged area, families, including this older child seen here, eked out a living working from dawn until dusk, using every natural resource to its best advantage. (Courtesy of Tallulah Falls School.)

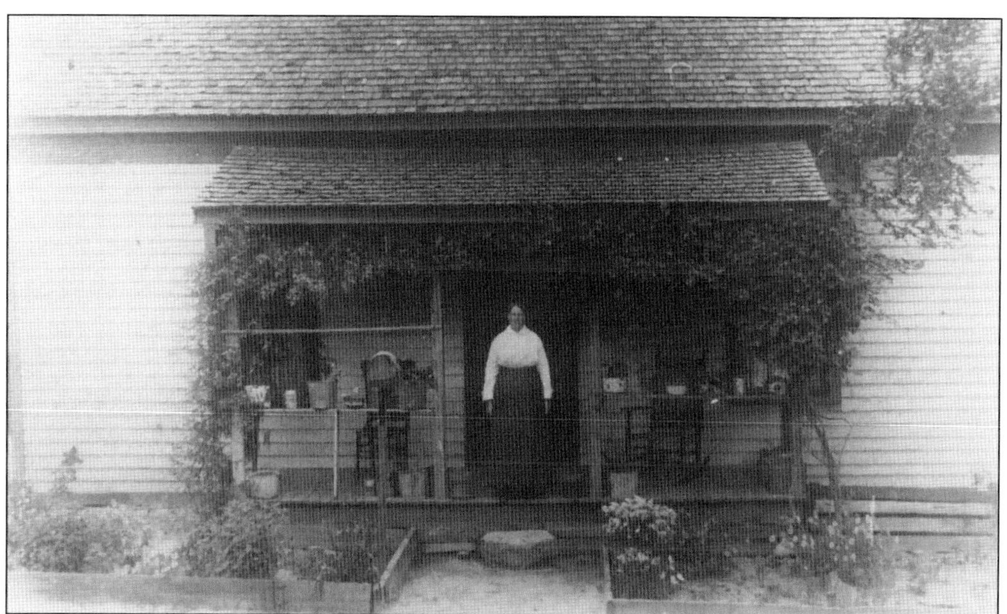

Later, some of the families were able to build larger cabins such as this home belonging to Mrs. Smith, built around the turn of the century. Other buildings on the farm might include a springhouse for storing butter or milk, a pig or chicken pen, and barn or tool shed. (Courtesy of Georgia Department of Archives and History.)

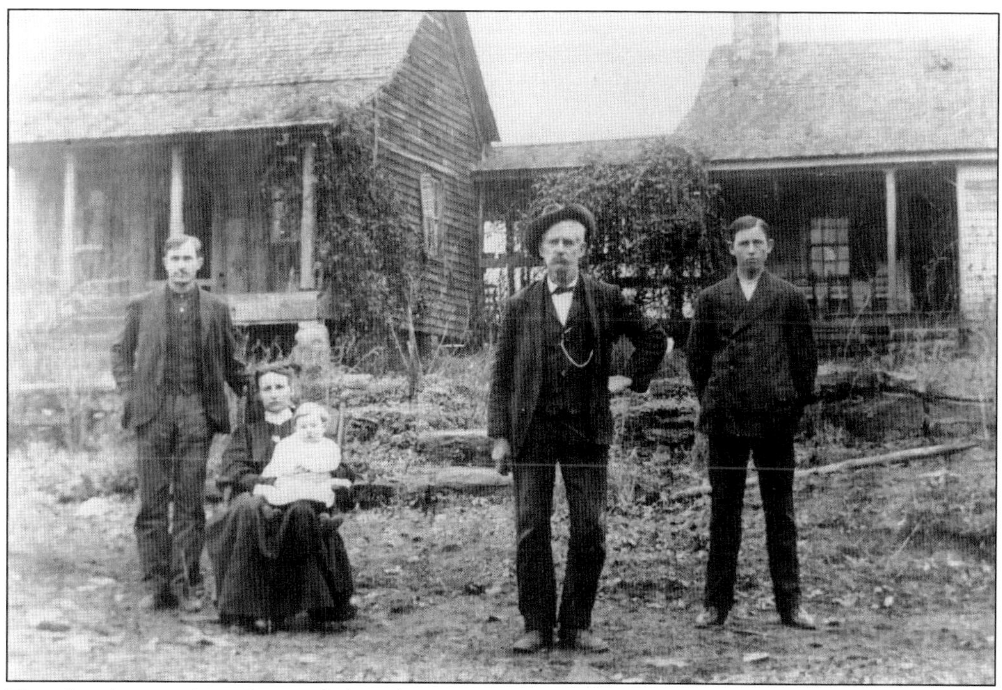

This family posed in front of their home *c.* 1906. The breezeway and additional structure were probably added as the family grew. The homesteaders matured and married young, and raised large families on self-sufficient farms. (Courtesy of Georgia Department of Archives and History.)

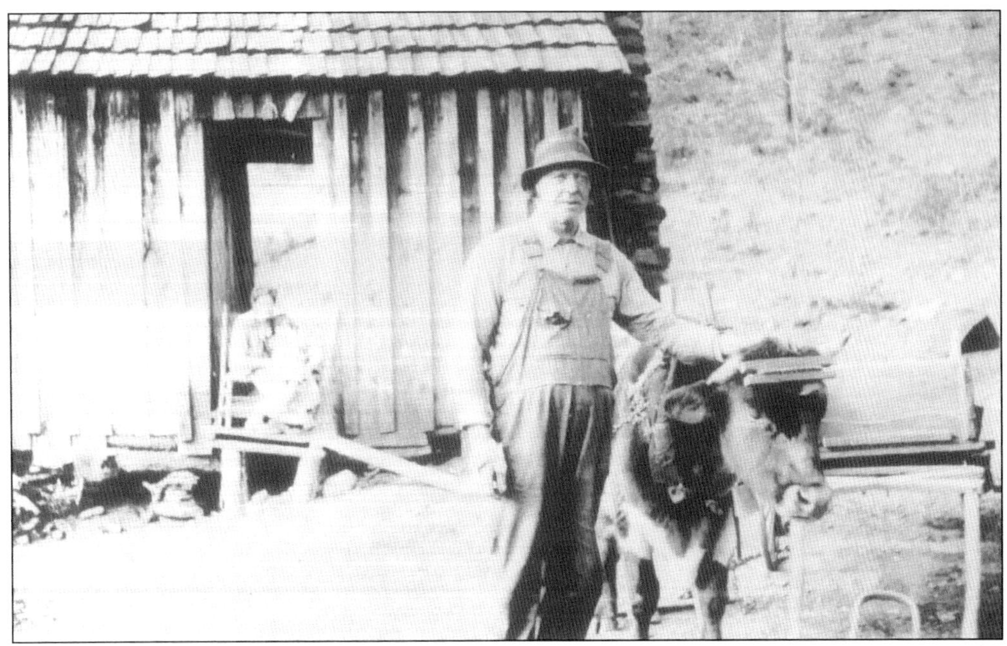

The farmer stands in front of his home displaying his family and cow, the prized possession. The settlers were primarily farmers with few and simple wants. With an axe a man cleared his land and built his cabin. With his mule and plow he cultivated the land, and with his rifle hunted abundant wild game to feed his family. (Courtesy of Tallulah Falls School.)

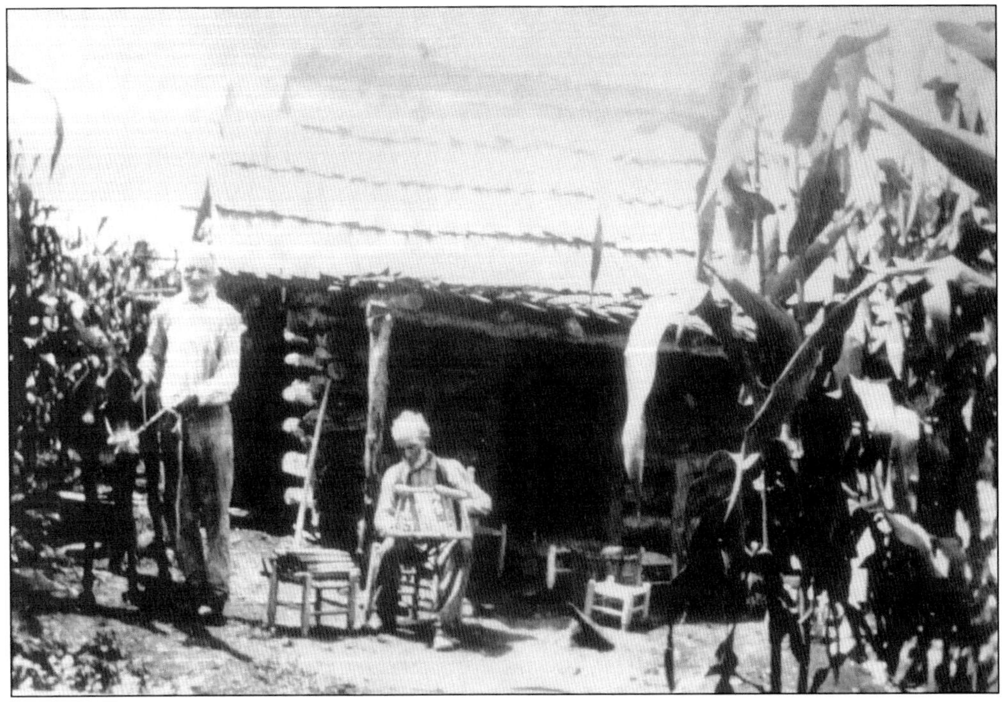

These farmers are probably crafting chairs or stools for trade, as "cash money" was rare. Shucks from the corn crop could be used for the seat bottoms. Corn was a staple of the mountain harvest, providing food to both the farmer and his livestock. (Courtesy of Tallulah Falls School.)

This farmer with his triple team of mules is working the land in the Persimmon community in the early 1930s. Mules were the farm animal of choice in rural north Georgia, as they both plowed the earth and served as a means of transportation. (Courtesy of Georgia Department of Archives and History.)

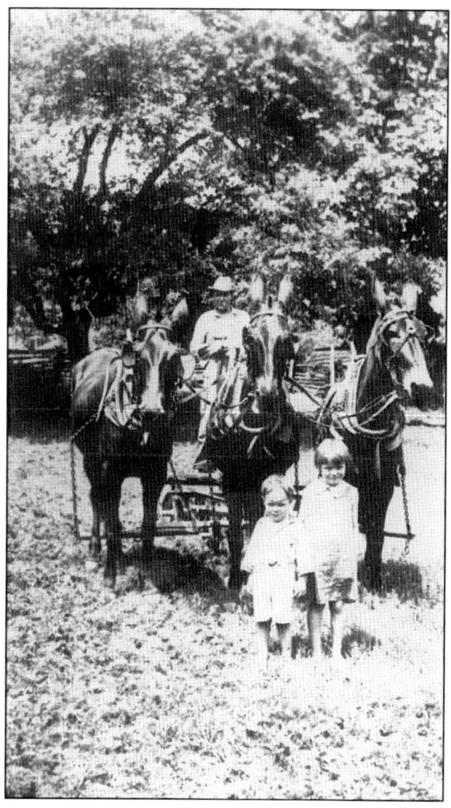

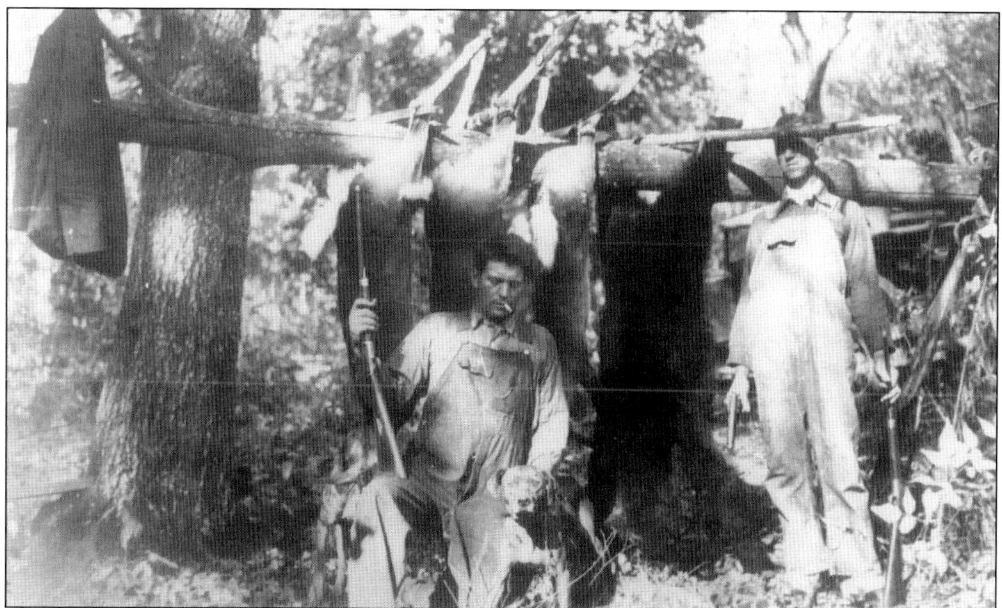

Hunting was a necessity for the mountain family. These men and their hunting dog display their trophies—two deer and a bear, *c.* 1920. Deerskin could be dressed into buckskin for clothing or cut into plowlines or bridles. Antlers were used for spoons or buttons and also made fine coat or rifle racks. (Courtesy of Georgia Department of Archives and History.)

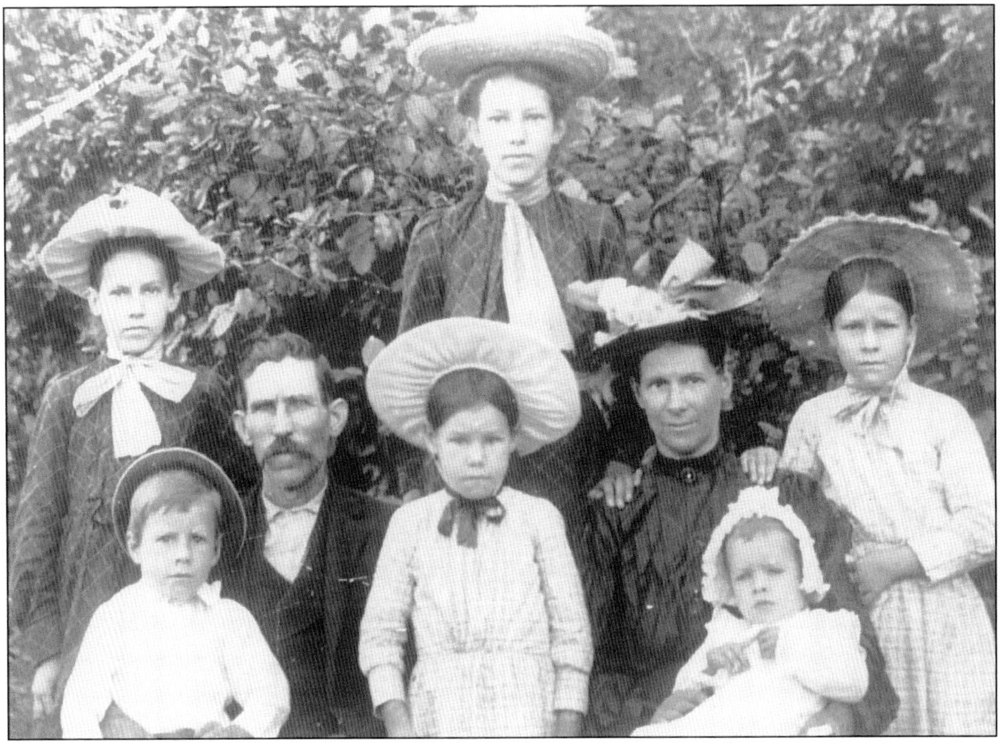

Families were large, such as the William Parker family pictured here in their best attire, hats included, in 1904. The hats were most likely made by the mother. Life was hard for the Appalachian woman. She spun, wove, sewed, and quilted the clothing, canned or preserved the fruits and vegetables, helped clear the land, cut timber, plowed, planted, and harvested. (Courtesy of Georgia Department of Archives and History.)

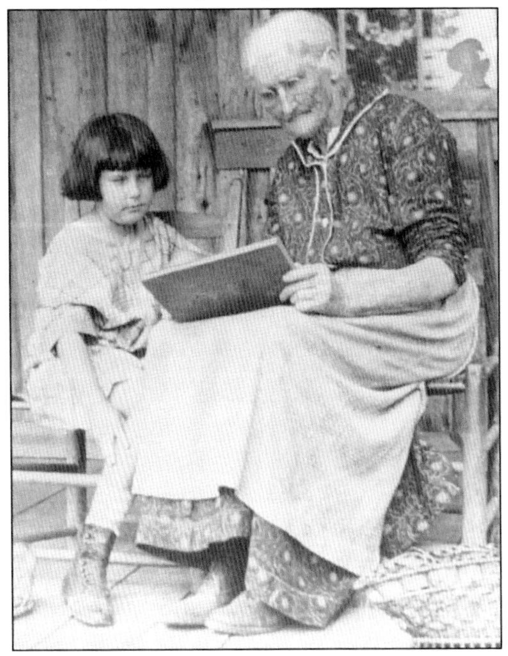

A member of the older generation teaches the young at home in this extended family. Note the "settin' " chairs and baskets which of necessity were produced by hand on the farm. These items are collectors' pieces today. (Courtesy of Tallulah Falls School.)

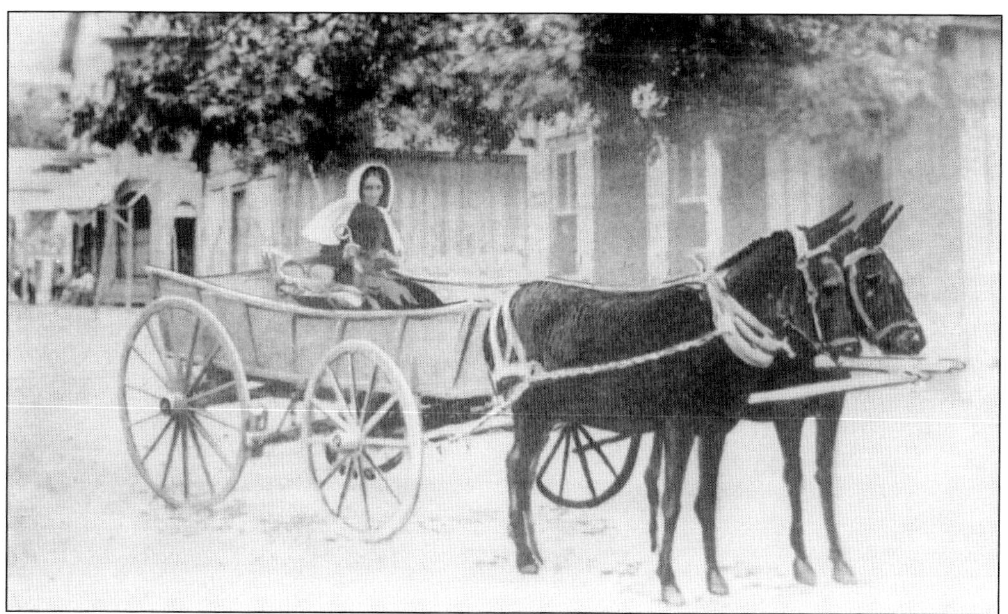

One of the early settlers, Fannie Picklesimer Kerby Smith, shown here on a trip to town to stock up on supplies, operated her home on Sinking Mountain as a guest house to travelers visiting Tallulah Falls. The home was built by her first husband, William R. Kerby, after their 1841 marriage. Later, as a widow she married Ambrose J. Smith and produced a total of 11 children. (Courtesy of Tallulah Falls School.)

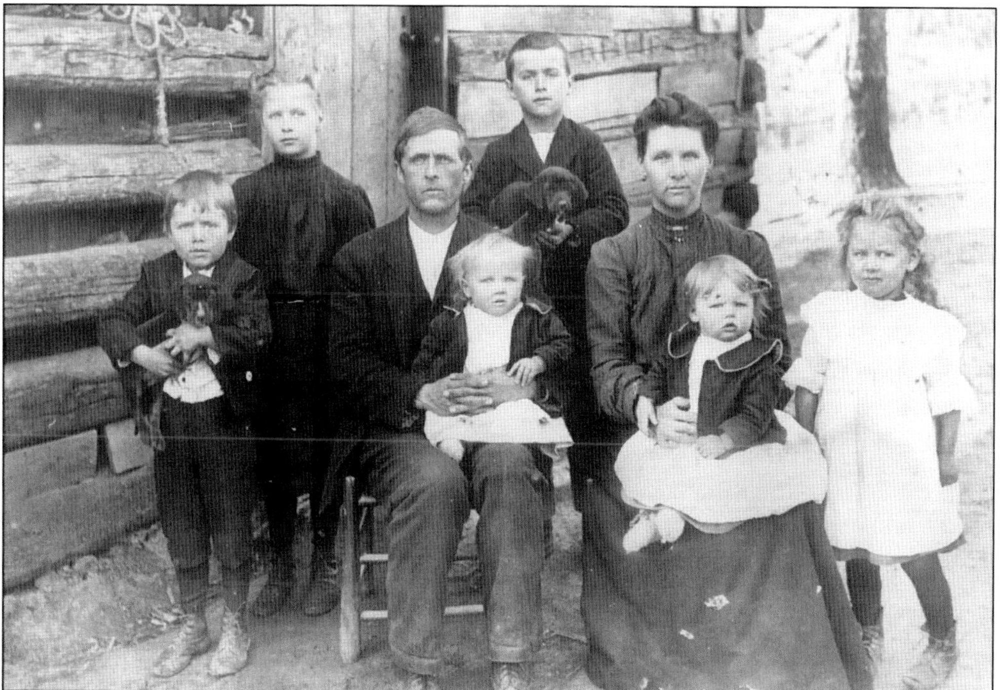

The Samuel Taylor family settled on Black Rock Mountain near Clayton, Georgia. This photograph of the family and puppies was taken in front of their log cabin around 1909. (Courtesy of Georgia Department of Archives and History.)

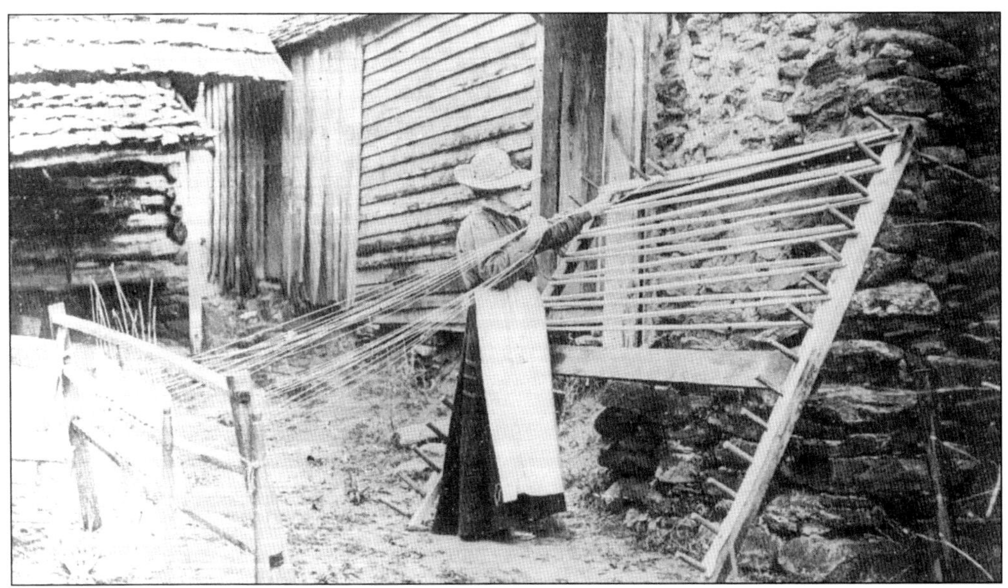

The natural raw materials of flax, cotton, or wool had to be grown, combed or carded, spun, and woven into cloth. This woman is preparing threads on the warping bars so they can be set on the loom to weave the cloth. (Courtesy of Gary Doster.)

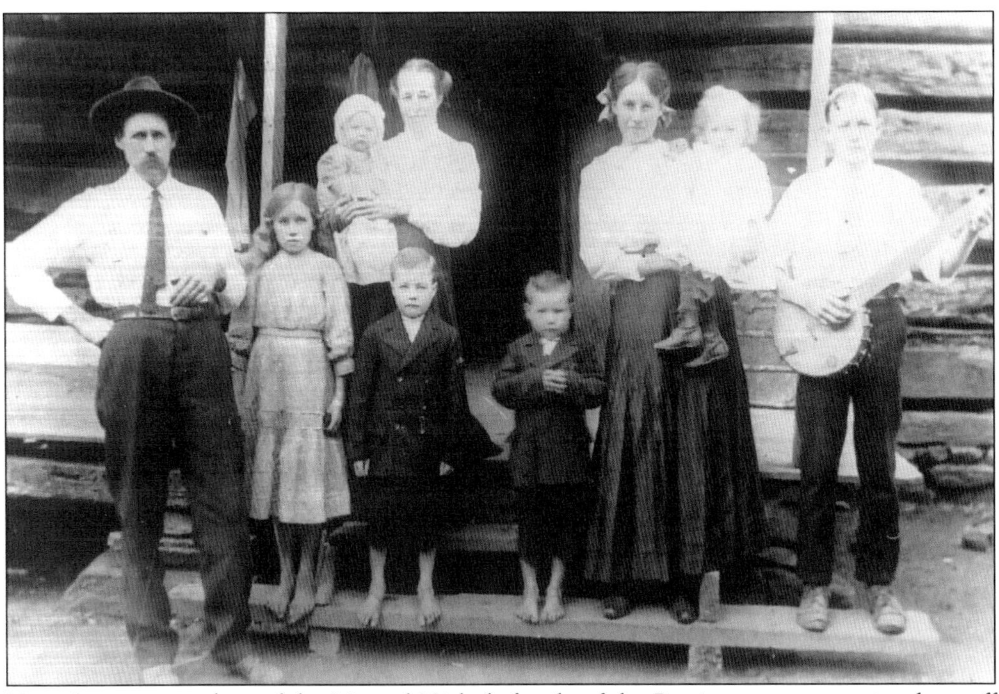

Here the nine members of the Manuel Nichols family of the Persimmon community show off their family, and banjo, c. 1910. Storytelling, music, and dance traditions from their ancestral roots provided entertainment. (Courtesy of Georgia Department of Archives and History.)

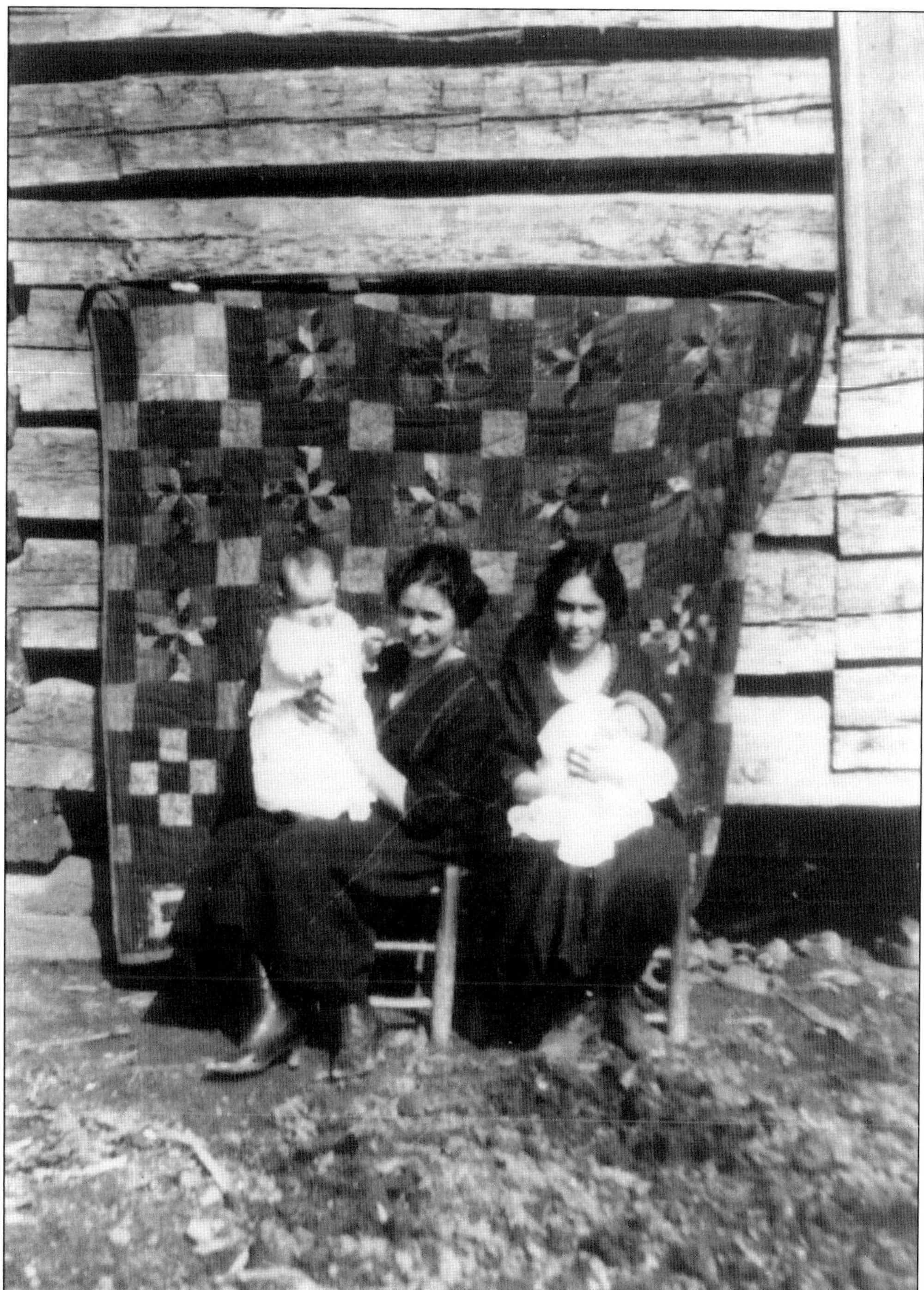

Neighbors were usually separated by distances, so gatherings often turned into social occasions. Weddings, funerals, barn-raisings, and quilting bees provided a sense of community. This photograph shows Lelar Thompson Coleman and Eula Coleman Parker in the Persimmon community in 1924. They proudly display their children and quilt against the side of a log cabin. (Courtesy of Georgia Department of Archives and History.)

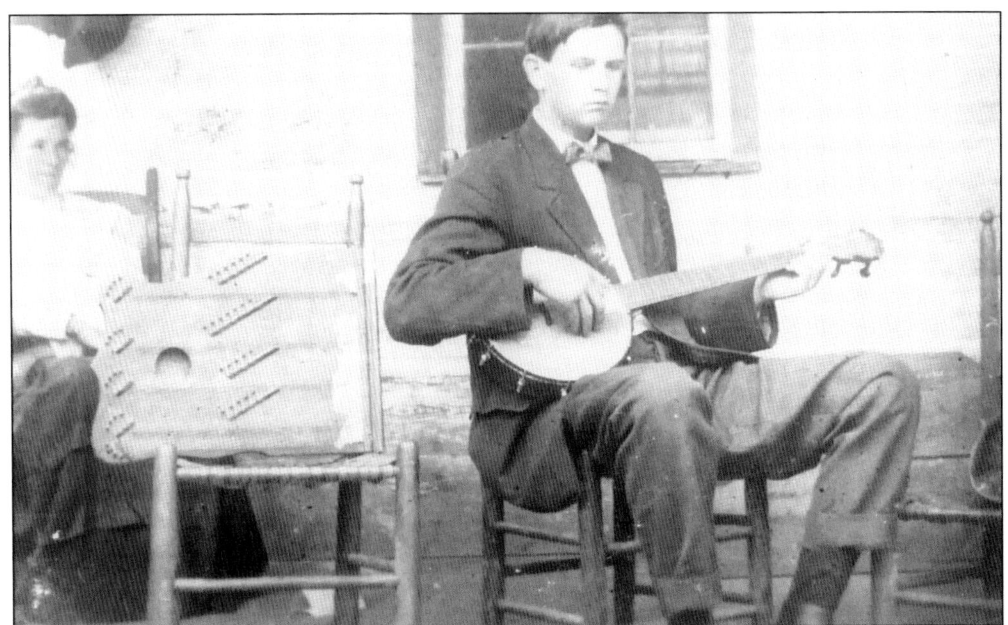

Music provided a release and recreation for the settlers. The banjo, based on a West African gourd instrument, became popularized in the South in the 19th century. Here Dock King plays a tune while Mrs. A.B. Forrester looks on. (Courtesy of Georgia Department of Archives and History.)

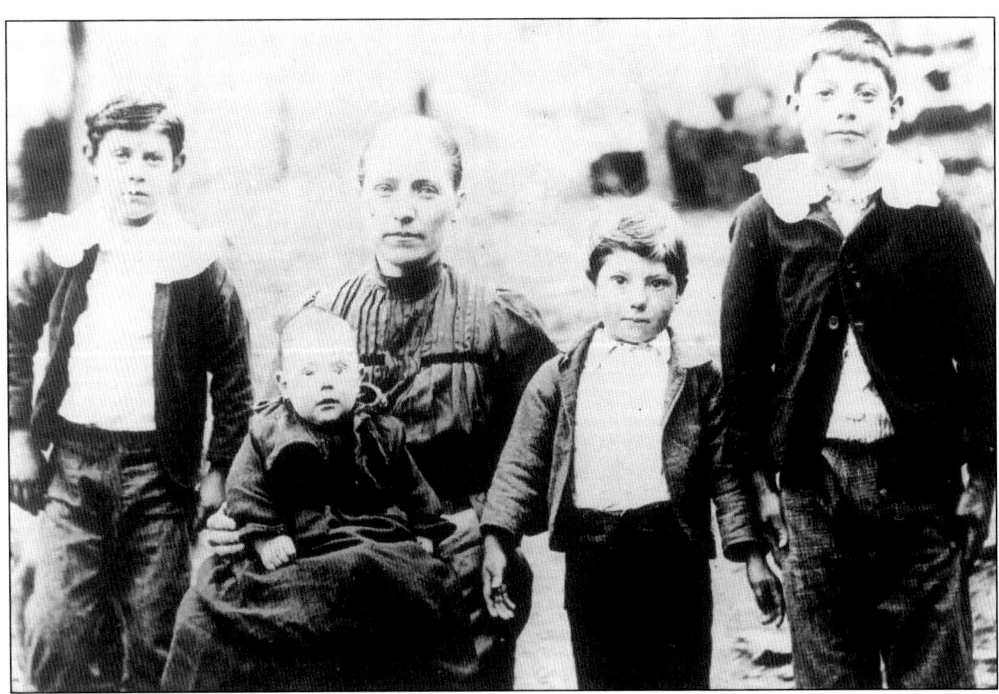

Mrs. Rose Kirby and her four bright-eyed children, (left to right) Lee, Jesse, Carie, and Frank, lived in the Persimmon community of north Georgia *c.* 1905. (Courtesy of Georgia Department of Archives and History.)

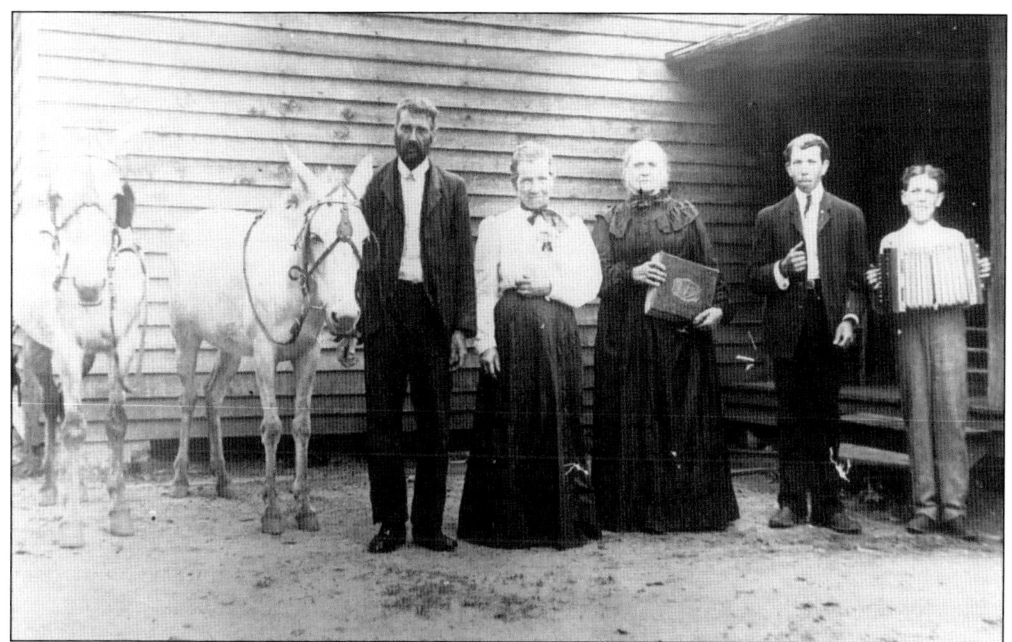

In what is likely their only photograph, the family brings out all of their prized possessions. William Smith shows off his two fine mules, while the son displays his accordion. Grandmother Blalock is holding the family Bible. The settlers were independent people, strong in their religious faith, which was essential because illness and death took a toll on many, with only home remedies and natural medicines to combat diseases. (Courtesy of Georgia Department of Archives and History.)

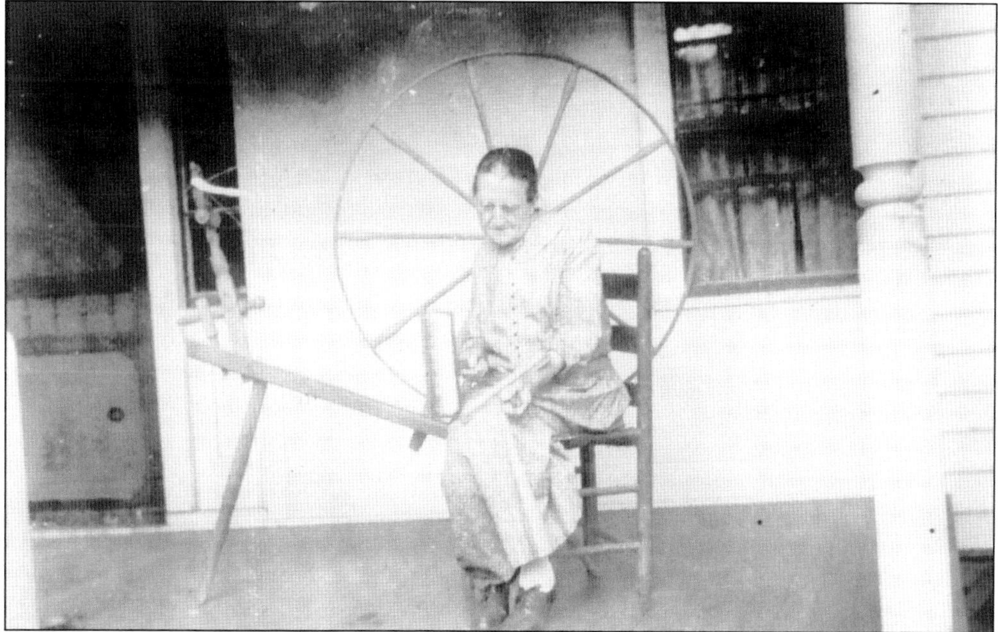

Mary Ritchie Dillard cards either cotton or wool before spinning on her porch, c. 1925. This may be the original Dillard House, which is well known today for its tradition of fine southern food. (Courtesy of Georgia Department of Archives and History.)

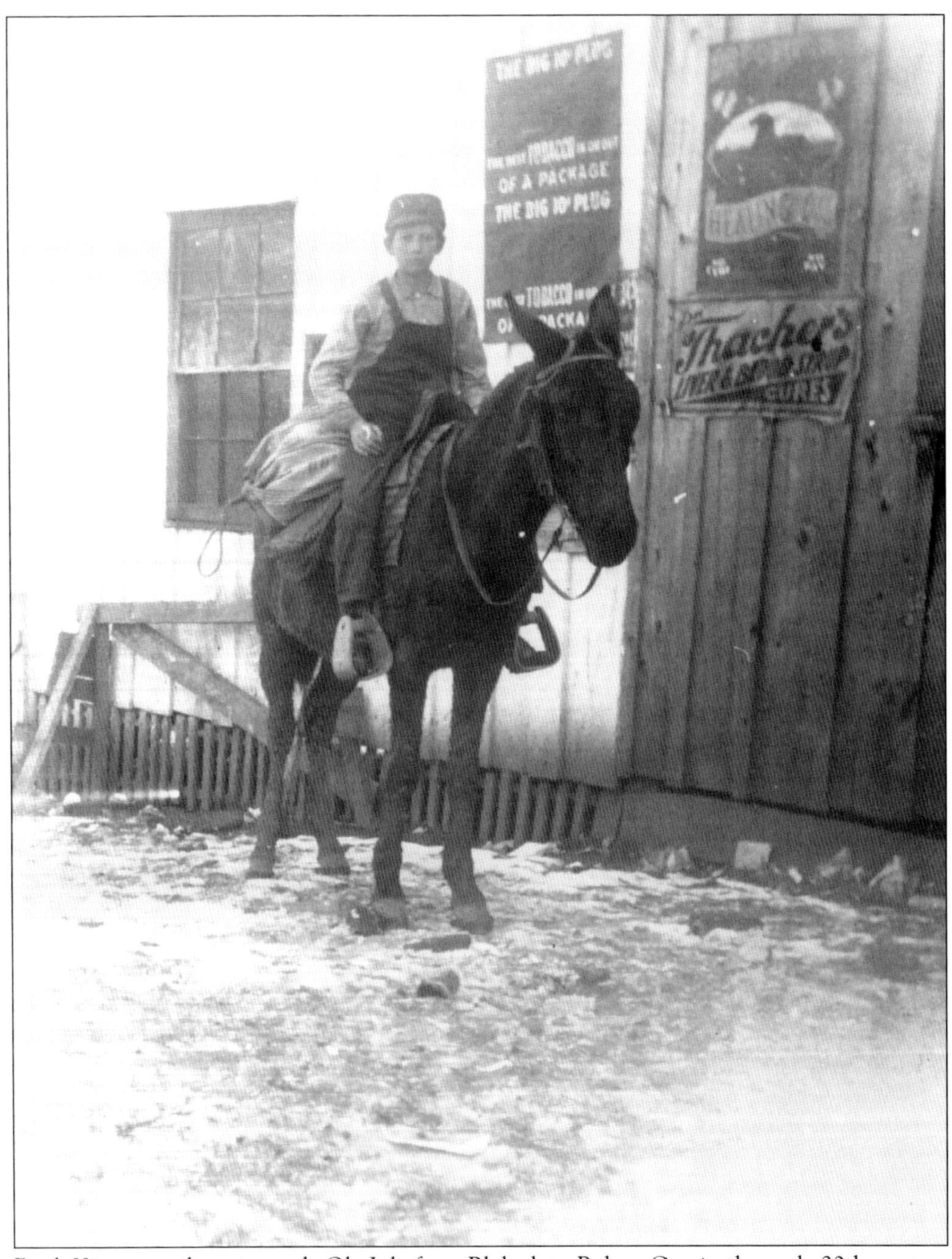

Dock King, a mail carrier, rode Ole Jule from Blalock to Rabun Gap in the early 20th century while on his deliveries. (Courtesy of Georgia Department of Archives and History.)

Three

Out of Necessity

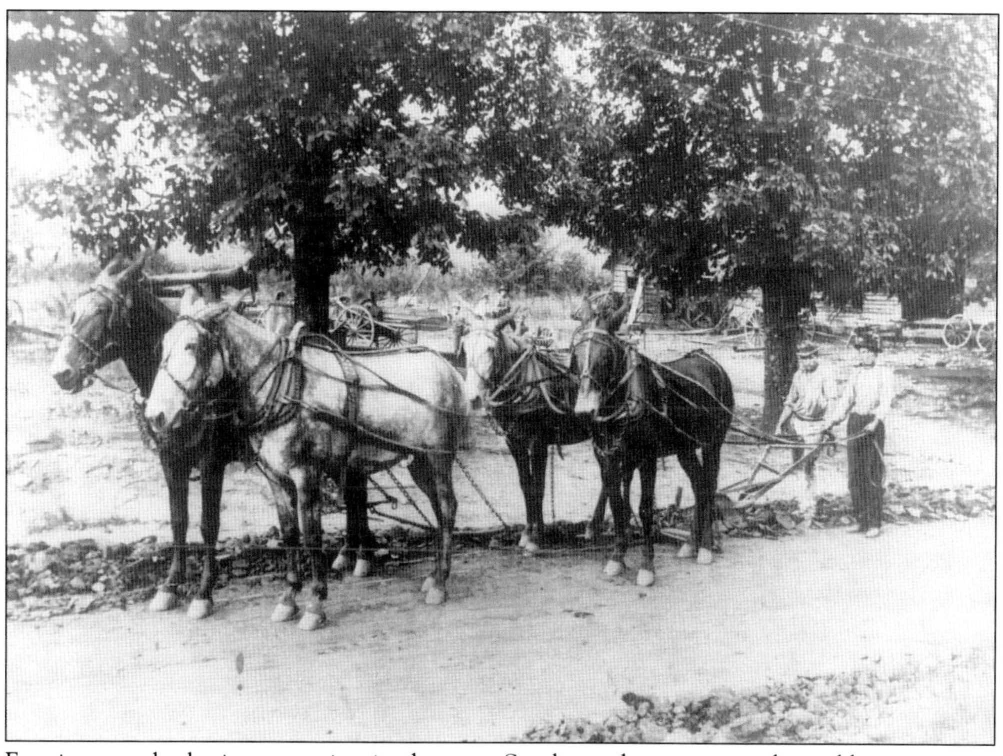

Farming was the basic occupation in the area. Staples such as corn, apples, cabbages, carrots, potatoes, onions, squash, and tomatoes fed the mountain people. During the heyday of the tourist era, farmers provided the hotels with plenty of fresh produce. These two men with their teams of mules do not lack for wagon wheels, as noted in the background, c. 1900. (Courtesy of Georgia Department of Archives and History.)

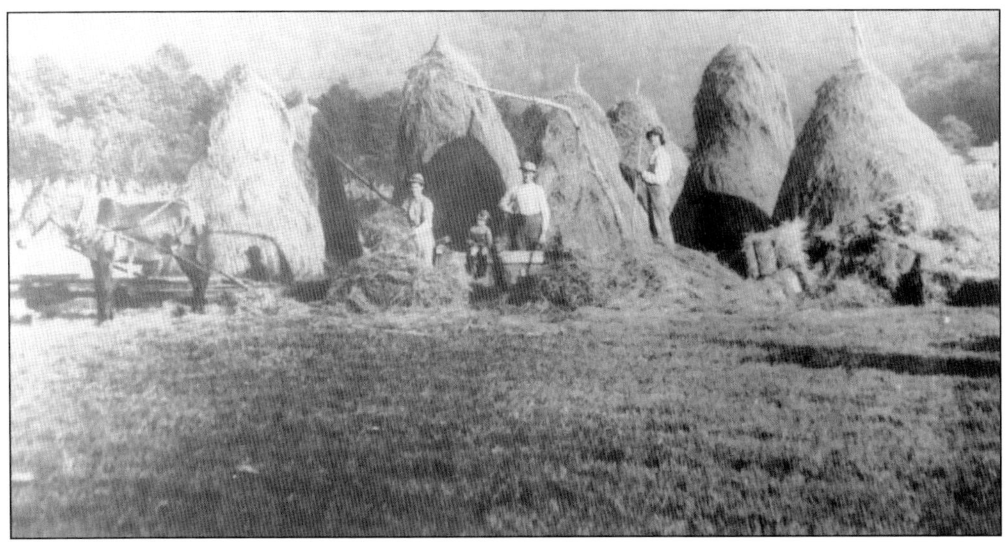

Farm laborers are pictured beside haystacks on the farm of the York House in Rabun County, probably in the 1890s. Hay fed the livestock throughout the winter months. (Courtesy of Georgia Department of Archives and History.)

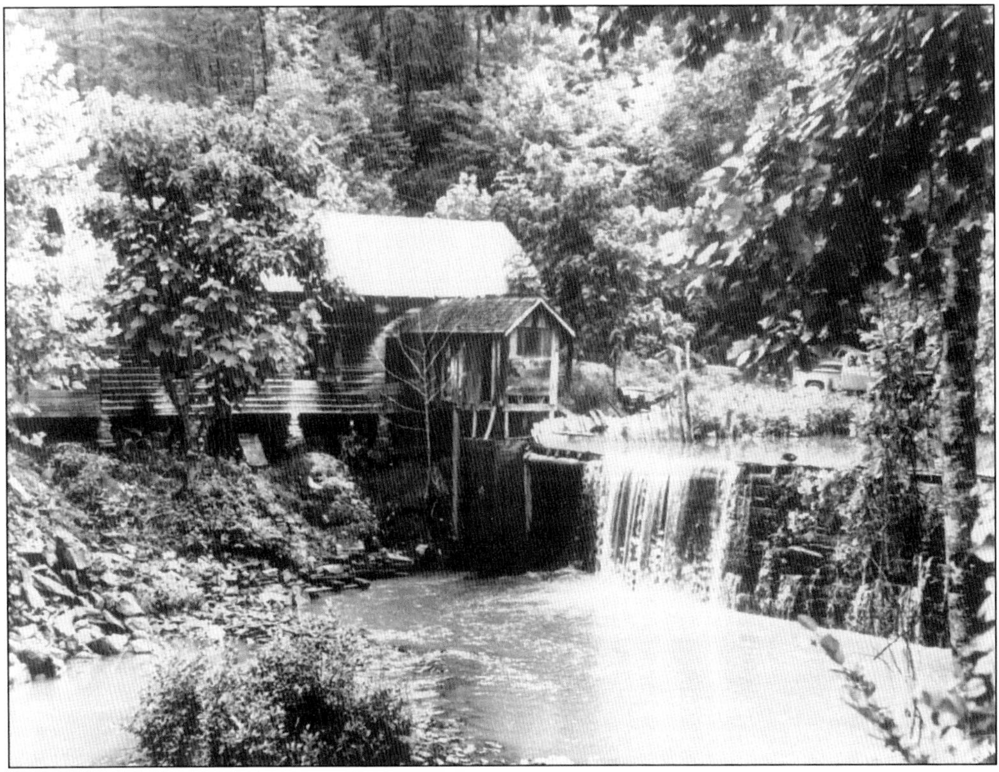

Wherever farming occurred, milling establishments were necessary. Gristmills for grinding grains, primarily corn, were a labor-saving device. These water-powered mills dammed creeks and rivers in many places in north Georgia. This image of an early gristmill located in Habersham County was made about 1950. (Courtesy of Georgia Department of Archives and History.)

Dr. Arnold and three out-of-state visitors observe gold mining by the placer method, which utilizes a long wooden box. Gold was first discovered in Rabun County prior to the Civil War on Dick's Creek, and was later mined on Moccasin and Wild Cat Creeks. The Civil War brought to a halt extensive gold mining and other types of industrial development in the county. (Courtesy of Georgia Department of Archives and History.)

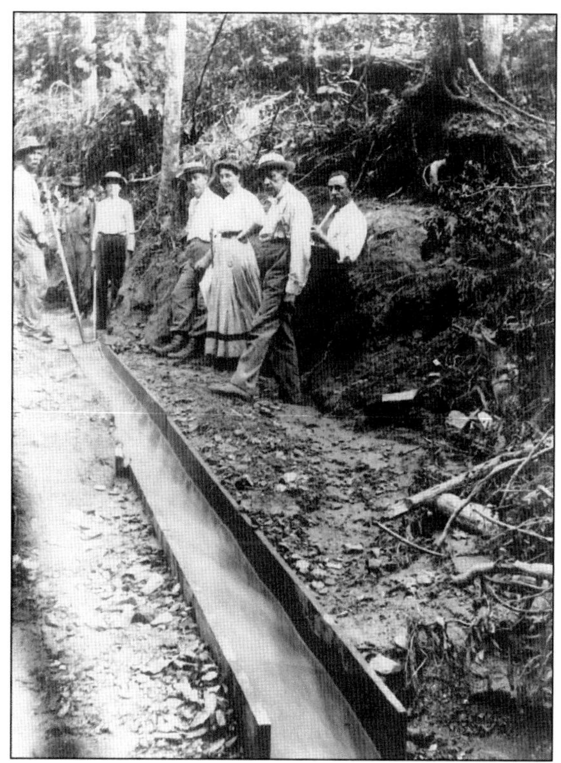

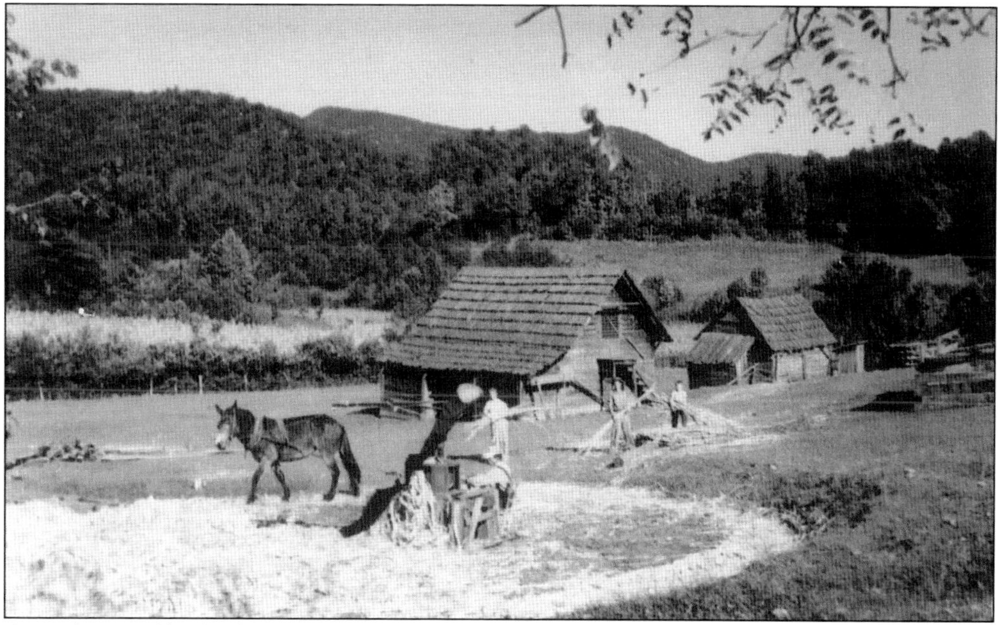

A sorghum mill, which ground sorghum into syrup, was traditionally powered by the farmer's mule. The mule provided the power to turn the stones that crushed the stalks of the sorghum plant. Some of this distinctively flavored syrup, commonly served on hot biscuits, was shipped out of the region. (Courtesy of Edwards Studio.)

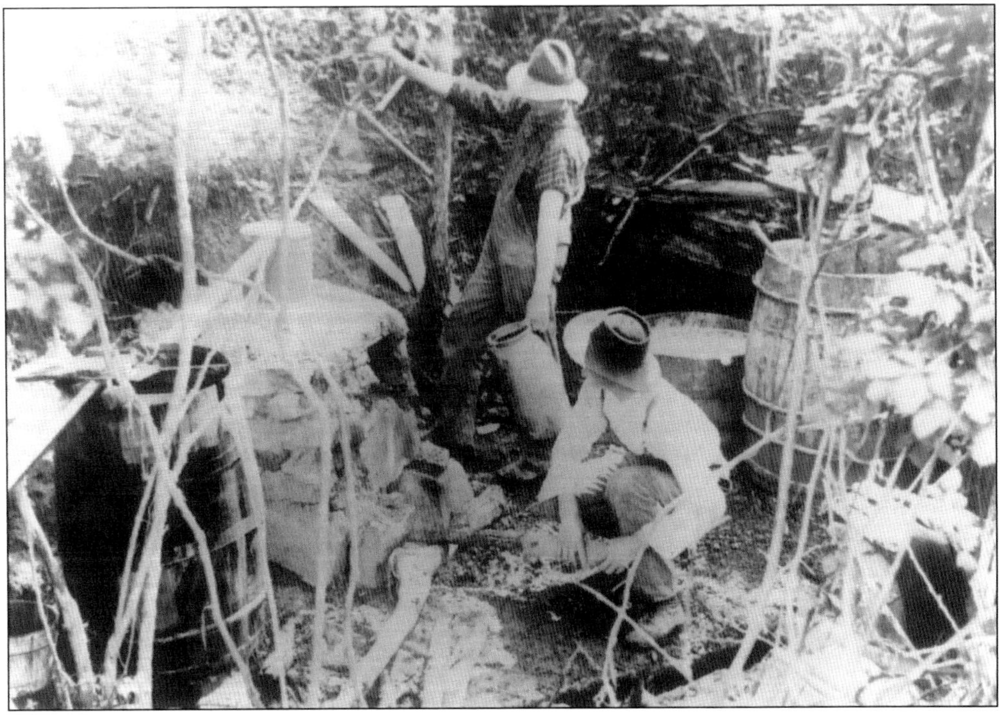

Moonshining, or the production of "white lightning" from corn, was practiced so widely it was practically a cottage industry in these hills. (Courtesy of Georgia Department of Archives and History.)

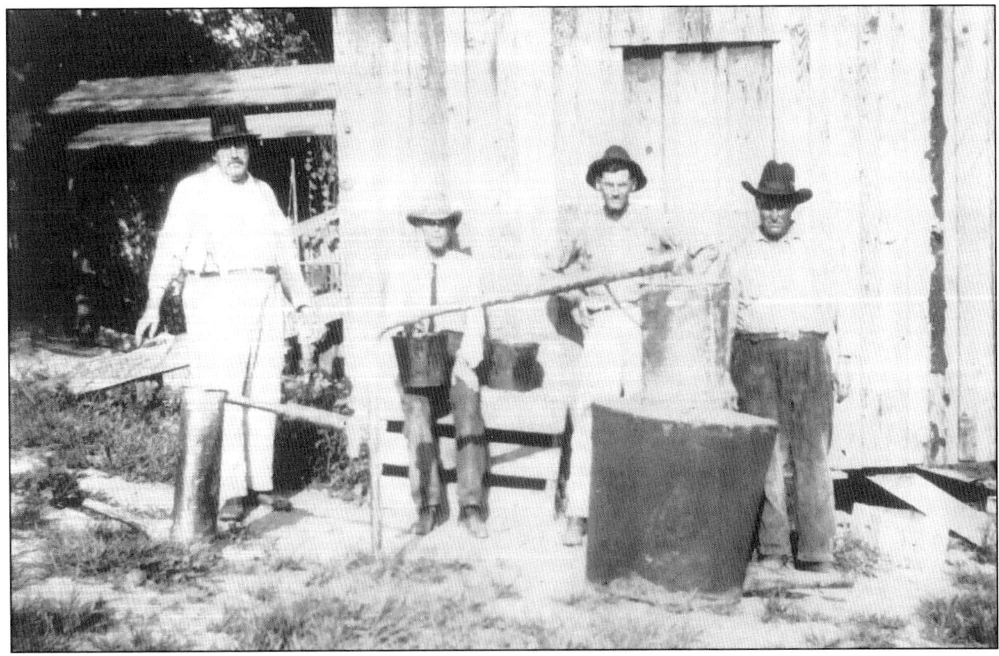

This is a moonshine still discovered in Rabun County. An advantage of turning corn into whiskey by distilling was that the corn crop was condensed for ease of transportation. (Courtesy of Ronald Vandiver.)

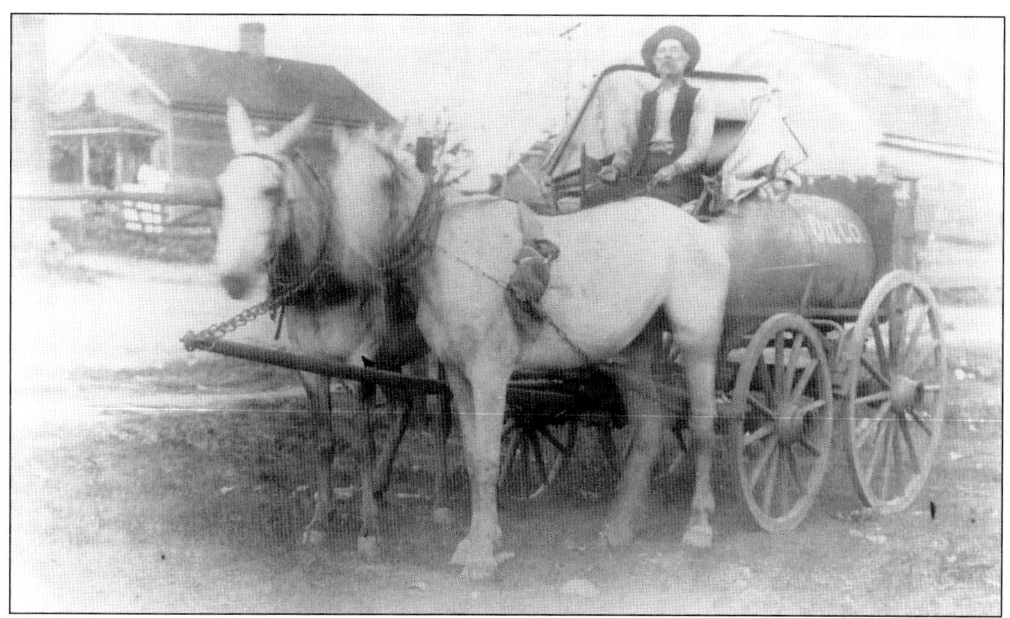

W.C. Hicks transported kerosene to mountain communities by way of wagon and mules. The holder in the wagon reads "Oil Co." The photograph was made *c.* 1900. (Courtesy of Georgia Department of Archives and History.)

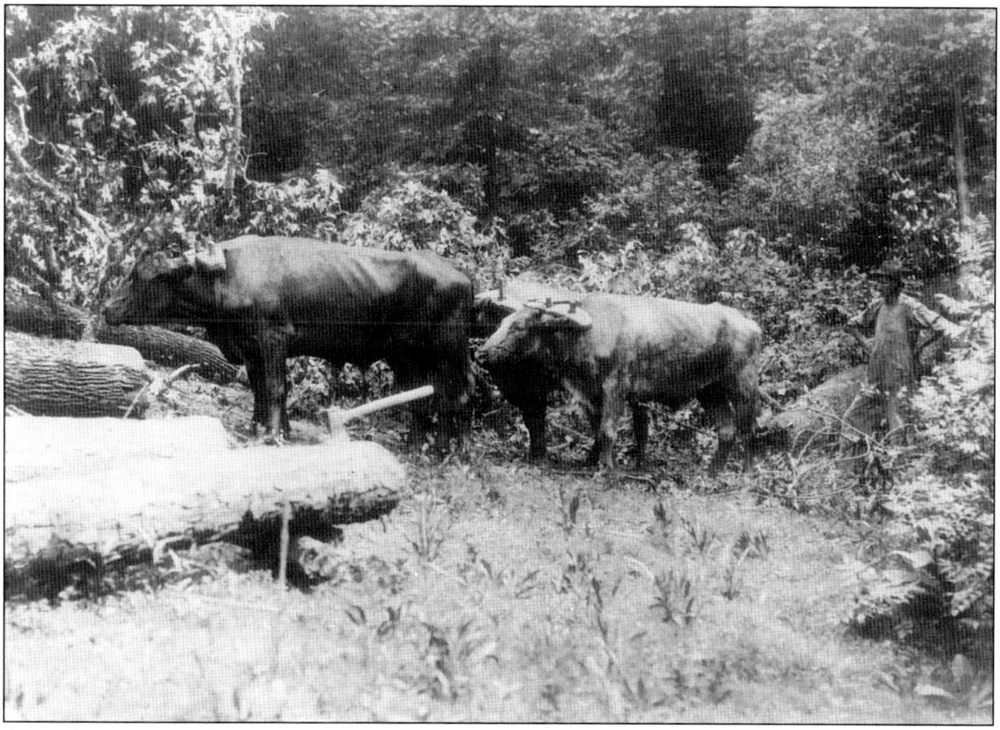

Oxen bring in timber for construction of Burton Dam, 1919. Georgia Railway and Power Company, later Georgia Power, became the major economic force in town during the construction of the dams. (Courtesy of Georgia Power Land Department Photo Archives.)

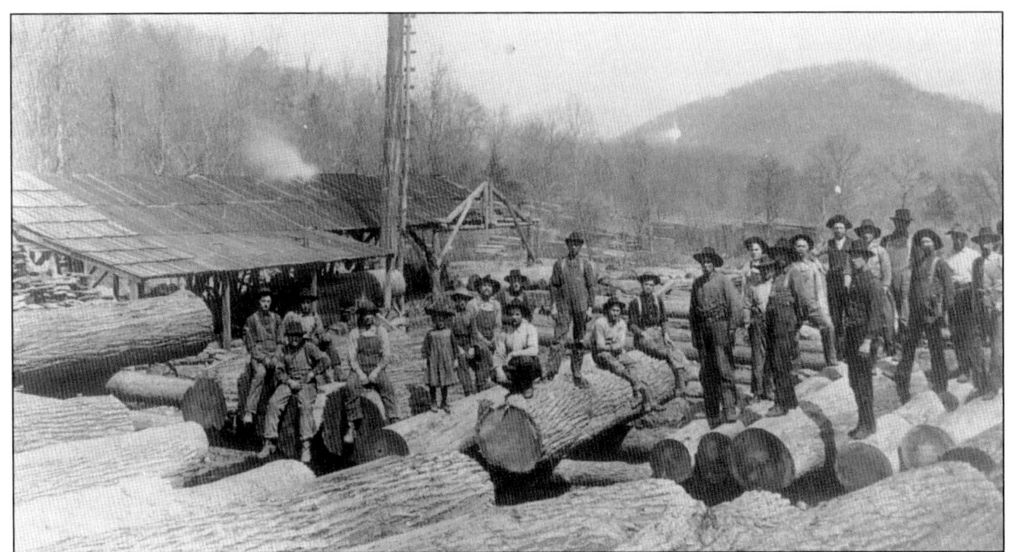

A large sawmill operation, shown here around 1900, temporarily halted production to allow workmen to be photographed on huge logs amassed in the yard. (Courtesy of Georgia Department of Archives and History.)

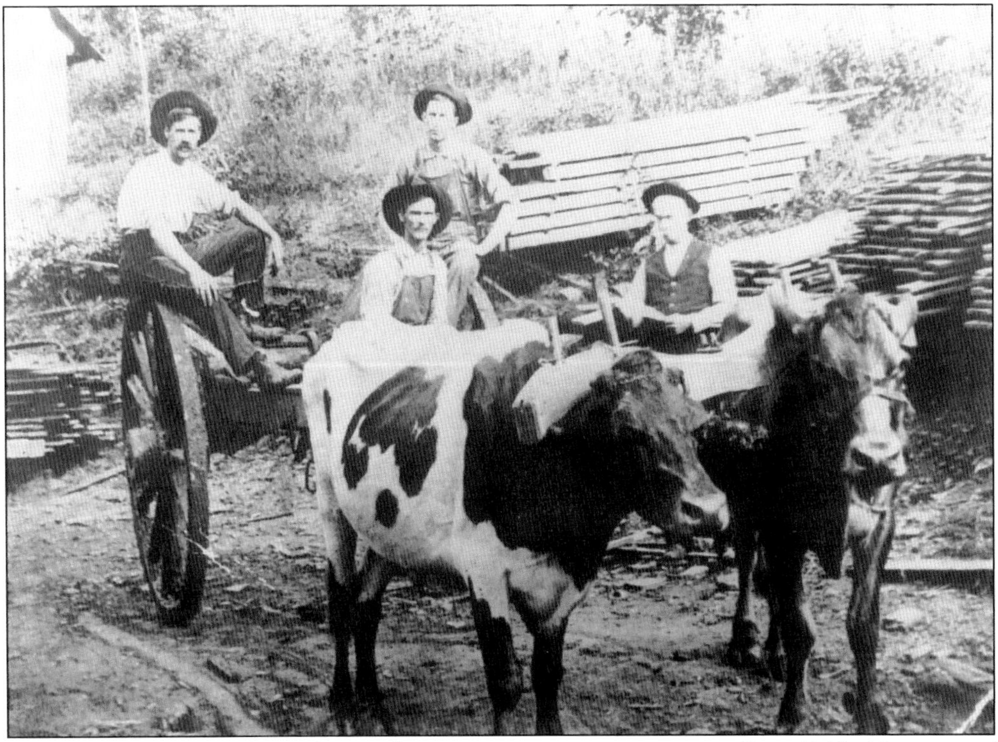

Cattle were used to pull lumber in this mountain community sawmill, *c.* 1915. (Courtesy of Georgia Department of Archives and History.)

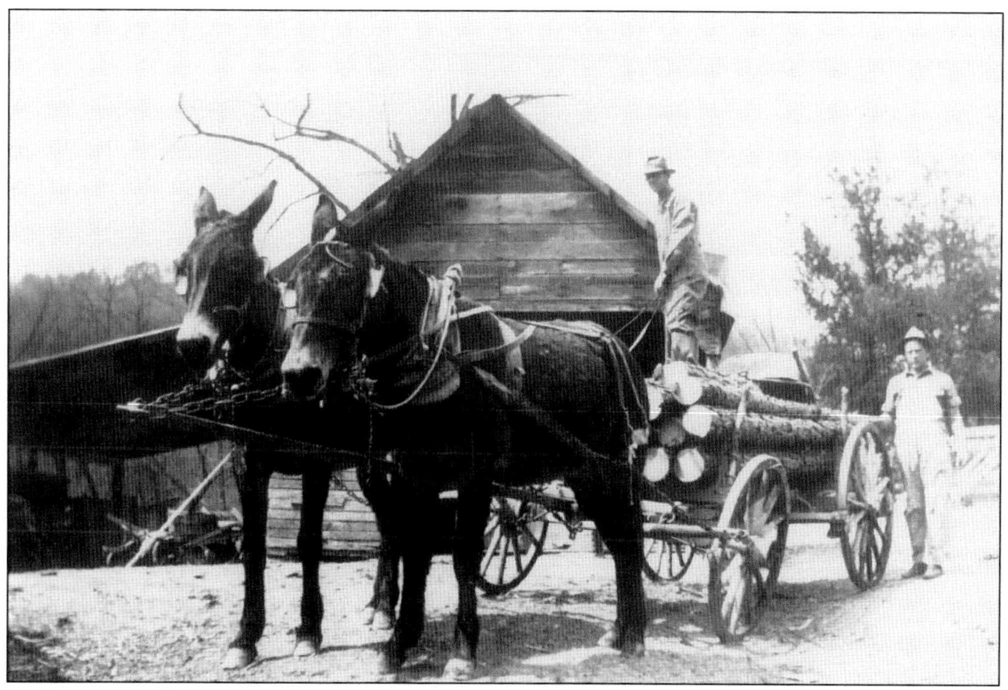

Carl Henry and Marion Kilby haul logs in this image from about 1930. Logging and lumbering benefited from the construction of the railroad, becoming one of the largest industries in the area. (Courtesy of Georgia Department of Archives and History.)

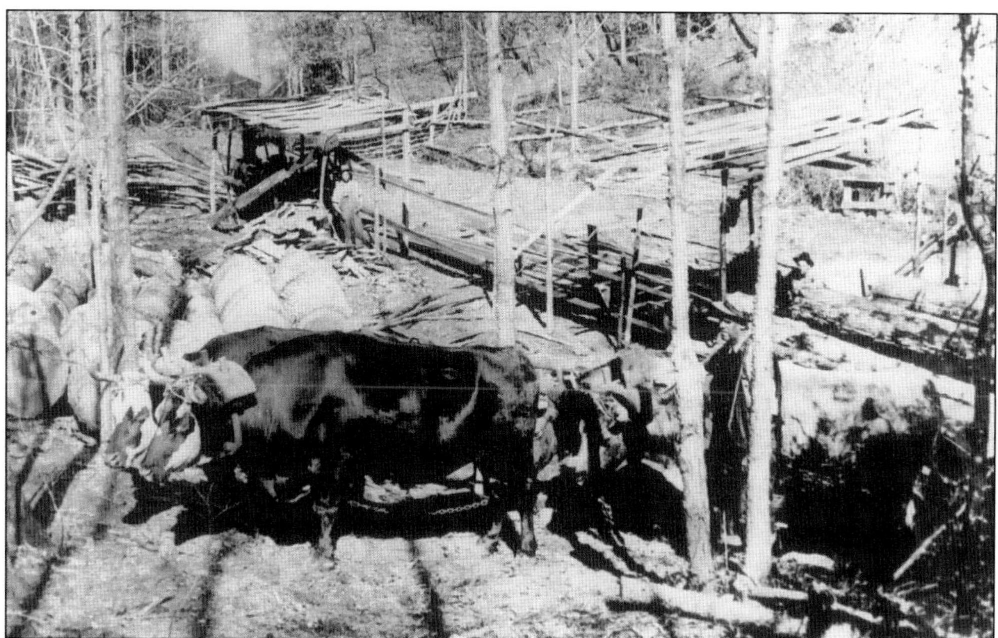

This is a Rabun County sawmill adjacent to Warwoman Dell, c. 1929. Powerful oxen moved the logs. Down the hill, right, is the finished lumber. (Courtesy of Georgia Department of Archives and History.)

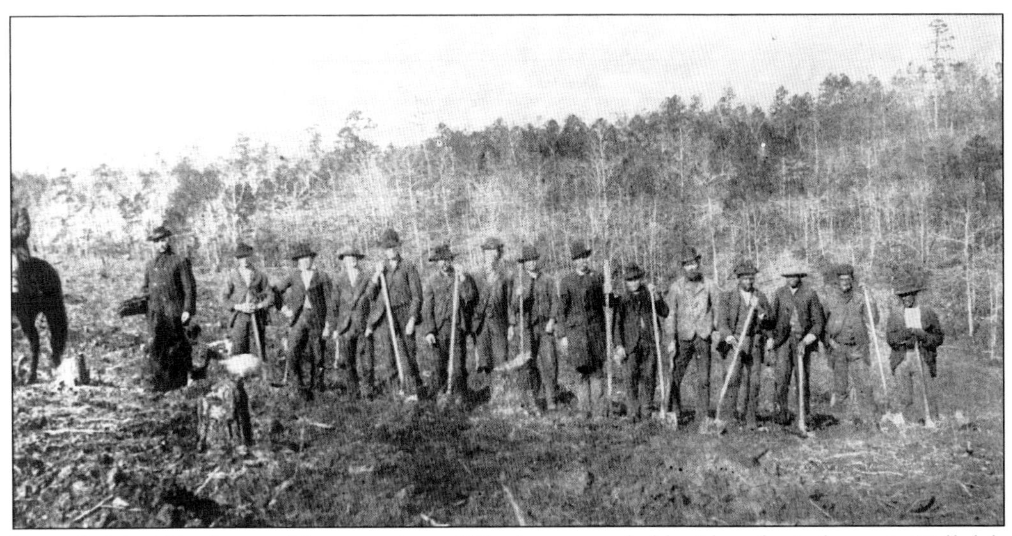

Louis B. Magid had one of the most incredible, but unworkable, ideas for industry in Tallulah Falls. Shortly after the turn of the twentieth century, he purchased approximately 3,500 acres for a silk plantation. In this publicity view, workers are shown ready to plant mulberry trees for Magid's Seri-Culture and Manufacturing Company. Magid is on horseback at left. (Courtesy of Archives, Library and Information Center, Georgia Institute of Technology.)

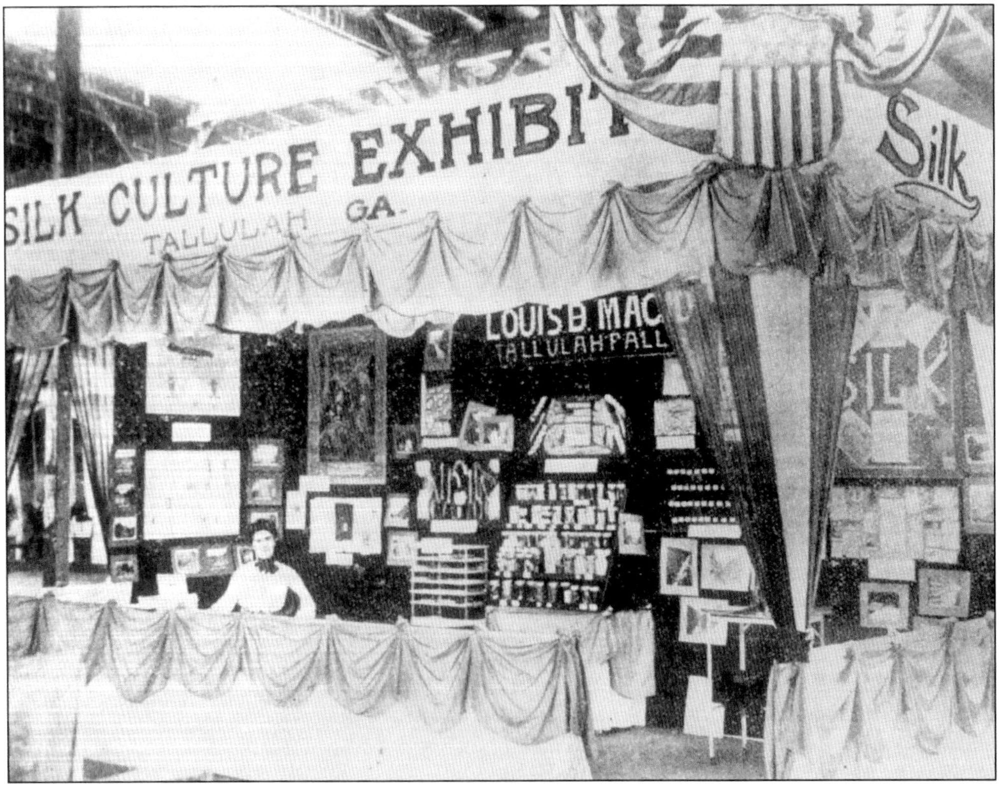

Magid widely advertised his enterprise in order to interest stockholders. He held an exhibit booth at a fair in New York c. 1905 to promote his venture. (Courtesy of Archives, Library and Information Center, Georgia Institute of Technology.)

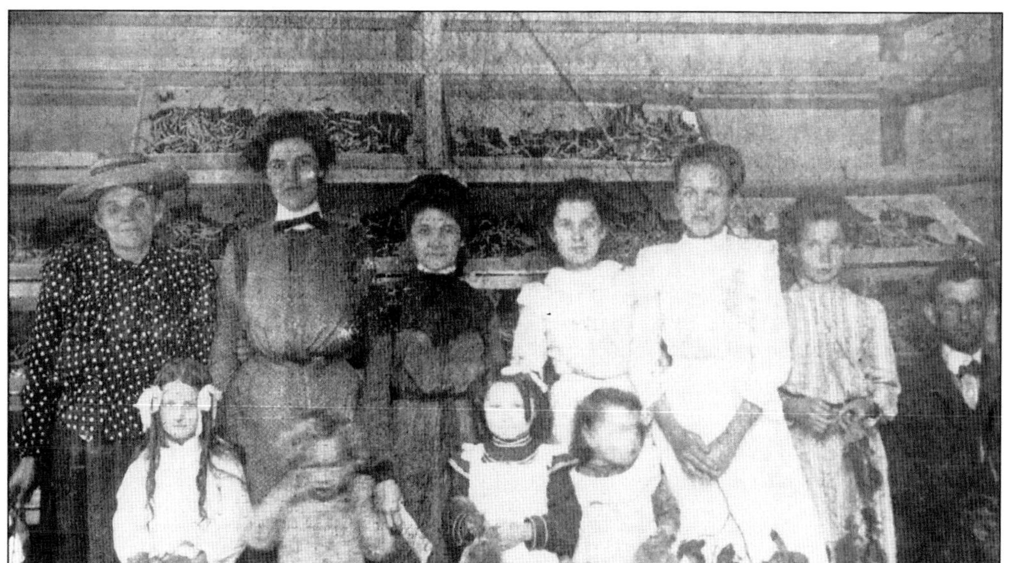

In this publicity photograph, leaf gatherers and feeders are shown adjacent to the silkworms, with Magid on the right. Magid's plan was to move in a colony of people from northern Italy to raise silk. (Courtesy of Archives, Library and Information Center, Georgia Institute of Technology.)

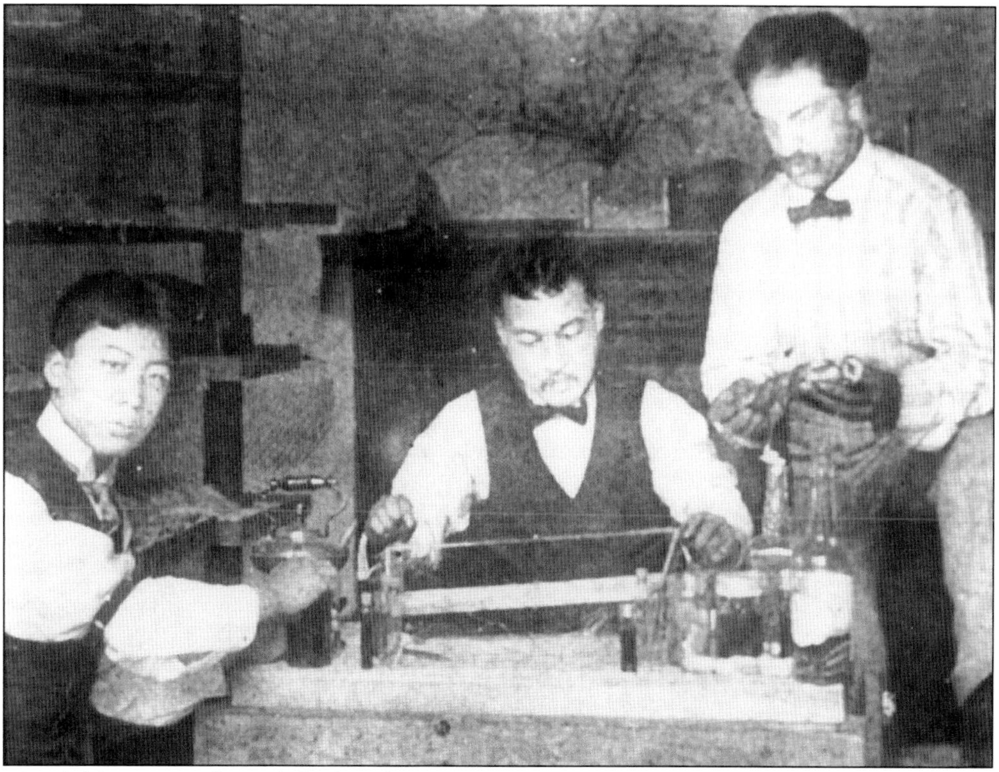

Magid (shown on the right) also planned to import technicians from Asia to assist in silk production. (Courtesy of Archives, Library and Information Center, Georgia Institute of Technology.)

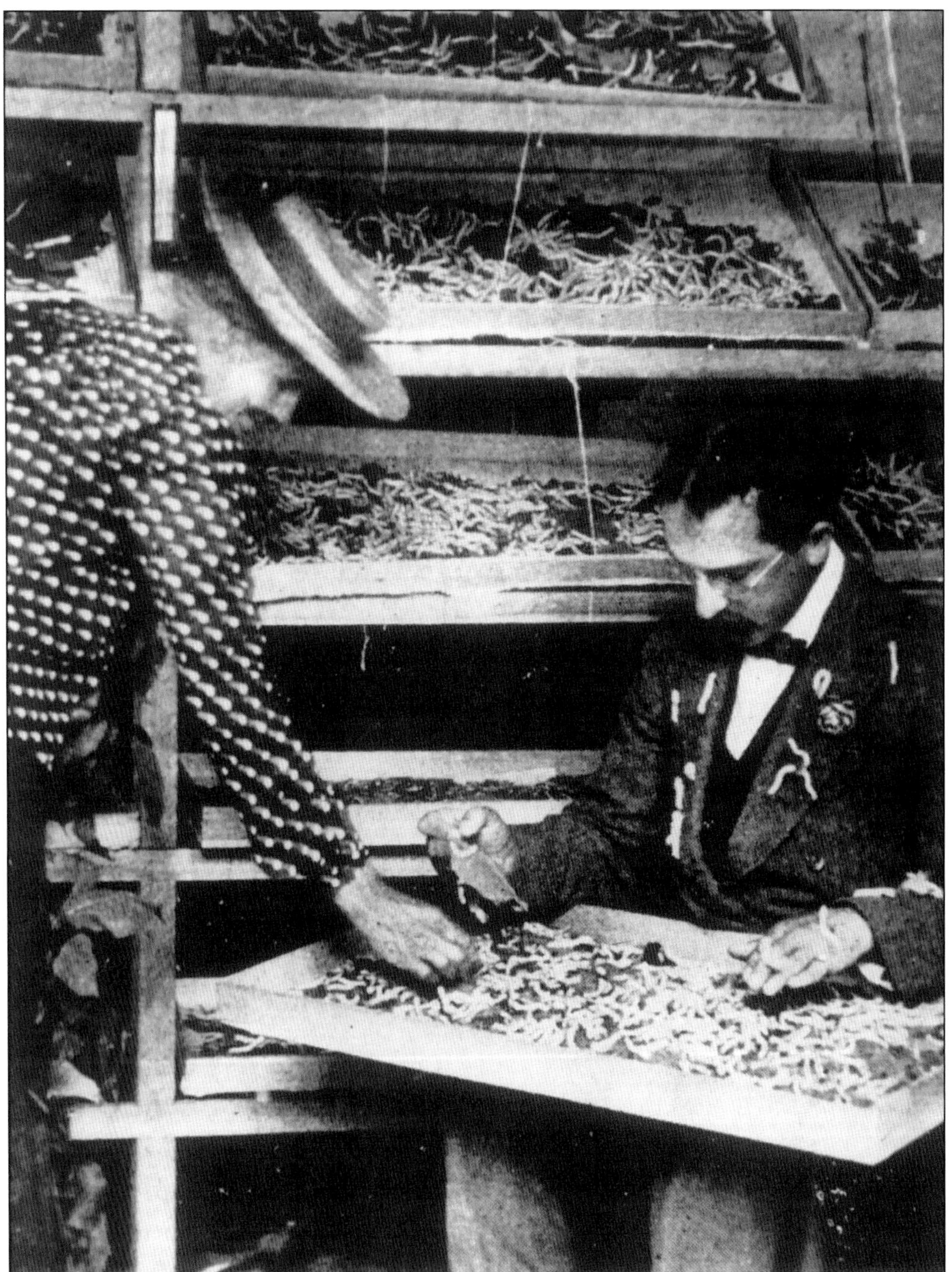

Louis Magid and a feeder are inspecting silk worms at close range at a cocoonery. Magid was a visionary and a dreamer, but his plans did not materialize. Silk manufacturing never thrived in Tallulah Falls or anywhere in Georgia. (Courtesy of Archives, Library and Information Center, Georgia Institute of Technology.)

Four

The Short-line Connection

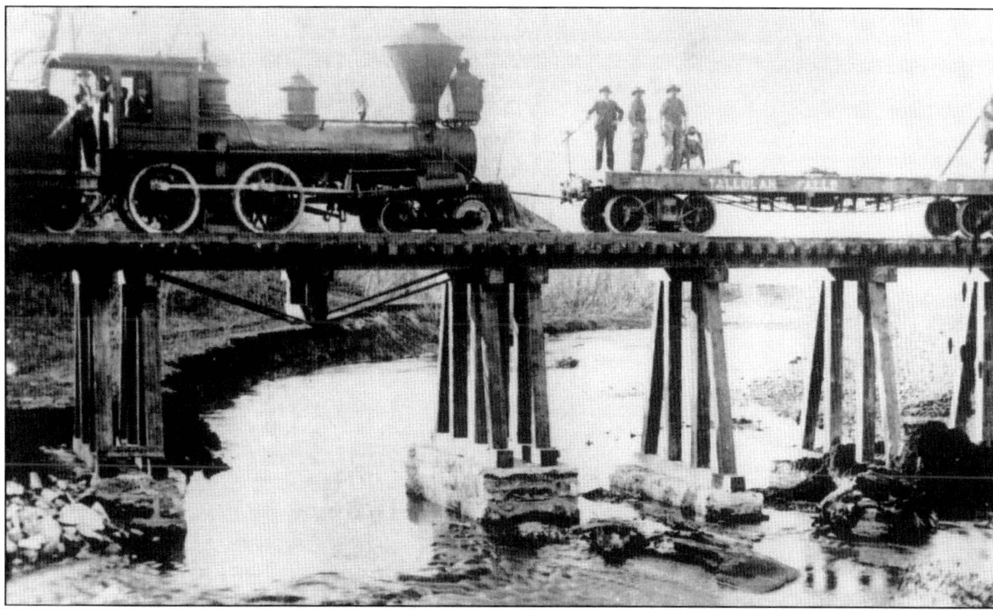

A Tallulah Falls Railroad locomotive and flatcar are shown on the railroad trestle near Dillard, Georgia, *c.* 1910. The mountainous country of northeast Georgia and western North Carolina was a remote region prior to the coming of the railroad. In those early days, directions for travel to Rabun County were: "Go one day by railroad, the next day by horse and buggy, a third day on horseback, a fourth day on foot, and then on all fours until you climbed a tree, and when you fell out, you'd be in Rabun County."—*Sketches of Rabun County History*. (Courtesy of The Foxfire Fund, Inc.)

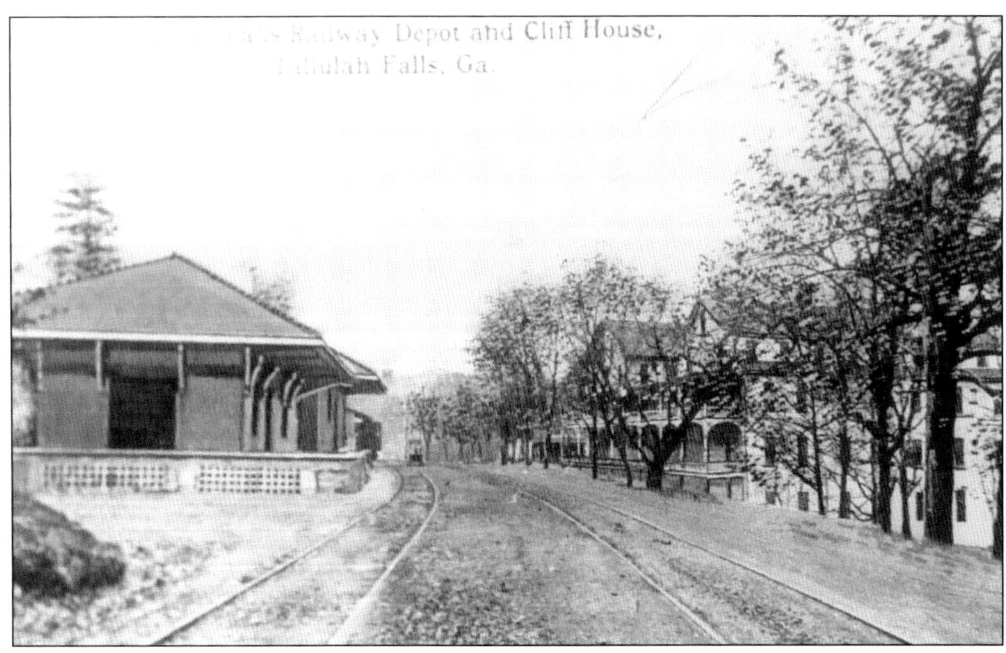

In this image, the Tallulah Falls Railroad depot is on the left and the Cliff House Hotel is on the right. The convenience of rail transportation directly to the hotel later caused its demise, as sparks from a wood-burning locomotive started a fire which burned the hotel to the ground in 1937. (Courtesy of Tallulah Falls School.)

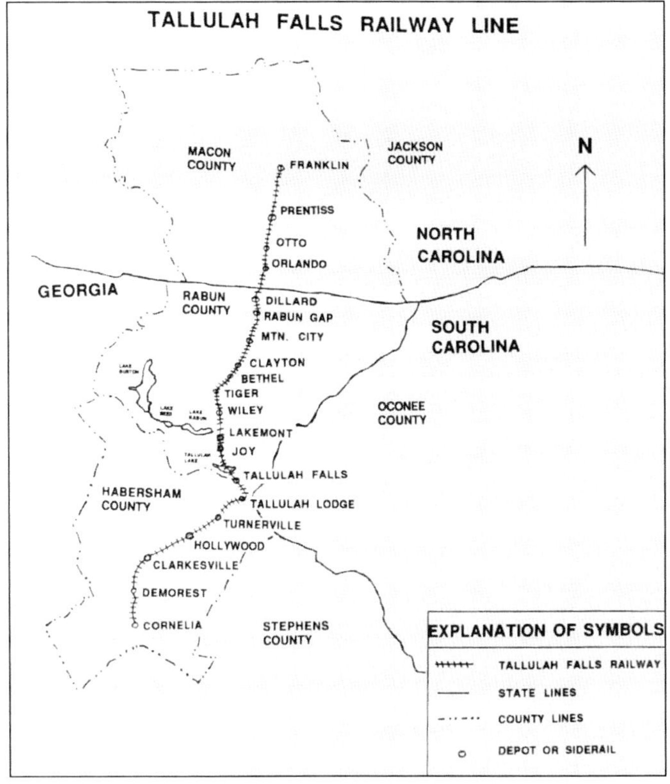

The Tallulah Falls railway line was a short-line railroad originating in Cornelia, Georgia and terminating in Franklin, North Carolina. It served the people of Habersham and Rabun Counties, Georgia and Macon County, North Carolina for 54 years. The railroad touched most facets of people's lives in the surrounding territory along the route. (Courtesy of The Foxfire Fund, Inc.)

A short-line railroad had limited miles of track and was dependent upon larger railroads for the transfer of freight and passengers. In 1907 the railroad was extended to Franklin, North Carolina. Mrs. Edmondson (standing) and Mrs. Riley are shown in the doorway of the car at Franklin in 1913. (Courtesy of Gary Doster.)

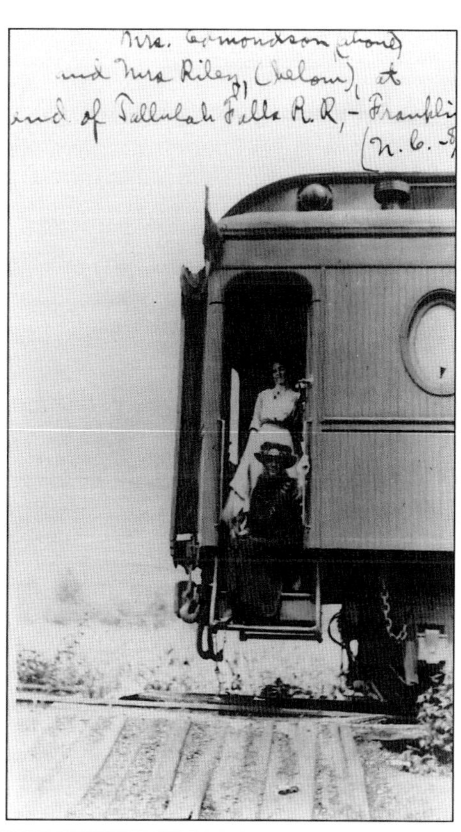

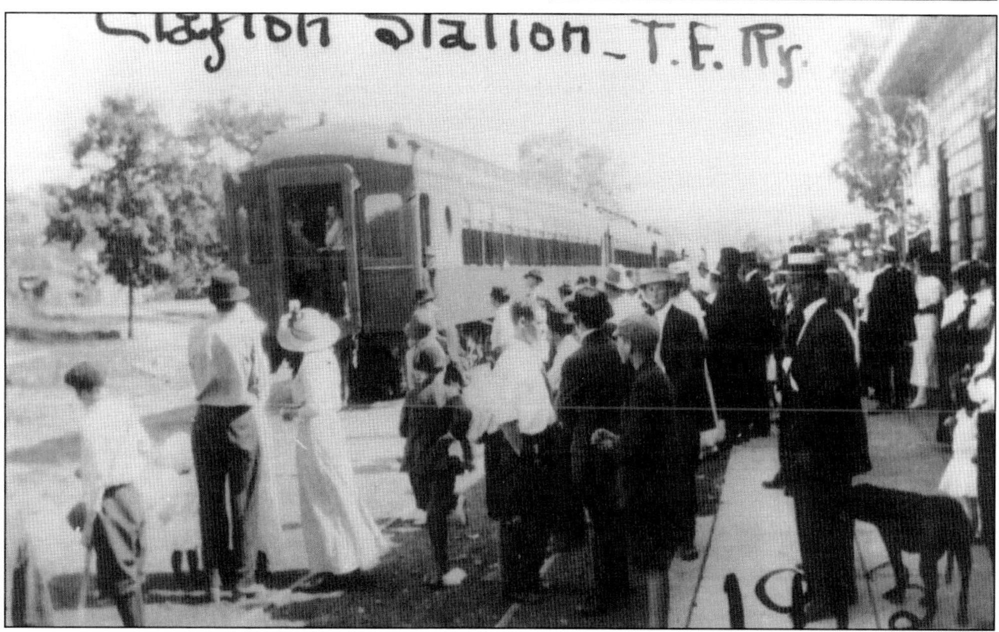

Crowds, including children and pets, wait at the Clayton Station of the Tallulah Falls Railroad in 1913. The arrival of a train was an event. The Tallulah Falls Railroad was the major link to the outside world for people of the area. (Courtesy of Georgia Department of Archives and History.)

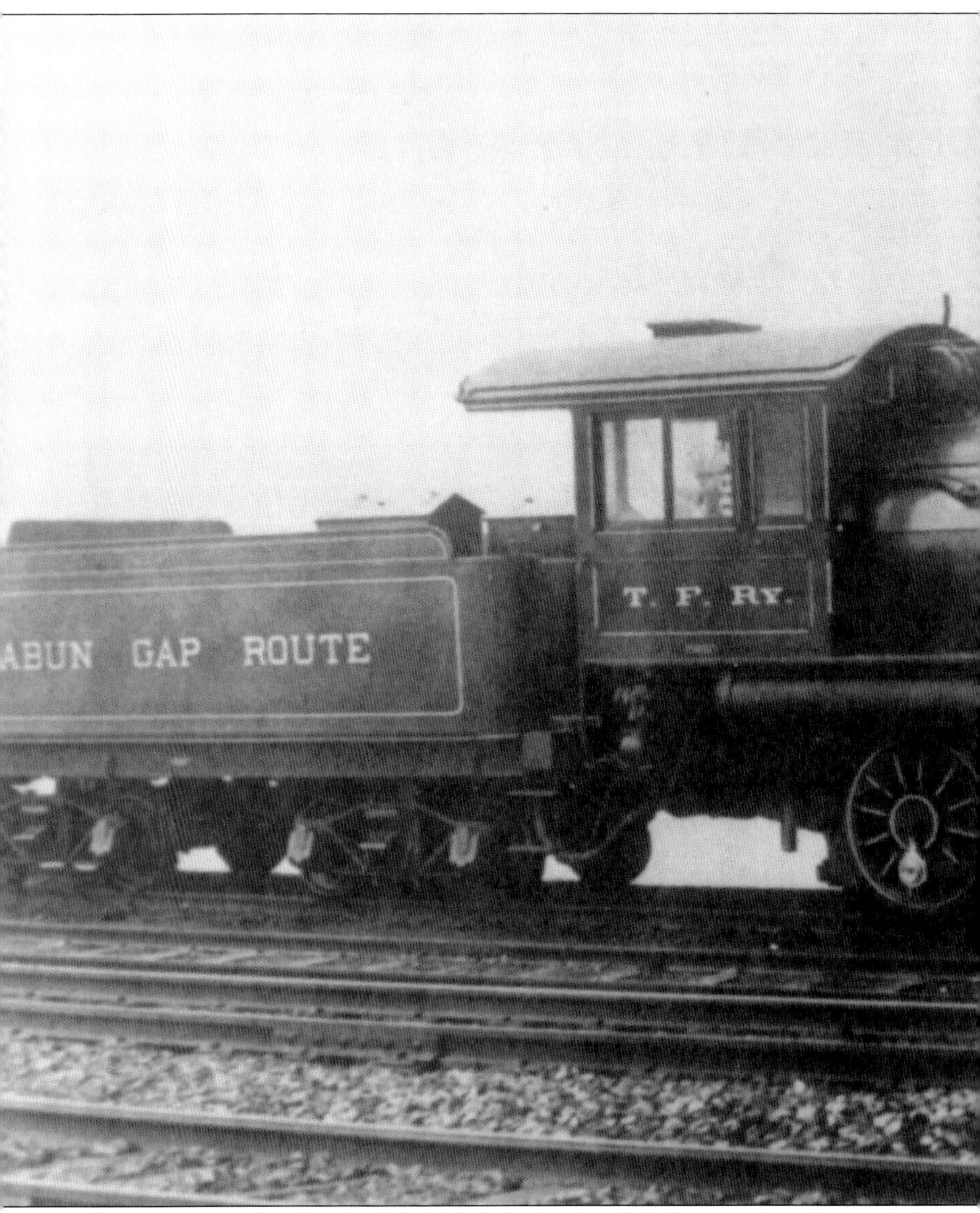

This is engine number 75 of the Tallulah Falls Railroad, *c.* 1905. Plans for this railroad, which originated in Cornelia, Georgia, included an extension to Bryson City, North Carolina to

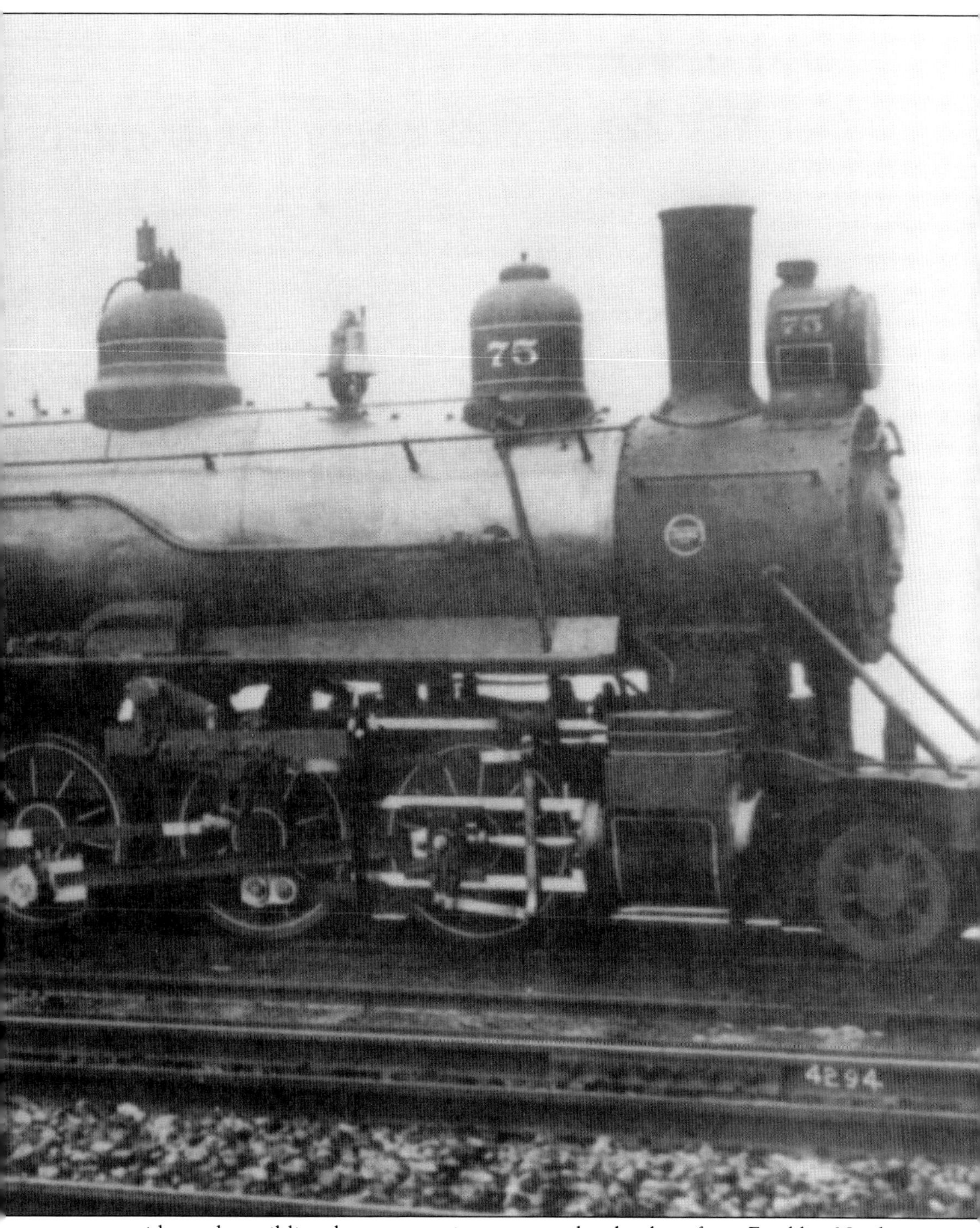

connect with another rail line, but construction was completed only as far as Franklin, North Carolina, and it became a dead-end line. (Courtesy of Edwards Studio.)

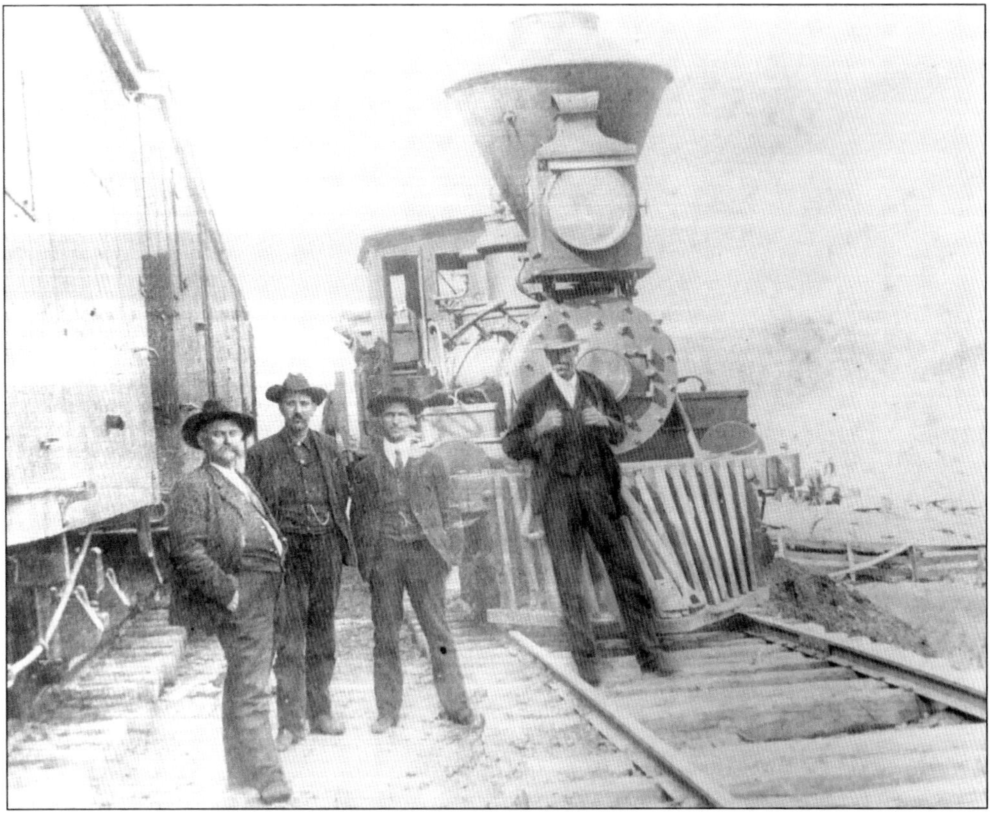

Rabun County Sheriff Tom Carver stands with a group in the railroad yard of the Tallulah Falls Railroad in 1906. From left to right are: Hugh Pickens, Sheriff Carver, Frank Singleton, and Tom McWhorter (far right, in front of the locomotive's cow-catcher). (Courtesy of Georgia Department of Archives and History.)

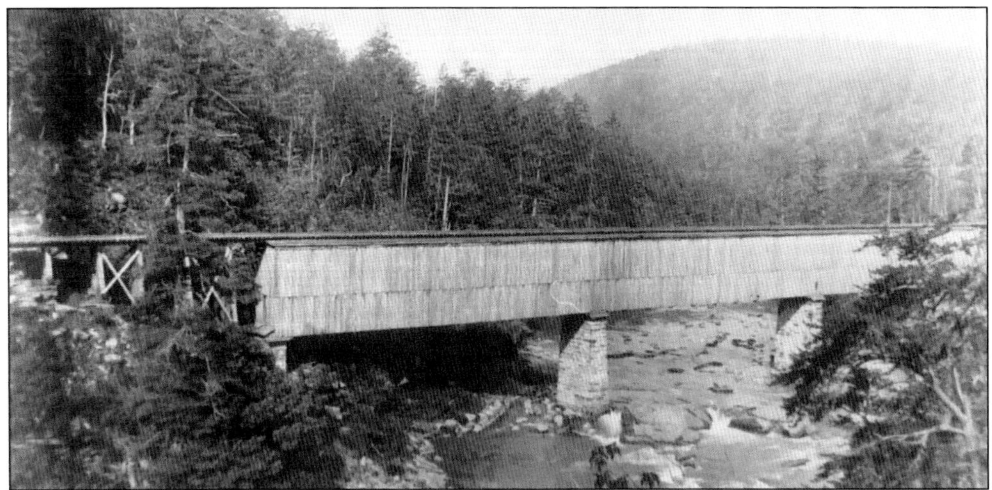

Pictured is the original Tallulah Falls Railroad bed and bridge prior to 1913. When Georgia Railway and Power Company constructed the Tallulah Falls power plant to generate electricity, the railroad bridge was raised by the power company to make way for filling of the lake basin. (Courtesy of Georgia Power Land Department Photo Archives.)

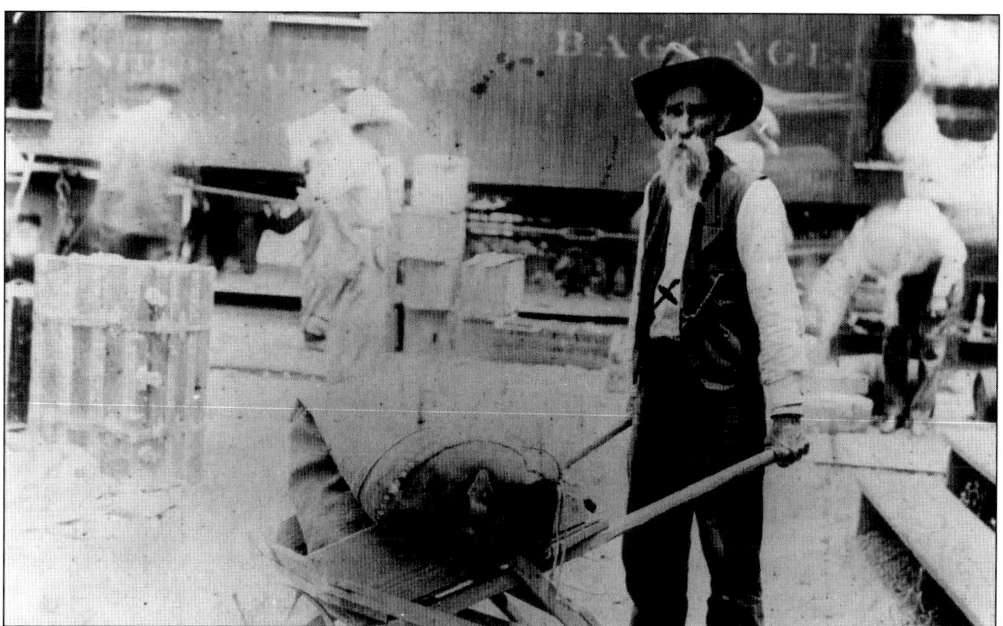

Wiley Pitts was the mail carrier for Tallulah Falls. Using a wooden wheelbarrow, he collected the mail at the depot. The train delivered the mail on a daily basis. (Courtesy of Georgia Department of Archives and History.)

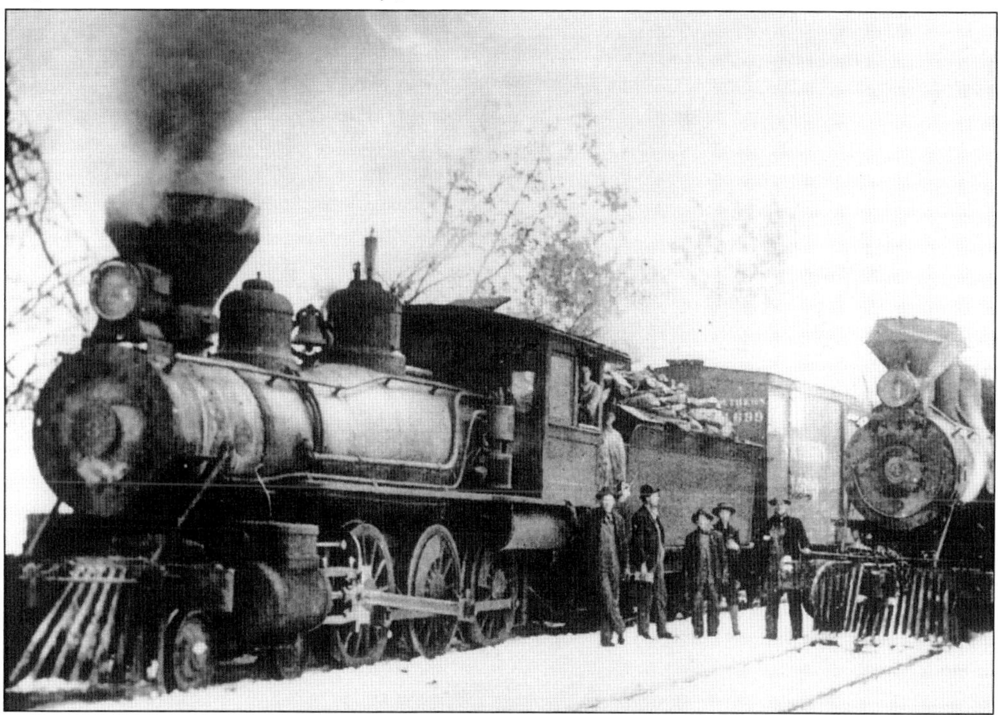

The photograph shows an operating steam locomotive with wood car attached, plus the crew of the Tallulah Falls Railroad. The early locomotives were wood-burning engines which emitted clouds of black smoke. Note the railroad bell and steam whistle atop the engine. (Courtesy of The Foxfire Fund, Inc.)

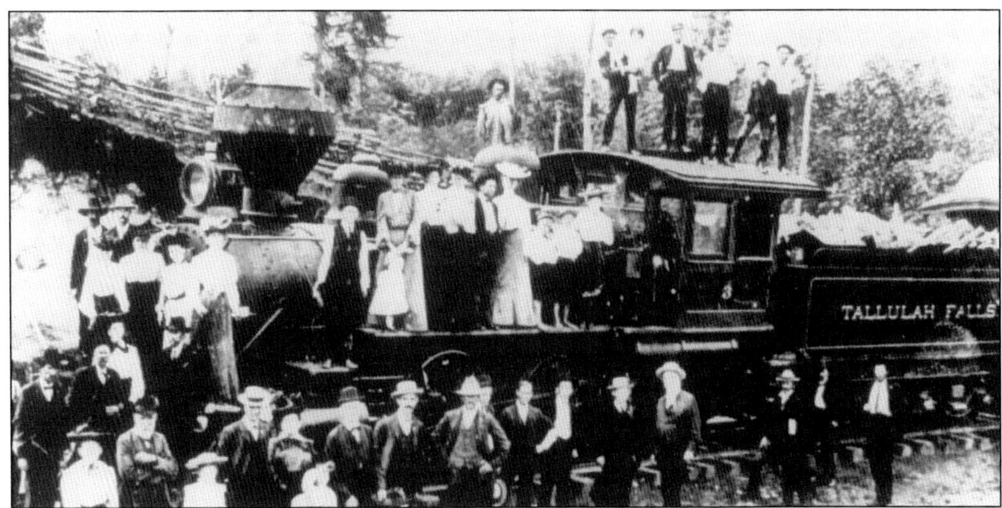

Tourists would often ride the Southern Railroad from Atlanta to Cornelia and change to the Tallulah Falls Railroad for outings. This image shows an excursion train from Cornelia to Tiger in 1904 on the Tallulah Falls Railroad track. (Courtesy of Tallulah Falls School.)

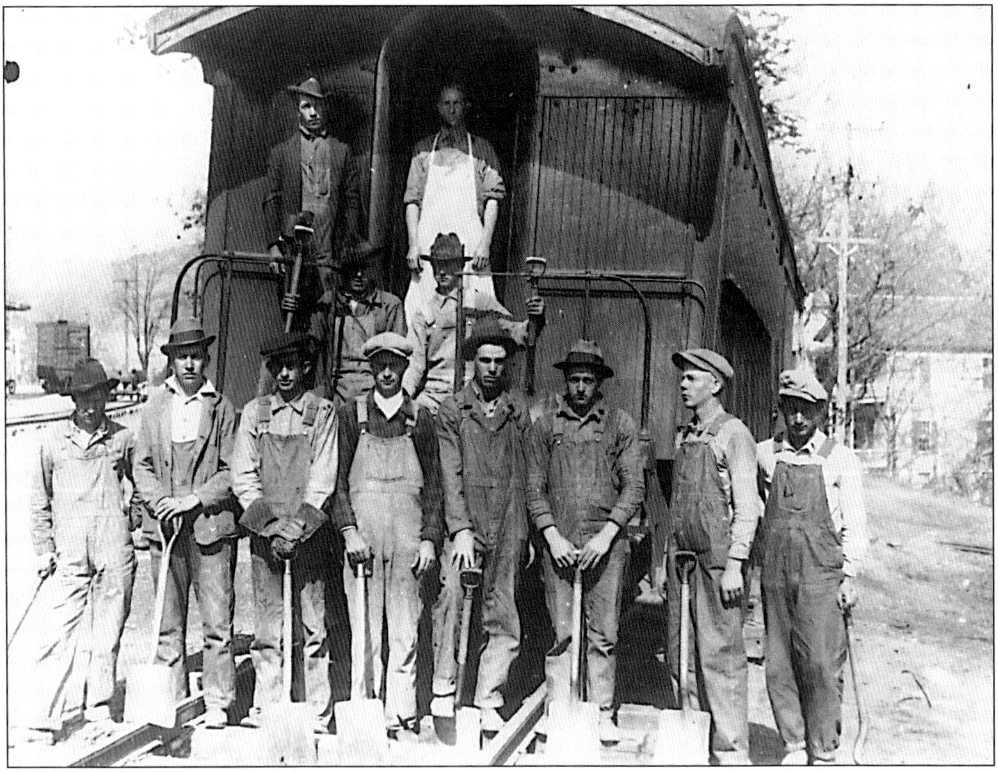

A great deal of the construction work on the Tallulah Falls Railroad was physically demanding. A ten-hour day of backbreaking labor was not uncommon. The cook is in the doorway and laborers below, probably the bridge crew, in this photograph. A shanty car, later called a work or camp car, was where a railroad gang stayed and lived while building the rail bed and laying tracks. (Courtesy of The Foxfire Fund, Inc.)

This timetable is from the *Clarkesville Advertiser* which printed the train schedule for the Tallulah Falls Railroad each week, as did other area newspapers. The train ran daily between Cornelia, Georgia and Franklin, North Carolina with a total of 20 stops. (Courtesy of The Foxfire Fund, Inc.)

United States Railroad Administration

W. G. McADOO, Director General of Railroads

TALLULAH FALLS RAILROAD

TIME TABLE NO. 17

Effective Sunday, Oct. 20th. 1918, 6:00 A. M., Eastern Time.

SOUTHBOUND			Eastern Standard Time	NORTH BOUND		
5 2d class	11 1st class		STATIONS.	12 1st class	6 2d class	Capacity of Tracks in Cars
Tuesday Thu. Sat.	Daily	Mi		Daily	Monday Wed. Fri	
A. M.	P. M.		Lv. Ar.	P. M.	P. M.	
8 00	2 10	58	Franklin	1 55	3 30	71
8 40	s 2 23	53	Prentiss	s 1 39	3 00	19
9 05	s 2 38	48	Otto	s 1 24	2 38	23
....	f 2 50	43	Orlando, N. C.	f 1 10	....	
9 40	s 2 56	42	Dillard, Ga.	s 1 05	1 50	17
9 45	s 3 00	41	Rabun Gap	s 1 00	1 35	52
10 05	s 3 09	38	Mountain City	s 12 50	1 15	16
10 30	s 3 19	35	Clayton	s 12 20	12 55	28
....	f 3 24	33	Bethel	f 12 10	....	
10 50	s 3 29	32	Tiger	s 12 12	12 12	17
10 10	s 3 43	28	Wiley	s 12 00	11 40	9
10 20	s 3 48	27	Lakemont	s 11 54	11 35	8
11 48	f 3 52	25	Joy	f 11 48	11 25	19
12 15	s 4 06	21	Tallulah Falls	s 11 36	11 00	21
12 20	s 4 11	20	Tallulah Lodge	s 11 31	10 45	18
....	f 4 16	19	Tallulah Park	f 11 28	....	3
12 40	s 4 26	16	Turnerville	s 11 19	10 20	15
12 55	s 4 34	13	Hollywood	s 11 10	10 00	8
....	f 4 39	11	Anandale	f 11 04	....	4
....	f 4 44	9	Hills	f 10 59	....	5
1 30	4 52	8	Clarksville	s 10 56	9 33	42
....	f 4 56	6	Habersham	f 10 48	....	5
1 50	s 5 03	5	Demorest	s 10 44	8 30	25
2 25	5 18	0	Cornelia	10 30	8 00	126
A. M. 5	P. M. 11		Ar. Lv.	A. M. 12	A. M 6	

All Northbound trains have right of track over trains of same class in opposite direction.

S—Regular stop. F—Stops only when flagged.

Riverside M. P. 50, Norton M. P. 45, York M. P. 40, Parkers M. P. 34, Bovard M. P. 30, Burton Jct., M. P. 28 1-2 not shown on Time Card, are Flag stops for trains 11 and 12.

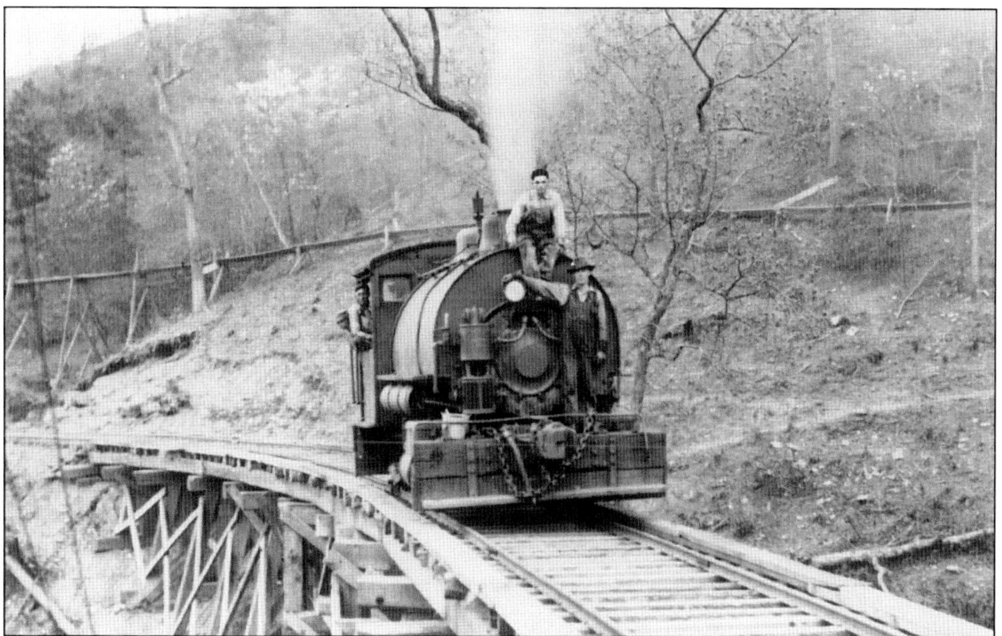

This locomotive, on the Burton spur of the Tallulah Falls Railroad, is enroute to pick up railcars loaded with construction materials. Machinery and materials were transported on spur lines built by the power company in order to access hydroelectric plant construction sites. The Burton spur made possible the construction and completion of Burton Dam in 1919. Note the water line in the background. (Courtesy of Tallulah Falls School.)

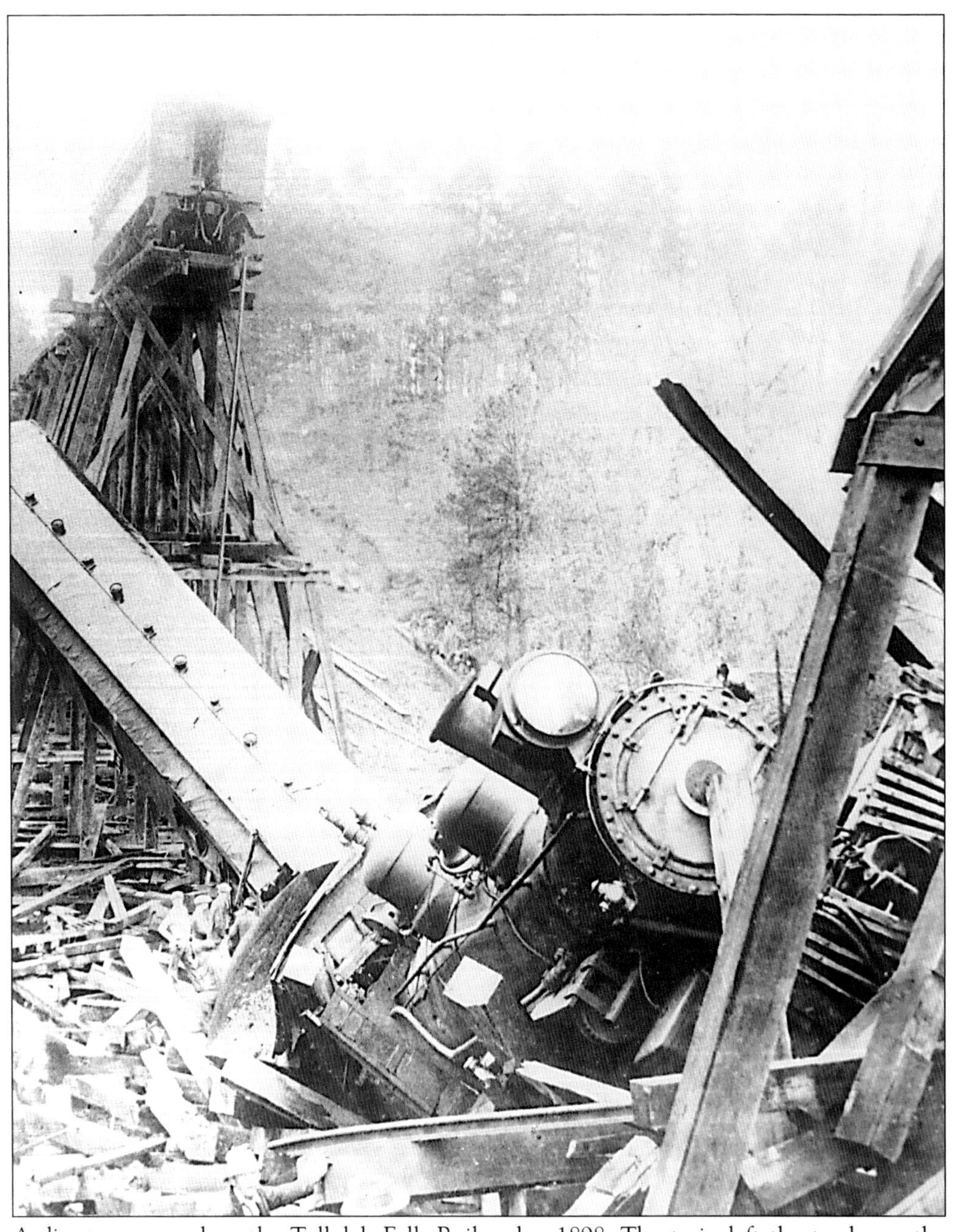

A disaster occurred on the Tallulah Falls Railroad *c.* 1898. The train left the tracks on the trestle at Hazel Creek and crashed below. (Courtesy of Edwards Studio.)

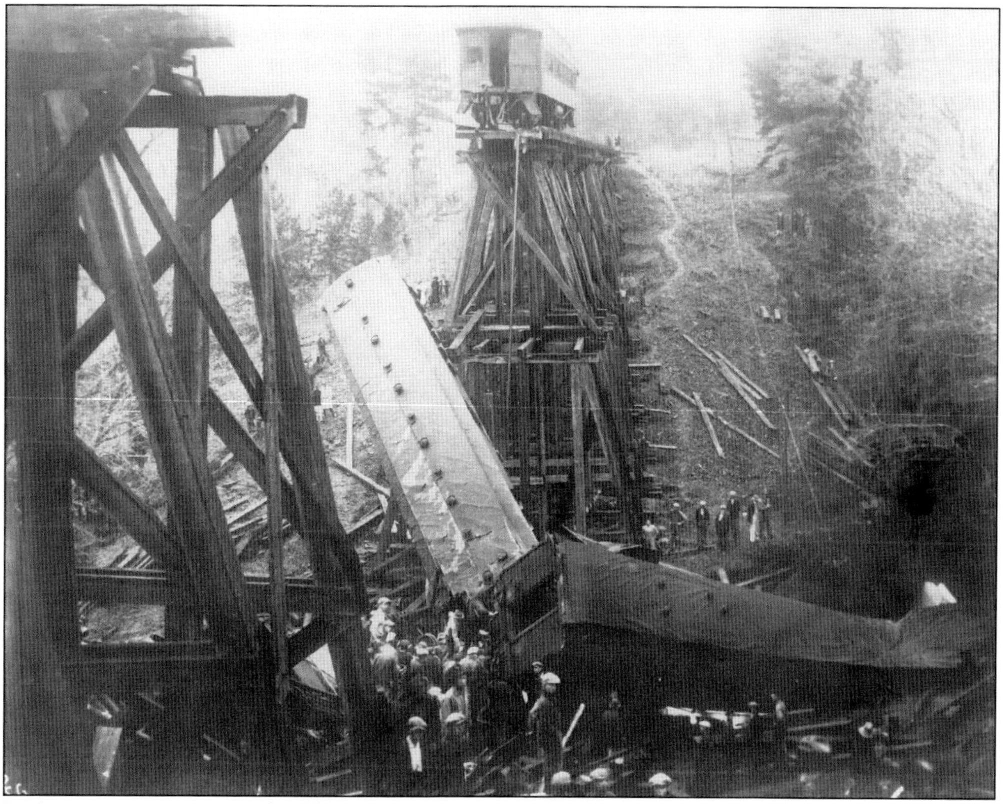

In this mountainous area, building wooden trestles was cheaper than blasting through mountains. However, even with frequent repair trestles sometimes collapsed, as this Hazel Creek one did, apparently due to human error. (Courtesy of Edwards Studio.)

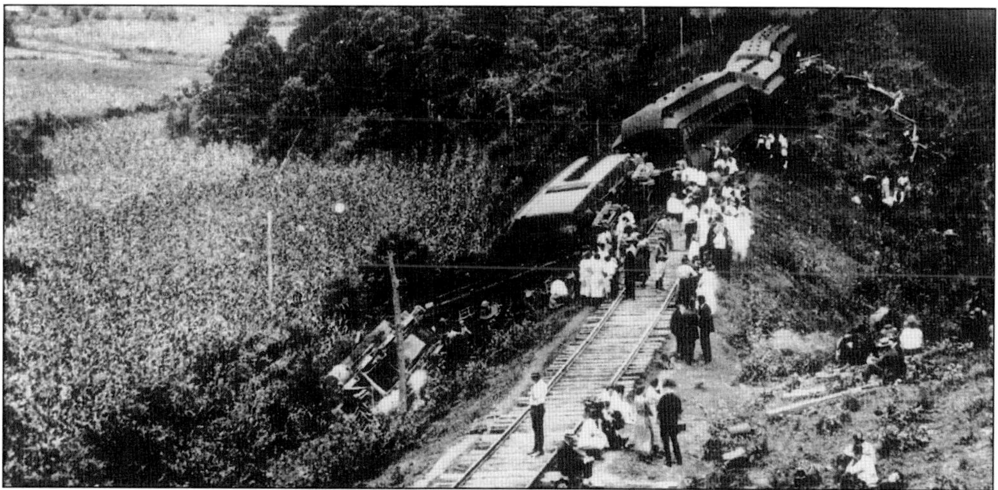

A train on the Tallulah Falls line loaded with summer campers jumped the track near Wiley, Georgia on August 23, 1920. The engine and baggage car turned over. Fortunately, none of the camp girls were injured, but it cost the life of the engineer, John Harvey. In addition, the fireman, Caloway Gibby, was severely burned. (Courtesy of The Foxfire Fund, Inc.)

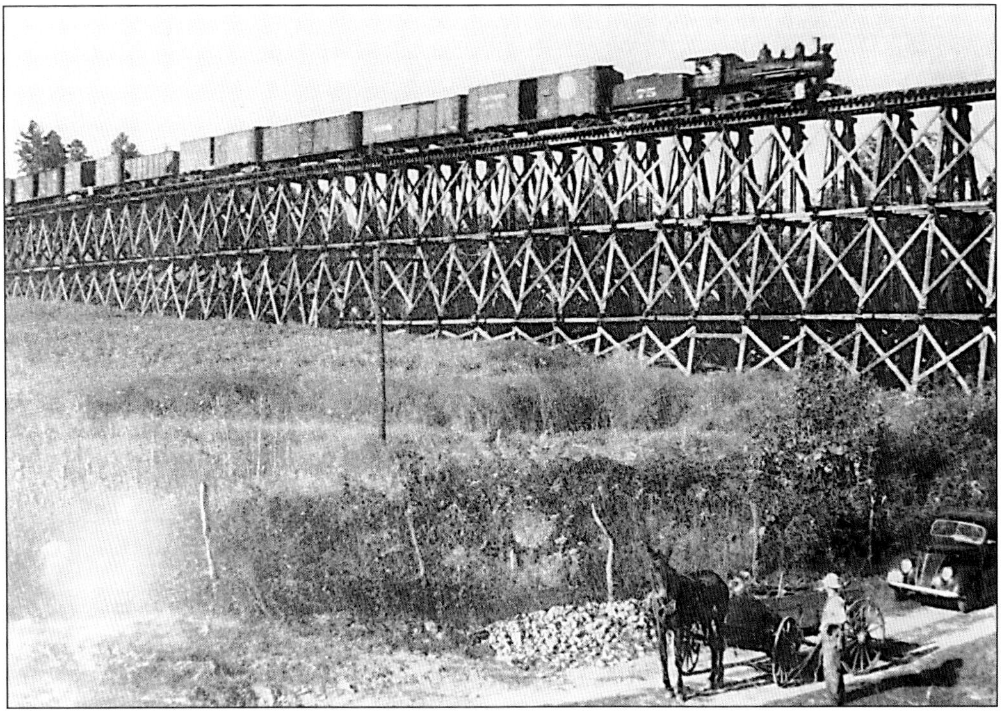

Three modes of transportation are noted in this photograph taken at the Tallulah Falls Railroad trestle in Wiley, Georgia in 1939. Railroad transportation was a great improvement over the mule and wagon, but both were eventually superseded by the automobile. (Courtesy of Georgia Department of Natural Resources.)

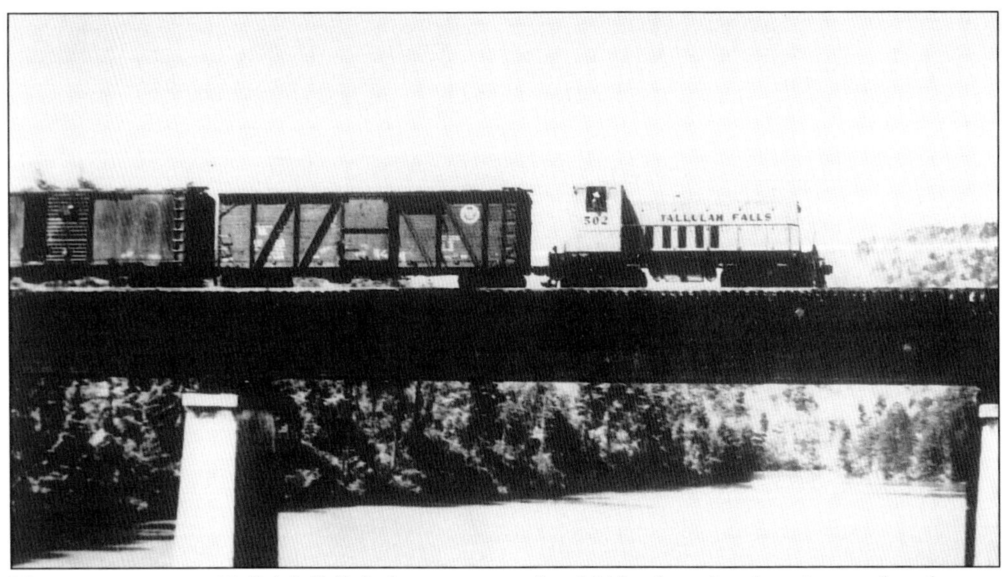

The train is crossing Tallulah Falls Lake sometime after 1948, when diesel engines replaced steam locomotives on the line. The entire line operated from 1907 to 1961, providing a dependable connection to other areas. It was discontinued due in large part to competition from automobiles, trucks, and the construction of highways. (Courtesy of The Foxfire Fund, Inc.)

Five

The Grand Era

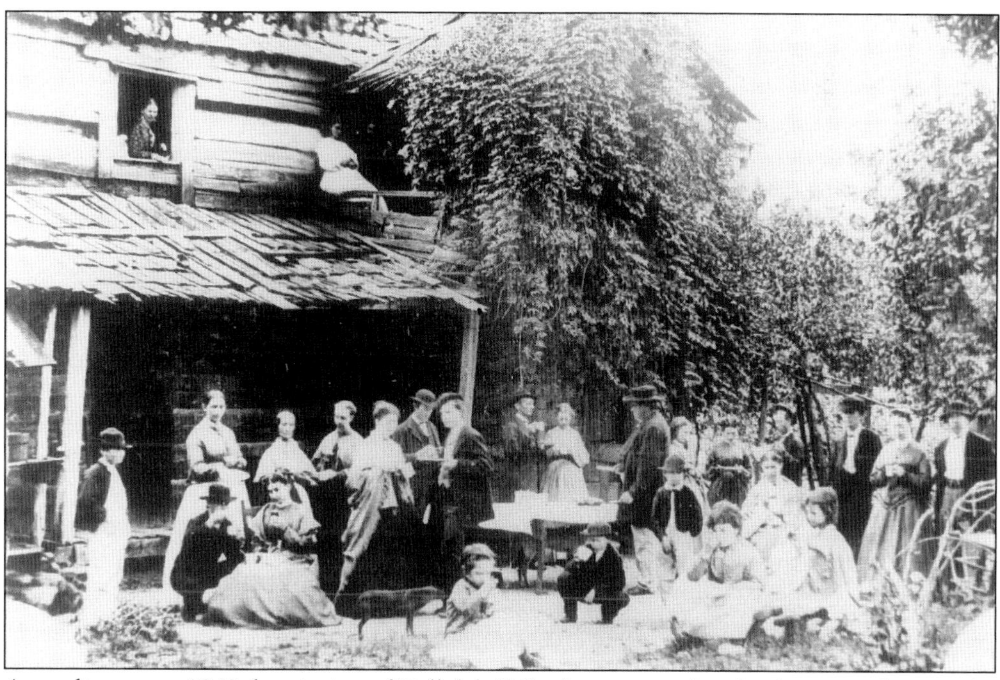

According to an 1848 description of Tallulah Falls there was only a log house in the area for tourists to stop for food and lodging. This may have been the Beale House, depicted here. A traveler in 1849 wrote of passing the night there: "Filled by the roar of the distant cataract, I strove to sleep, but strove in vain. I tried to forget my woes by counting the stars which glistened through the many cracks in the roof, but through those same cracks the wind, cold and chilling, came whistling through two holes, cut to let in the light, in which there was no sign of glass. Shivering, shaking, was my song during the whole night long, and happy was I when morning dawned."—*The Knickerbocker*, 1849. (Courtesy of Georgia Department of Archives and History.)

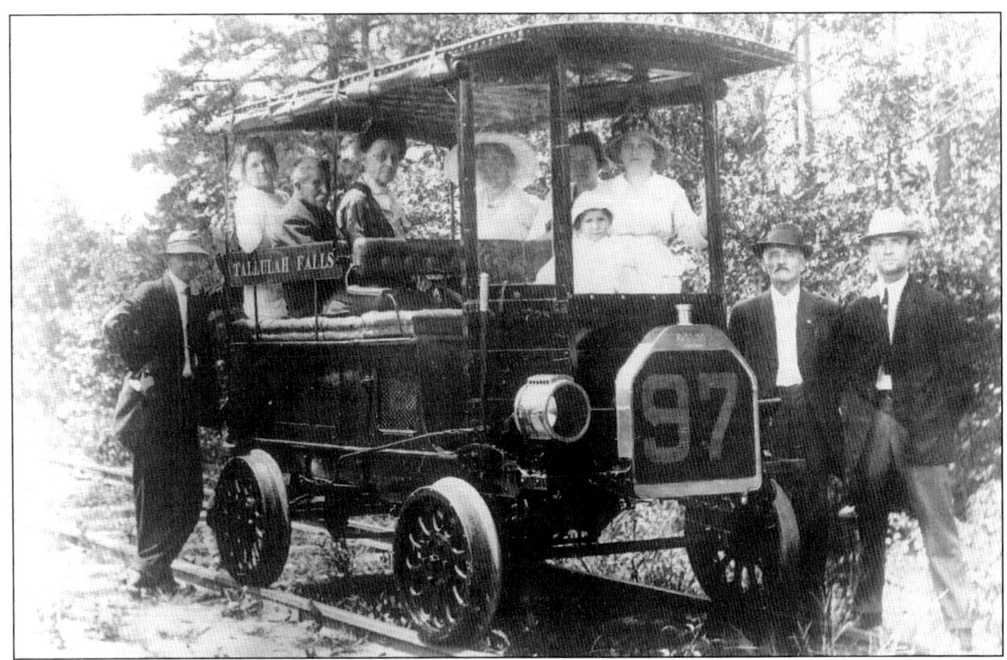

The Tallulah Falls Railroad executive rail car transported guests to their hotels in style. The arrival of the railroad in 1882 turned a remote natural wonder named Tallulah Falls into what hotel brochures termed the "Niagara of the South," and ushered in a grand era of tourism which lasted well into the 1920s. Tallulah Falls became a favorite destination for many of the well-traveled Victorians. (Courtesy of Georgia Department of Archives and History.)

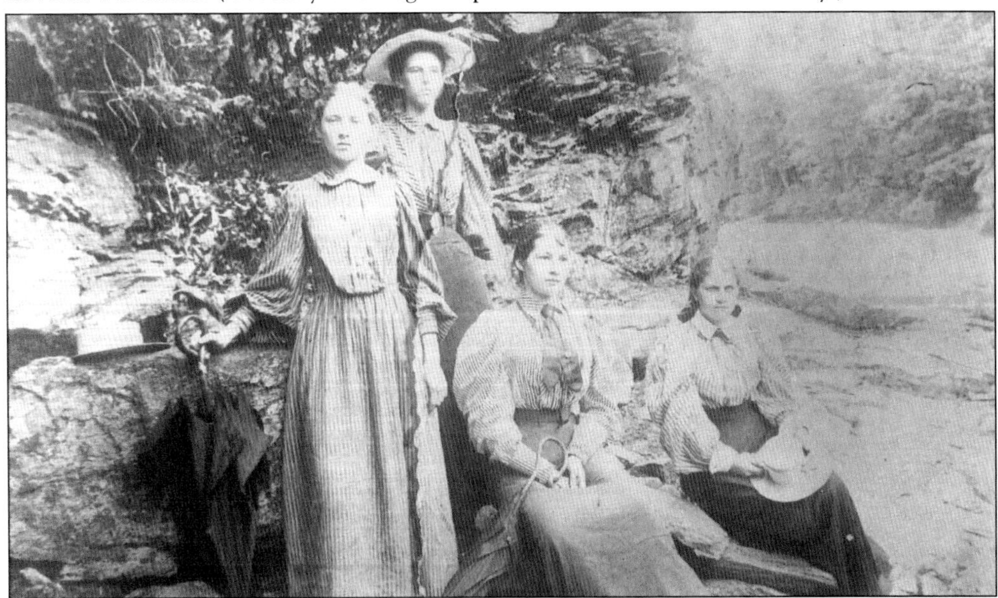

By 1890, hotels, cottages, and boarding houses provided lodging for the ever-increasing numbers of visitors to the gorge. Guides led groups of fashionably dressed tourists to the dramatic points of interest. Here a group of women, all dressed in striped attire, have their adventure recorded on film in 1895. They are, from left to right: Ruby Ritchie, Cleo Erwin, Anna Ritchie, and Leila Ritchie. (Courtesy of Georgia Department of Archives and History.)

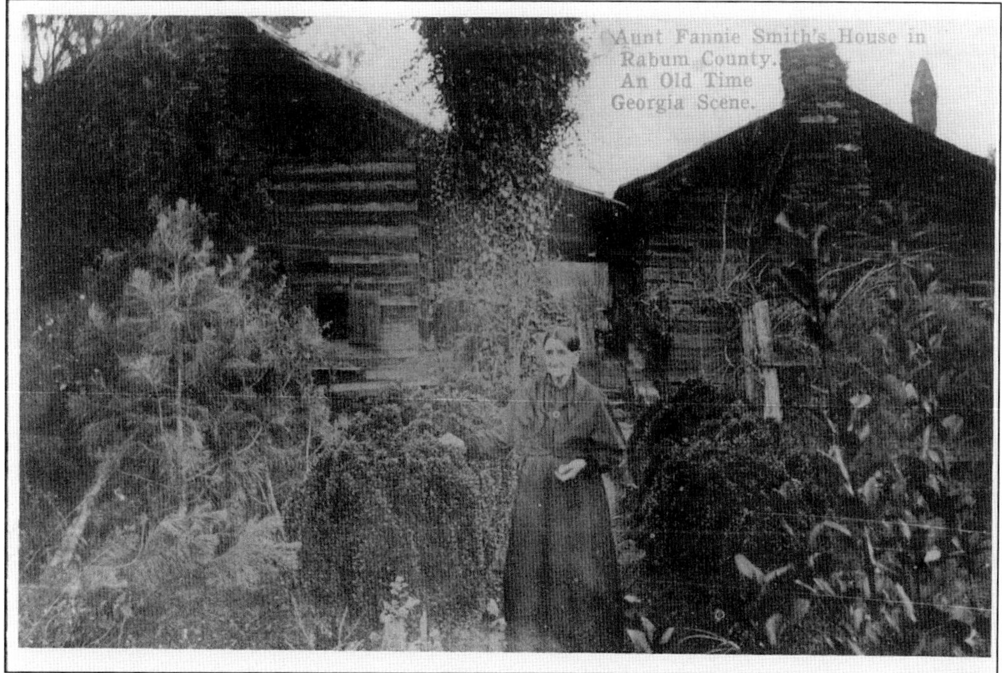

A favorite excursion was a day or overnight trip to nearby Sinking Mountain to enjoy fried chicken and ham at Aunt Fannie Smith's Cabin. The 7-mile trip was made on horseback, by buggy, or on foot to the 1840s home which served as both lodging and meal house. (Courtesy of Gary Doster.)

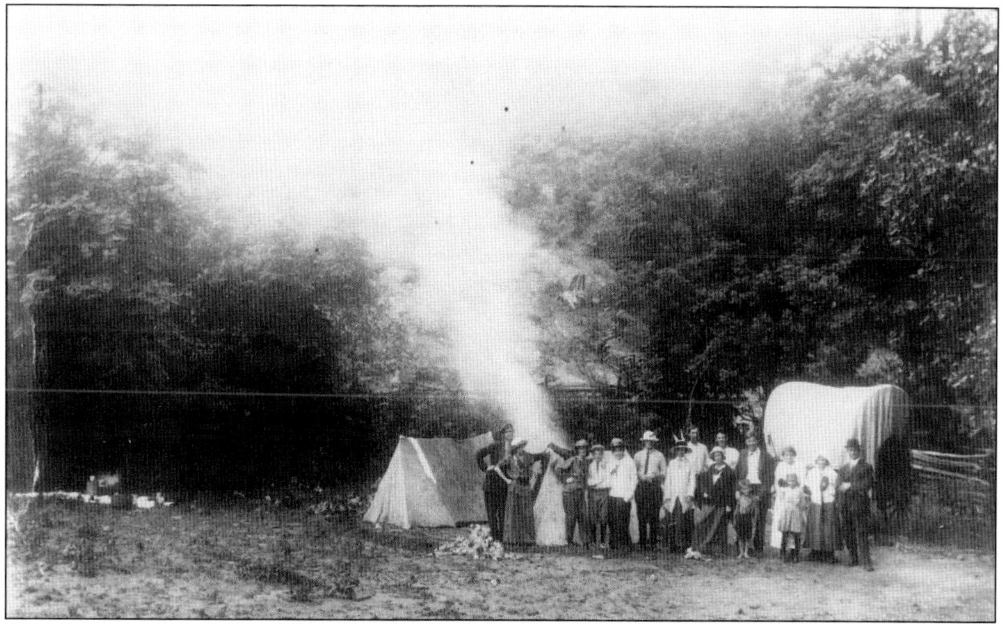

Overnight camping to nearby points of interest was fashionable in the 1890s, as attested to by this group of guests from the York House. The York House, built in 1841 as a private residence, was a boarding house for the railroad after 1896 and still accommodates travelers today. (Courtesy of Georgia Department of Archives and History.)

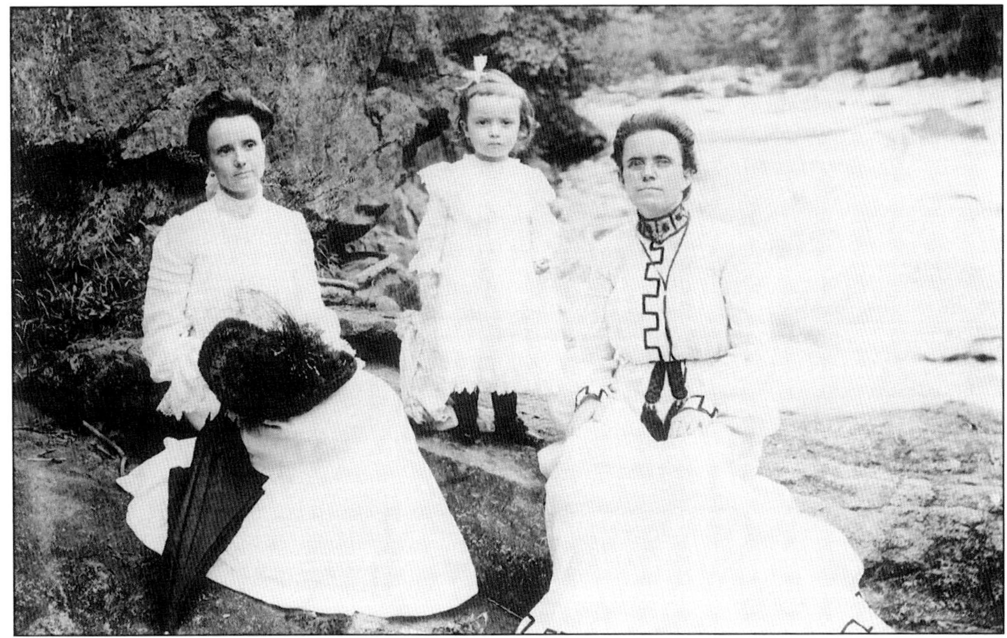

Three generations of Georgians on a trip to Tallulah Falls in 1905 included grandmother Mattie Moring Coleman (Mrs. John C.), mother Luck Coleman Mitchell (Mrs. Frank), and daughter Mattie Moring Mitchell (later Mrs. W.H. Flanders) of Swainsboro. (Courtesy of Luck Flanders Gambrell.)

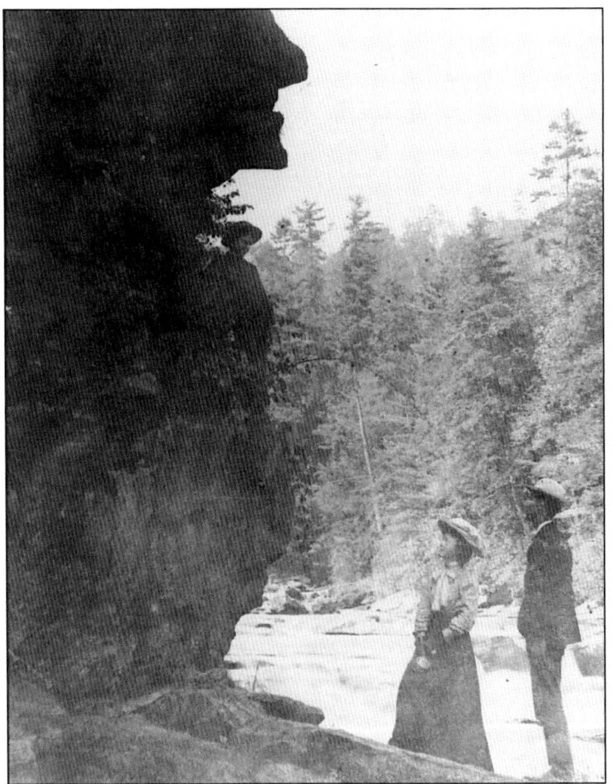

For many years in this grand Victorian era, newlyweds flocked to the falls, had their photographs taken at Witches Head, and named their children "Tallulah." The image of this couple, with their son perched under the witch's "chin," dates from the 1890s. (Courtesy of Rope Roberts.)

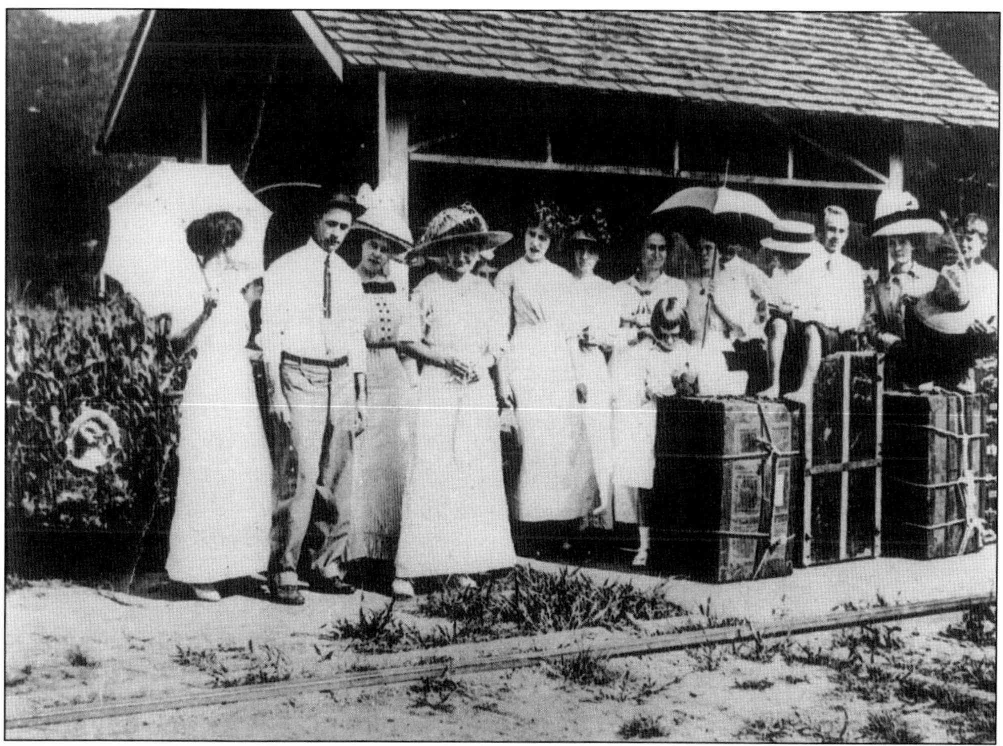

Excursions and day trips could be planned for trips farther up the railroad line from Tallulah Falls. This group is enjoying an outing c. 1910 and is shown at a railroad station, probably Mountain City. Note the parasols and trunks. (Courtesy of Georgia Department of Archives and History.)

SUMMER RESORTS.

NOTICE TO

TOURISTS, INVALIDS

—AND—

Pleasure Seekers.

TALLULAH HOTEL,

Tallulah Falls, Ga.

Is now open for the season. Low rates of board will be given visitors and tourists seeking health and pleasure amid the cool retreat and grand scenery of the mountains, as follows:

Board per day	$1 50
Per week	8 00
Per month	20 00

(During the month of June.)

The accommodations will be first-class in every particular Amateur musicians will be engaged to discourse sweet music for the guests.

THE MINERAL SPRINGS

of Tallulah comprise Iron, Sulphur and Magnesia, and are well proportioned, and pronounced to be both curative and promotive of health.

Three hundred regular boarders can be accommodated. Special rates will be given large families.

W. D. YOUNG, Proprietor.

Tallulah, Ga., May 31, 1883

An advertisement for the Tallulah Hotel entices visitors with its mineral springs, first-class accommodations, and musicales. (Courtesy of Georgia Department of Archives and History.)

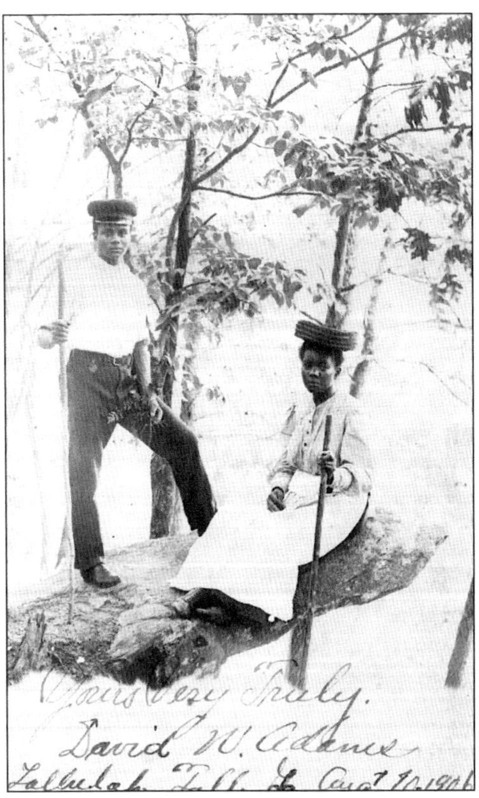

As a result of the Industrial Revolution, people had more money and the leisure time to spend it. Wealthy and working-class citizens took advantage of these changes and the better means of transportation to visit areas once thought inaccessible. (Courtesy of Gary Doster.)

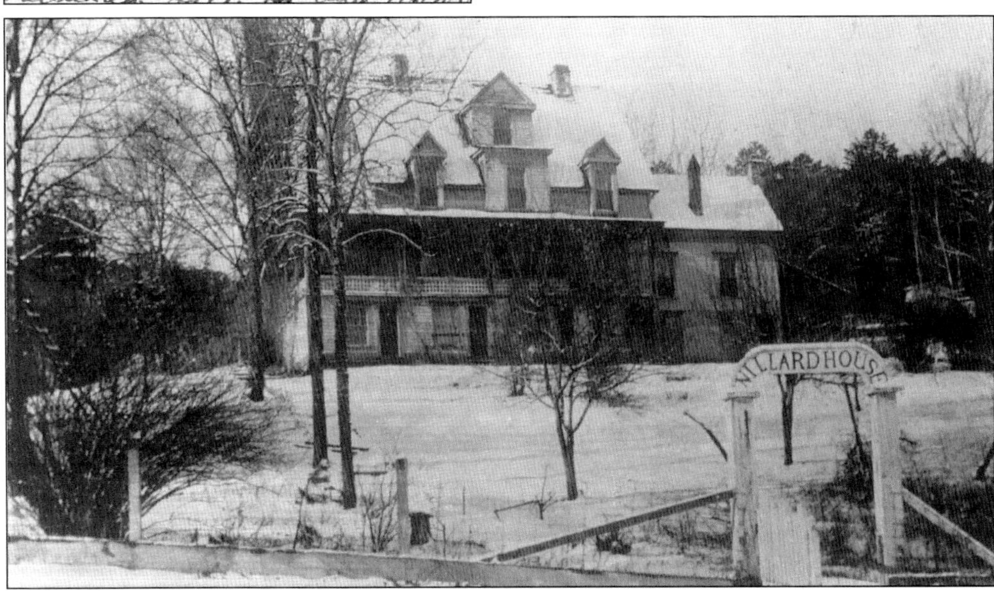

Hotels flourished as traveling increased. The Willard House Hotel, owned by W.D. Young, offered a band for nightly dancing, fishing, ten pins, and a good livery stable. Young also owned the Grand View Hotel, one of the largest in the area. Many small hotels such as the Pines, the Oaks, Chasm Brink, Maplewood Inn, Oak Haven, Taylor House, Arcadia, and King House also offered quiet, comfortable surroundings. (Courtesy of Georgia Power Land Department Photo Archives.)

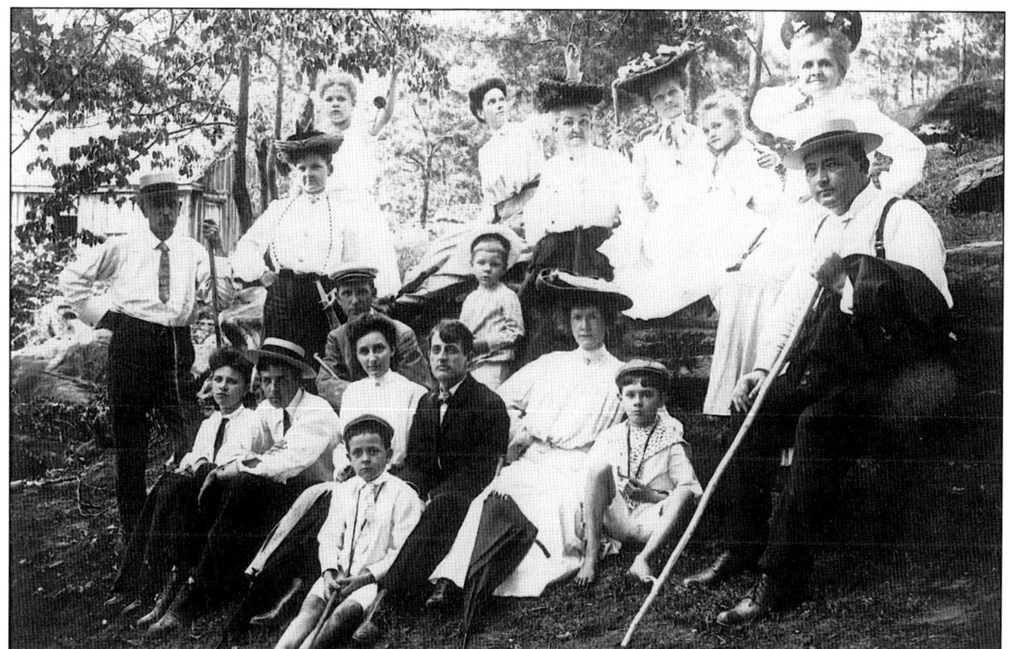

Outdoor activities appealed to people of all ages and income groups. Shown is the affluent Ellis/Lipscomb family hiking in 1904. Note the variety of fashionable hats worn. (Courtesy of Hargrett Rare Book and Manuscript Library/University of Georgia Libraries.)

ROBINSON HOTEL

At Tallulah is within 100 yards of the beautiful rapids and 200 yards of the mammoth falls, is located between the postoffice and depot, 100 yards from each. The Robinson Hotel is neatly furnished and keeps a good table. It is before the people that everybody that stops at the Robinson Hotel has a good time.

It is before the people that the Robinson Hotel is the place to go to spend the summer.

It is before the people that the Robinson Hotel has the finest grove of shade trees in Georgia and the coolest place in the mountains to sleep and have a good time. Rates reasonable.

T. A. ROBINSON,
Manager.

Blue Ridge and Atlantic Railroad.

TIME TABLE NO. 27.

In Effect September 6, 1896, 11 A. M.

11 Daily Ex. Sun	STATIONS.	12 Daily Ex. Sun
5 45pm Lv	....Tallulah Falls....Ar.	1 05pm
6 05pm	....Turnerville.....	12 45pm
6 25pm	.....Annandale.....	12 25pm
6 40pm	....Clarkesville....	12 10 m
7 00pm	.....Demorest......	11 50am
7 15pm Ar	....Cornelia.....Lv	11 35am

W. V. LAURAINE, Receiver.

Tom Robinson, local saloon owner, built the Robinson Hotel in the 1880s. Located near the head of Indian Arrow Rapids, it was a short distance from the roaring of the falls. An ad for the Robinson Hotel in the local paper even provides the railroad schedule. "The Robinson Hotel is neatly furnished and keeps a good table."—*The Tallulah Falls Spray*, July 1, 1897. (Courtesy of Georgia Department of Natural Resources.)

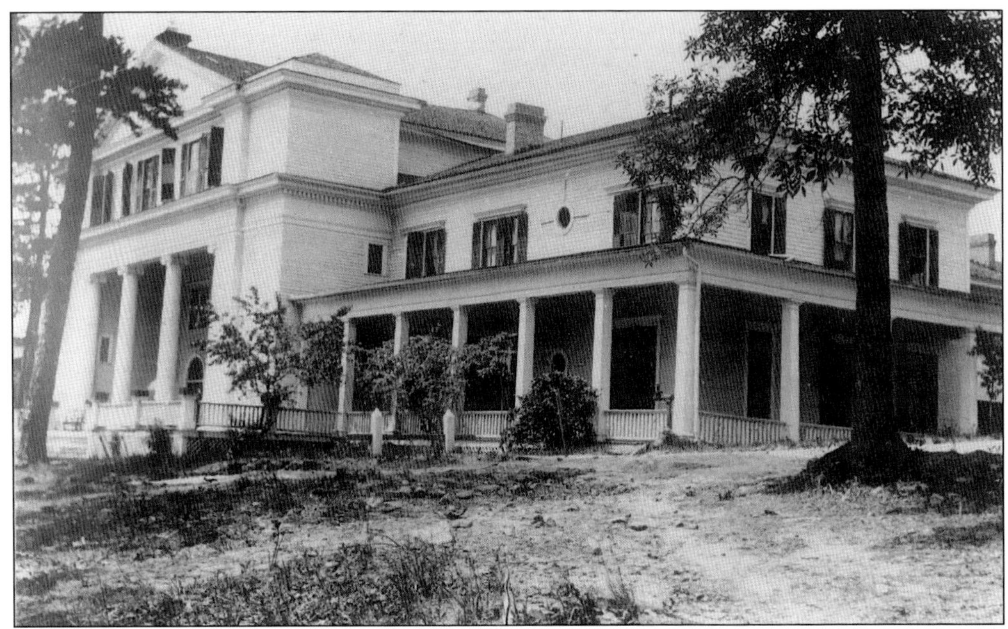

Tallulah Lodge, one of the major hotels, catered to wealthy guests. The Lodge offered tennis, ten pins, horseback riding, swimming, and mountain rambles by day, and card parties, dances, and musicales at night. Built around 1900, the "Tallulah Lodge sits like a dazzling diamond upon the head of the highest mountain in the foothills of the Blue Ridge."—*Athens Banner-Watchman*, July 19, 1903. (Courtesy of Georgia Power Land Department Photo Archives.)

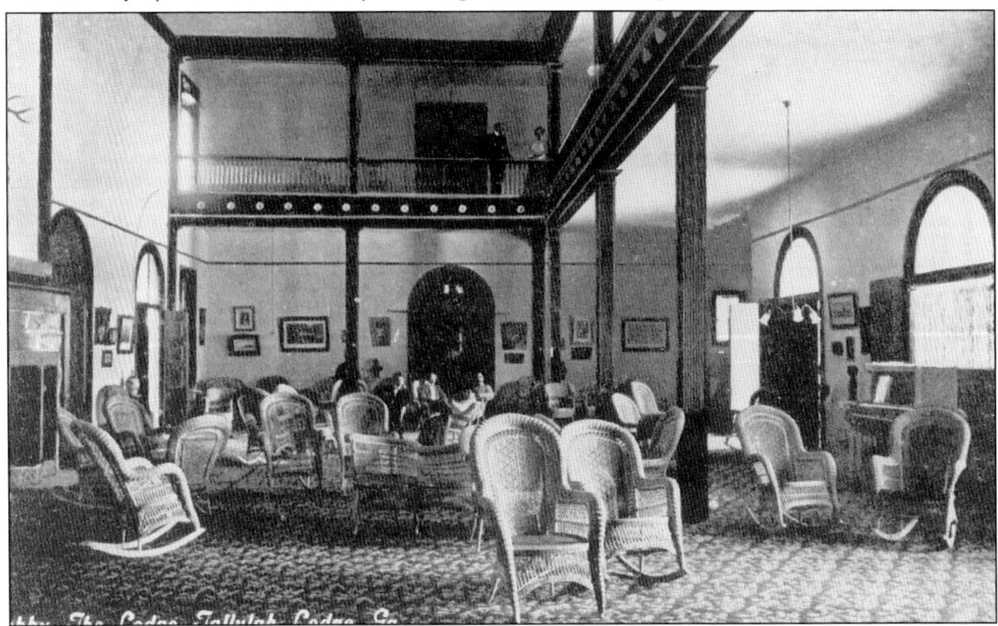

In what was perhaps the most elegant of the hotels in Tallulah Falls, the lobby of the Lodge boasted large wicker chairs and a rich carpet. It had over 100 bedrooms, half of which were equipped with private baths. The floor of the broad second-story hall was kept waxed for dancing. Located on the south rim just overlooking the gorge, it was the only hotel from which any view of the falls could be seen. (Courtesy of Gary Doster.)

This group of fashionably-dressed visitors enjoyed a hike to the bottom of the gorge c. 1898–1902. Note the walking sticks and the man with a camera leaning against the rocks on the far right. (Courtesy of Georgia Department of Archives and History.)

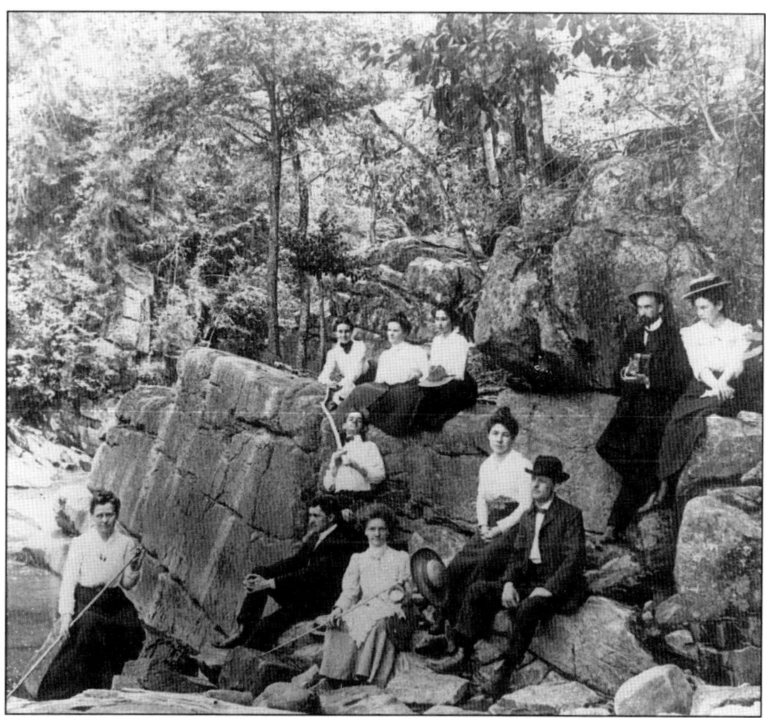

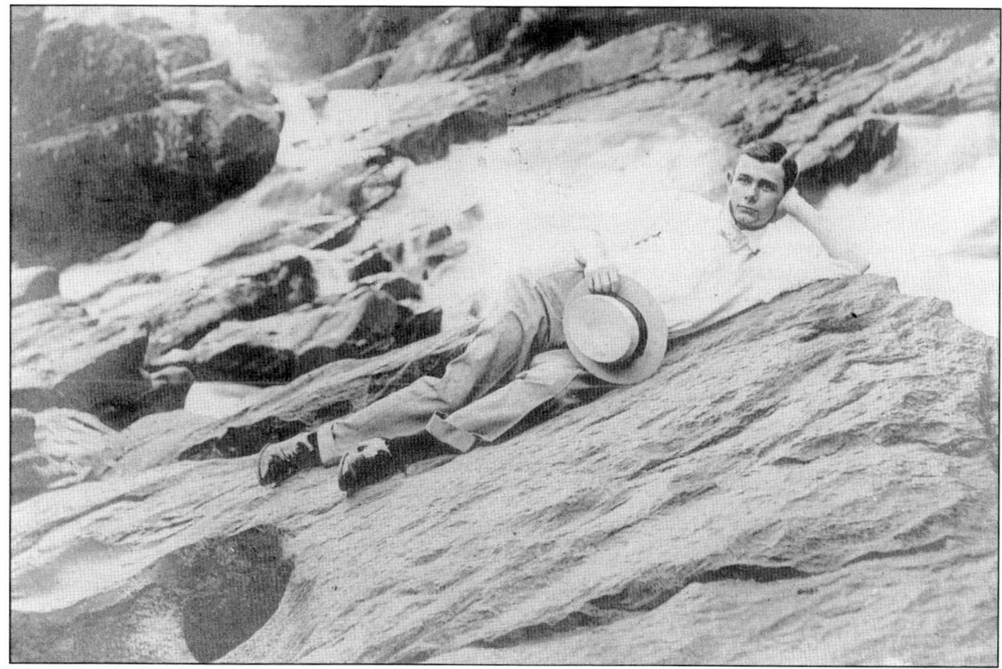

Leisurely days amid summer's heat inspire dreamy thoughts while resting on a rock near the rushing water at Indian Arrow Rapids. (Courtesy of Gary Doster.)

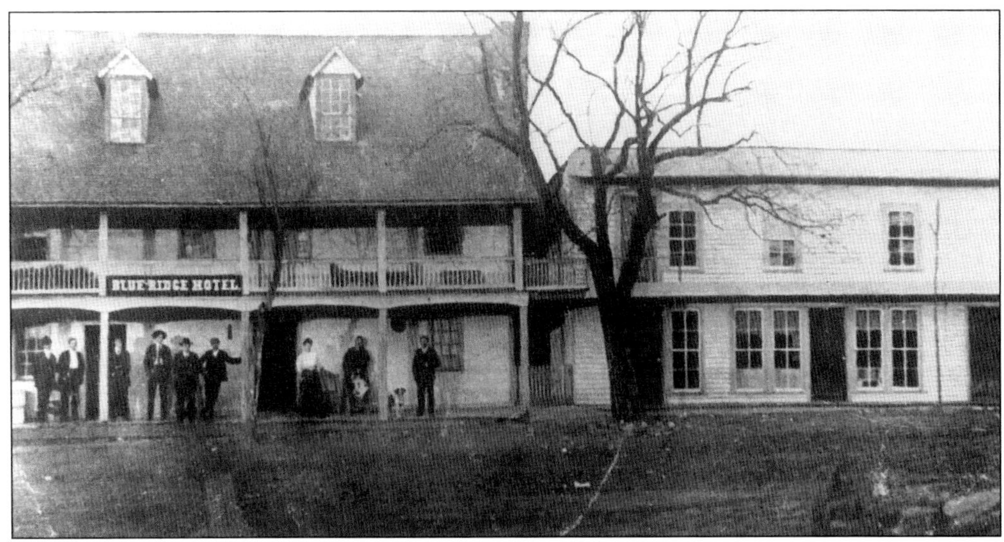

Located on Main Street in nearby Clayton, the Blue Ridge Hotel provided tourists an additional opportunity for relaxation in 1907. (Courtesy of Georgia Department of Archives and History.)

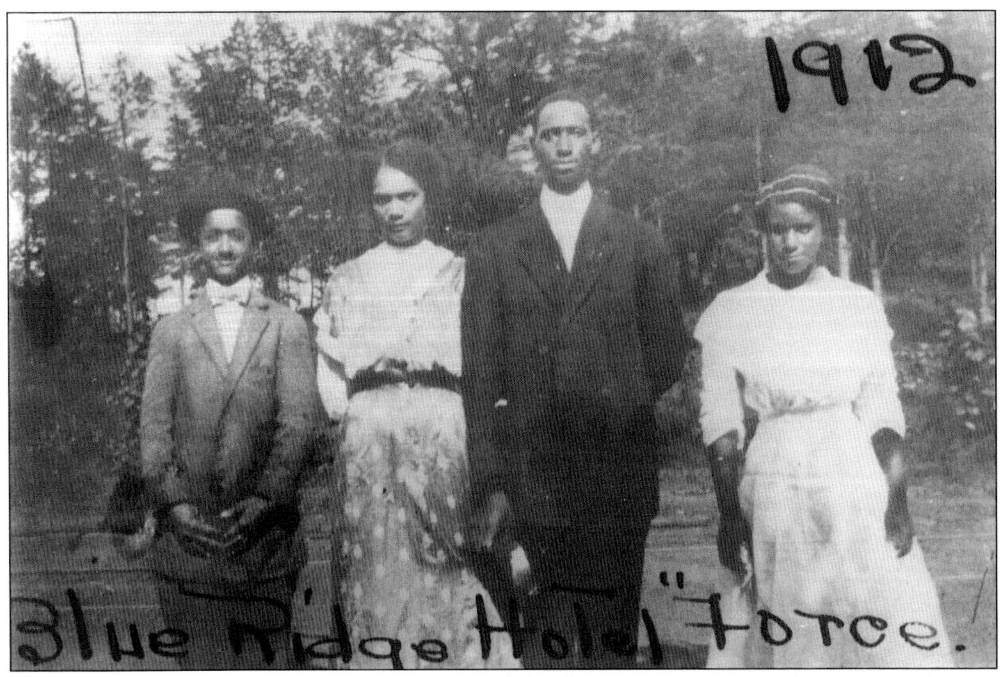

The working staff of the Blue Ridge Hotel stood for the camera in 1912. (Courtesy of Georgia Department of Archives and History.)

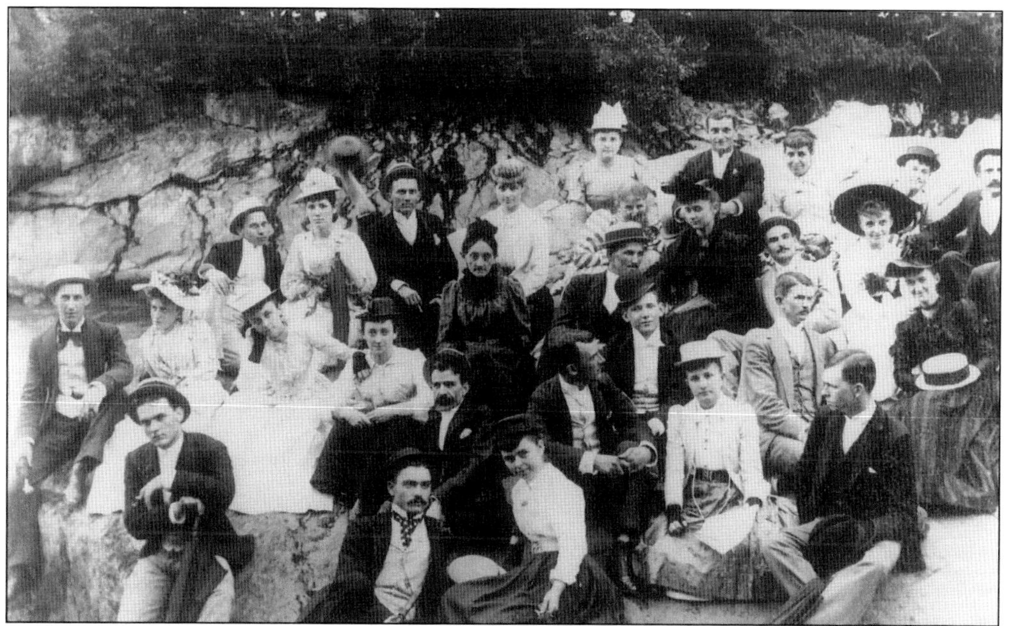

Mrs. Daniel Cornelius O'Keefe of Atlanta, in the center of the photograph, chaperoned an Atlanta group of young people, *c.* 1890. (Courtesy of Georgia Department of Archives and History.)

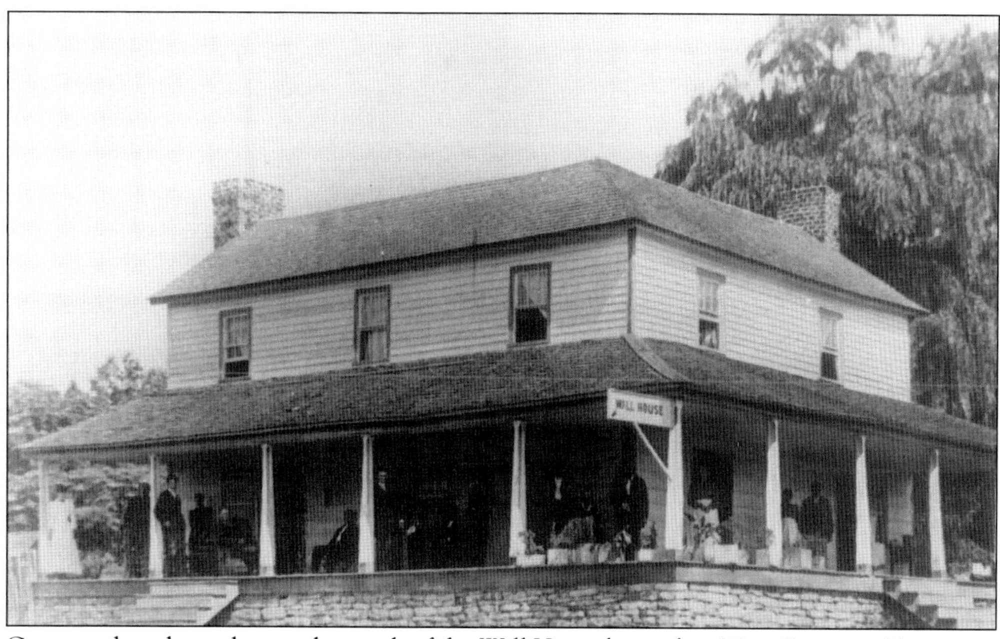

Guests gathered together on the porch of the Will House located on Main Street in Clayton, in 1910. The cooler mountain temperatures provided relief from the heat of other parts of Georgia and surrounding states. (Courtesy of Georgia Department of Archives and History.)

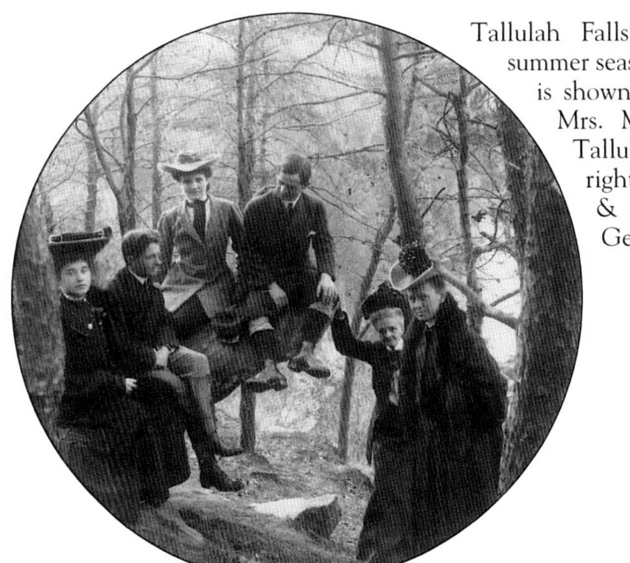

Tallulah Falls offered recreation beyond the summer season. This group, some from Athens, is shown hiking the gorge during the fall. Mrs. Mary Ann Lipscomb, founder of Tallulah Falls School, is second from the right. (Courtesy of Hargrett Rare Book & Manuscript Library/University of Georgia Libraries.)

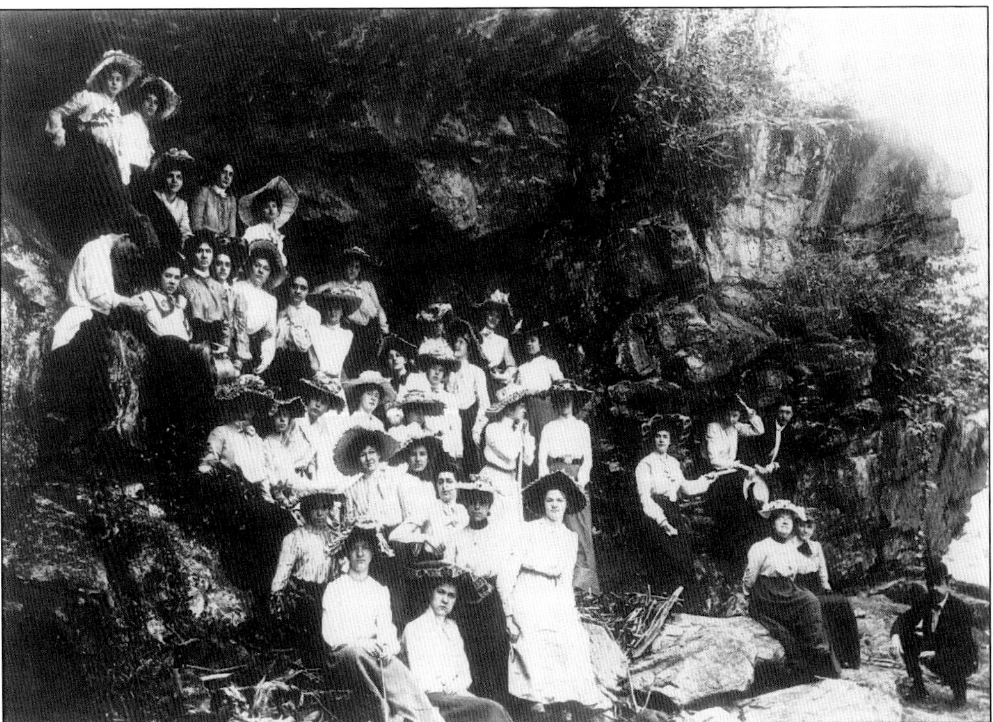

The natural features of the gorge were given dramatic names such as Hurricane Falls, Lover's Leap, Devil's Pulpit, and Point Inspiration. This group is shown below Witches Head, which can be seen at the upper right. (Courtesy of Hargrett Rare Book & Manuscript Library/University of Georgia Libraries.)

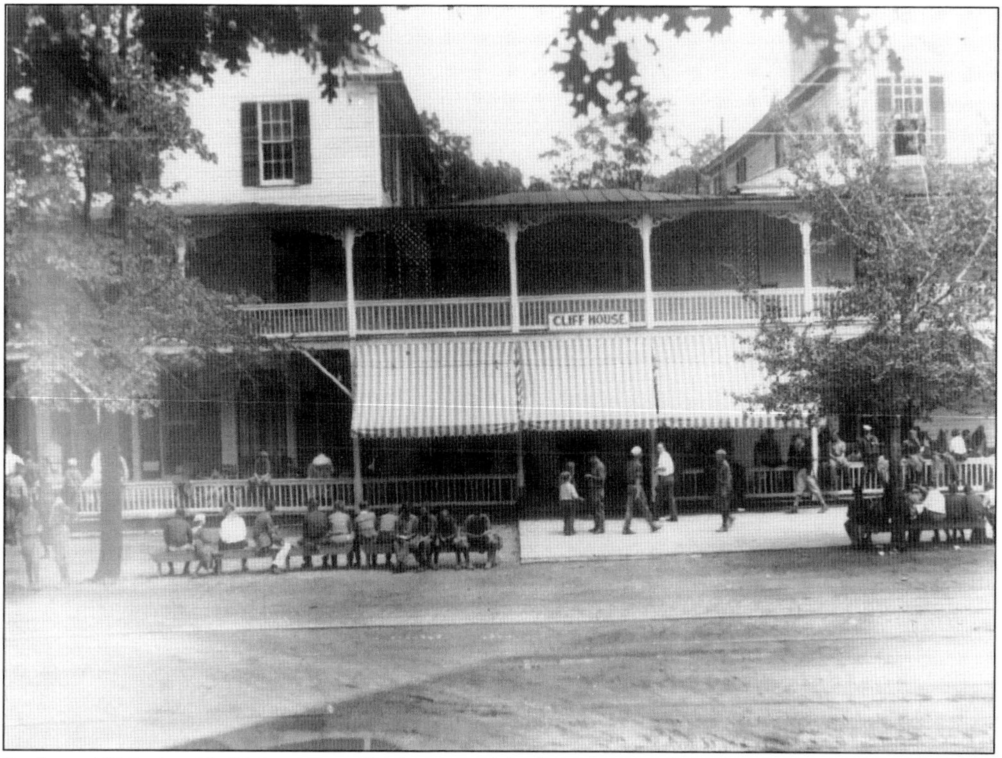

Built in 1882, the Cliff House was the largest of the hotels in Tallulah Falls. Located adjacent to the railroad tracks and just above Witches Head and Devil's Pulpit, this large hotel controlled the major access points into the gorge. Owned and operated by the Moss family for years, this 90-room hotel could accommodate 300 people on its 40-acre tract, with seating for 250 people in the dining room. (Courtesy of Rope Roberts.)

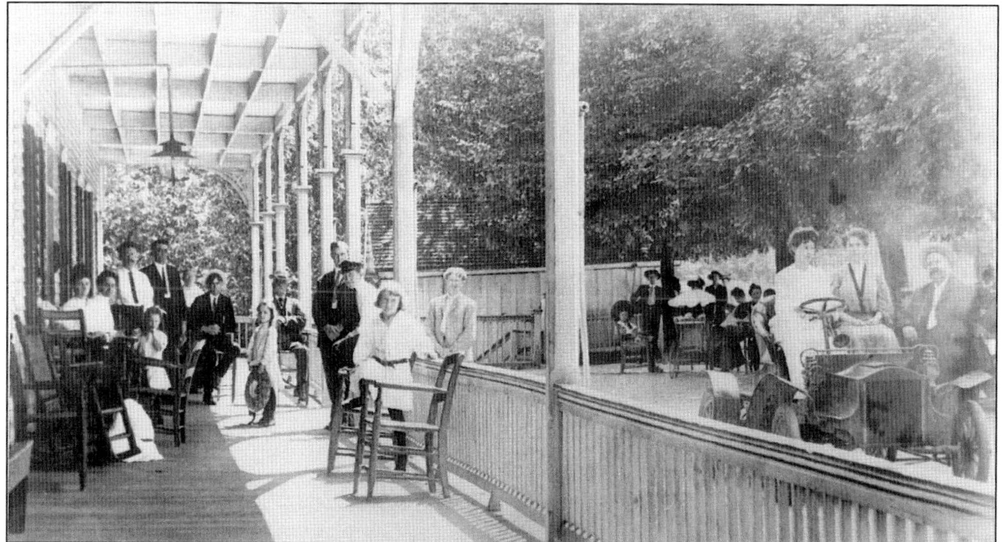

Named after the famous hotel in San Francisco, the Cliff House offered many opportunities for socializing, as seen in this image of the porch, c. 1906. (Courtesy of Georgia Department of Archives and History.)

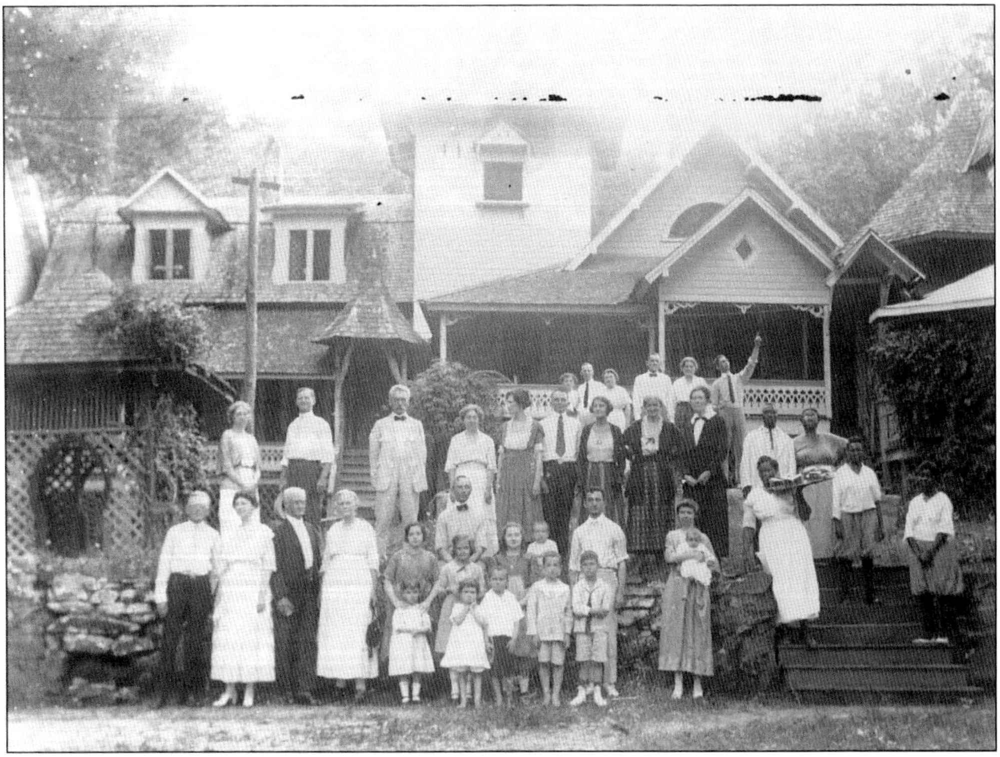

Dr. Count Piercy Norcop Duboeay built the Glenbrook as his home around 1894 on a hill overlooking Tallulah Falls. A native of France, Duboeay came to Tallulah Falls about 1888, and married a local girl, Sarah L. Hunnicutt. By 1897 he had enlarged his home to accommodate guests, many of whom congregated on the front lawn in this photograph. Note the cook on the right holding a tray of bread. (Courtesy of Rope Roberts.)

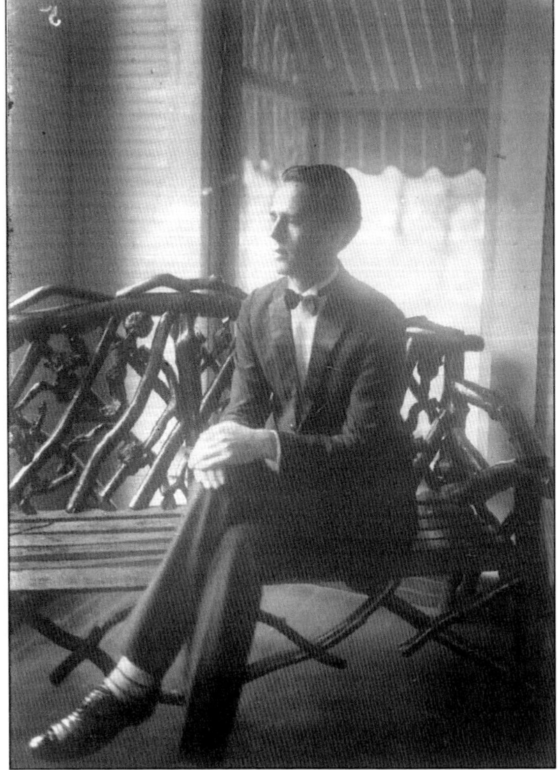

Reportedly, noted Tallulah Falls photographer Walter Hunnicutt used the lobby of the Glenbrook Hotel, shown here, as a backdrop for many of his photographs. This man is seated in a laurelwood chair probably crafted by Walter Hunnicutt. (Photograph by Walter Hunnicutt, courtesy of Jorene Lavender.)

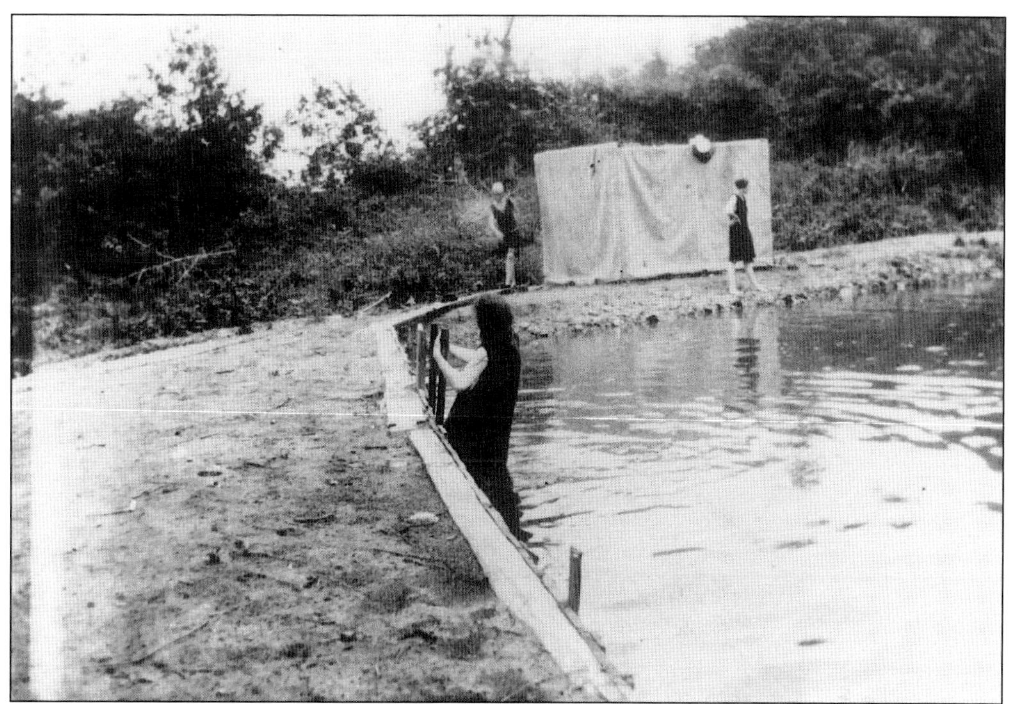

The Glenbrook Hotel had a swimming "hole" for its guests. The canvas changing room was very simple, as was the dirt apron around the pool. (Courtesy of Rope Roberts.)

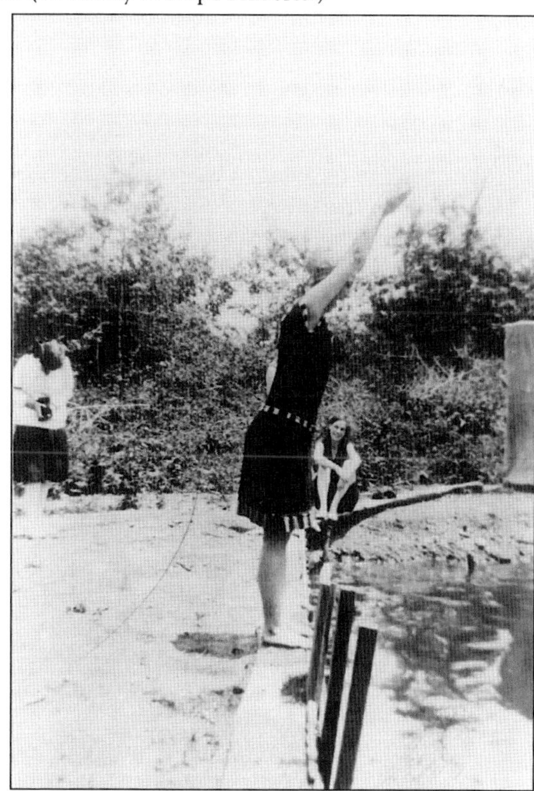

Glamorously attired in the conservative bathing fashions of the day, this young woman pauses before diving into the Glenbrook swimming hole. (Courtesy of Rope Roberts.)

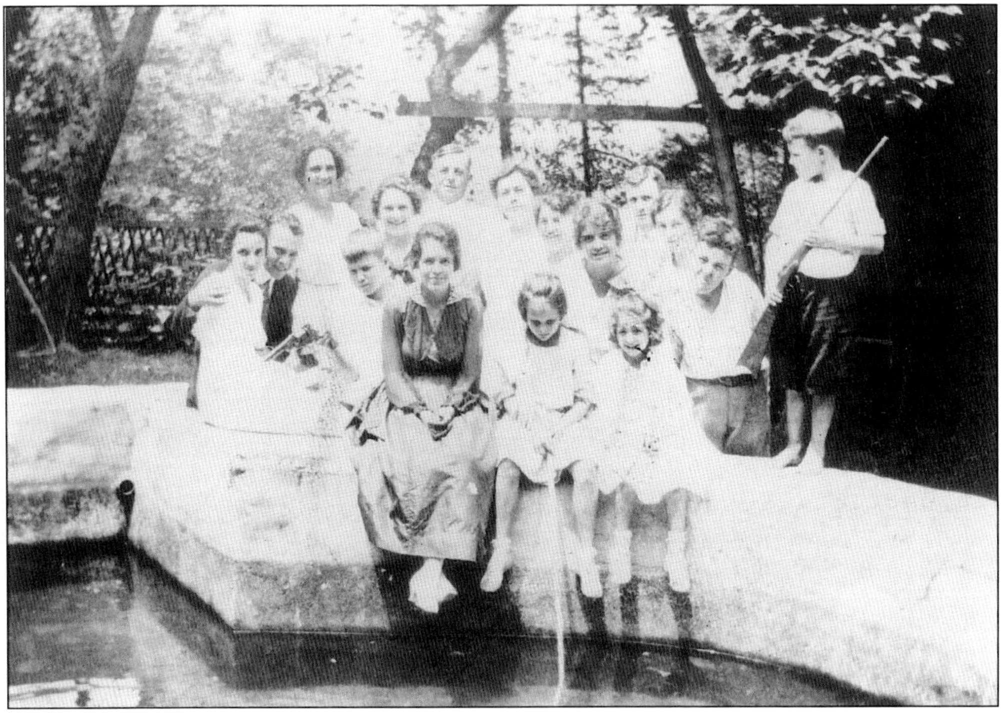

Surrounded by springs, the Glenbrook enclosed one of them to make a pond for the visitors' enjoyment. There were also places to sit or picnic nearby. (Courtesy of Rope Roberts.)

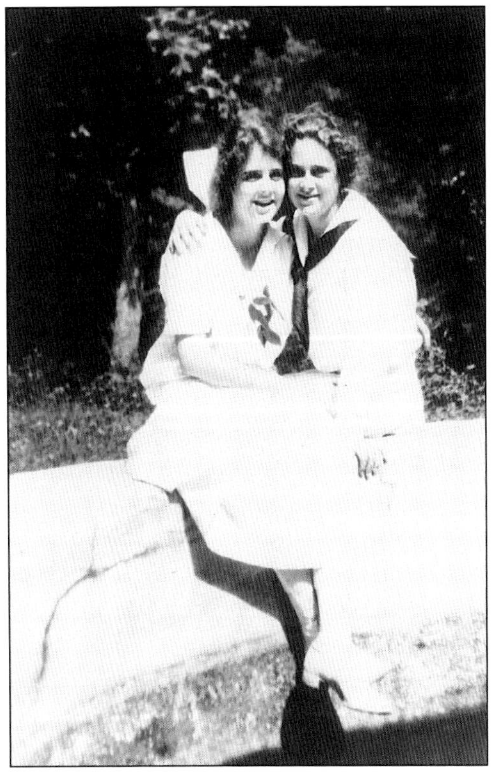

Sitting around the pond at the Glenbrook Hotel, these gals, probably sisters, enjoy the cool mountain air. The Glenbrook was the last of the hotels in Tallulah Falls to remain open, operating until the middle of the 20th century, long after the major era of tourism declined. A series of fires throughout the years, including a major fire in 1921, destroyed all of the other hotels in Tallulah Falls. (Courtesy of Rope Roberts.)

Six

The Wider Community

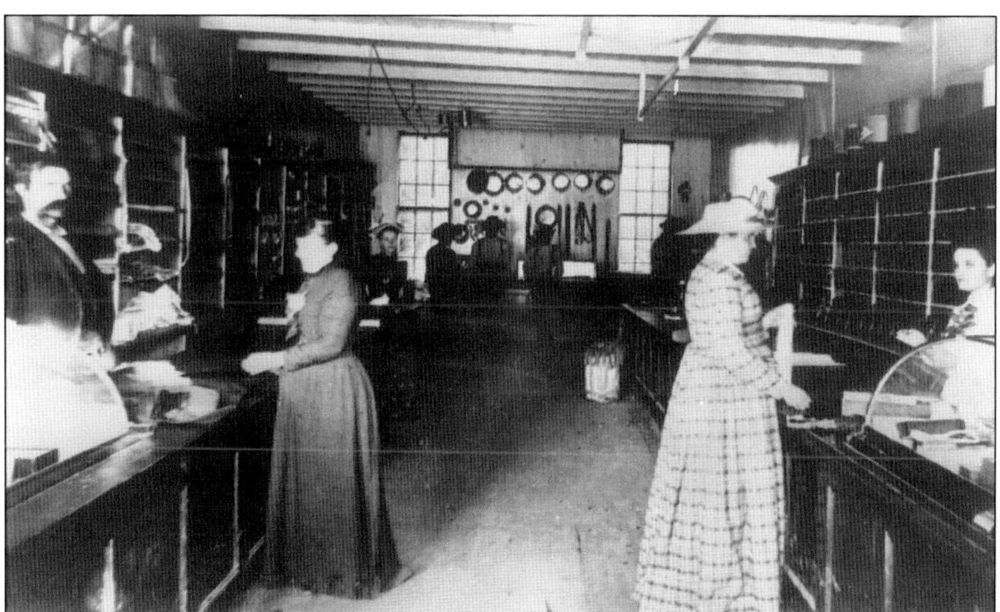

This image of a general merchandise store in Clayton dates from *c.* 1900. The nearby town of Clayton offered additional shopping for Tallulah Falls residents. Tallulah Falls was small and had to depend on neighboring communities for most essential goods and services. The Tallulah Falls Railroad provided convenient transportation for day trips to bank, shop, or run errands in Clayton and other adjacent communities. (Courtesy of Georgia Department of Archives and History.)

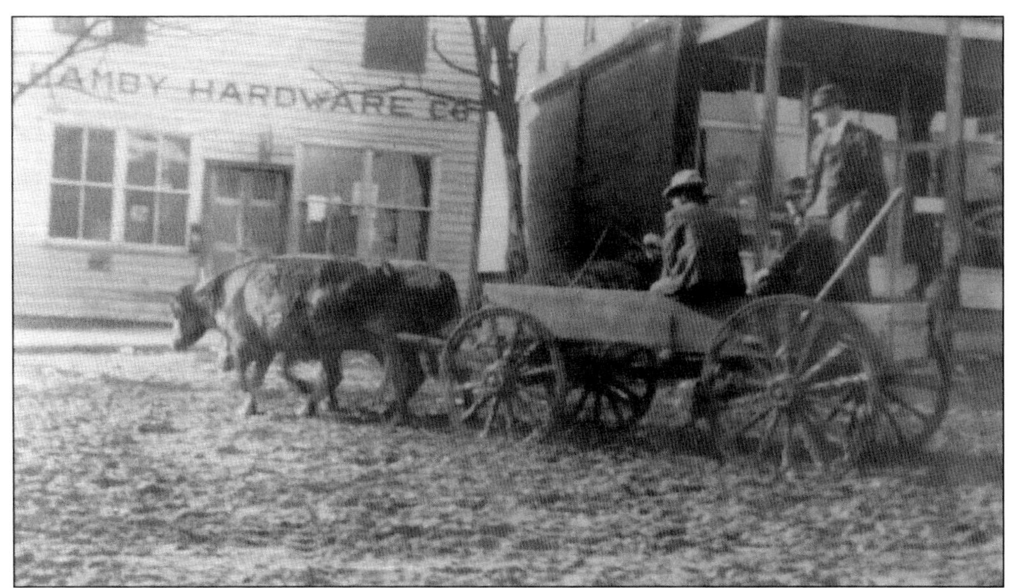

Oxen provided dependable transportation before paved roads. Note the mud beneath the wheels of the wagon as it heads to Hamby Hardware store, *c.* 1912. (Courtesy of Georgia Power Land Department Photo Archives.)

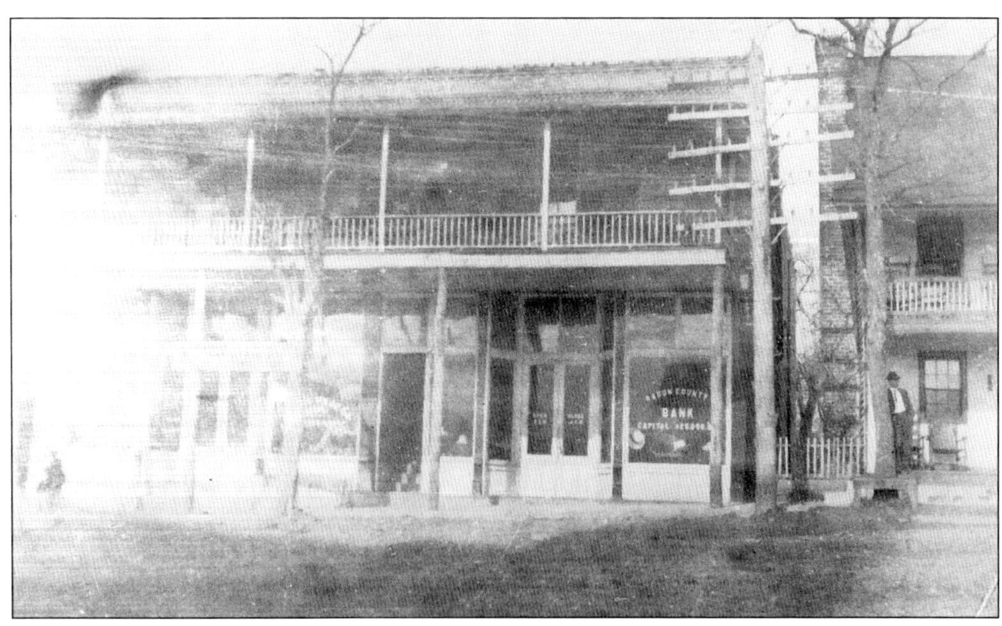

Banking services were available at the Bank of Rabun County in Clayton, *c.* 1912. (Courtesy of Georgia Power Land Department Photo Archives.)

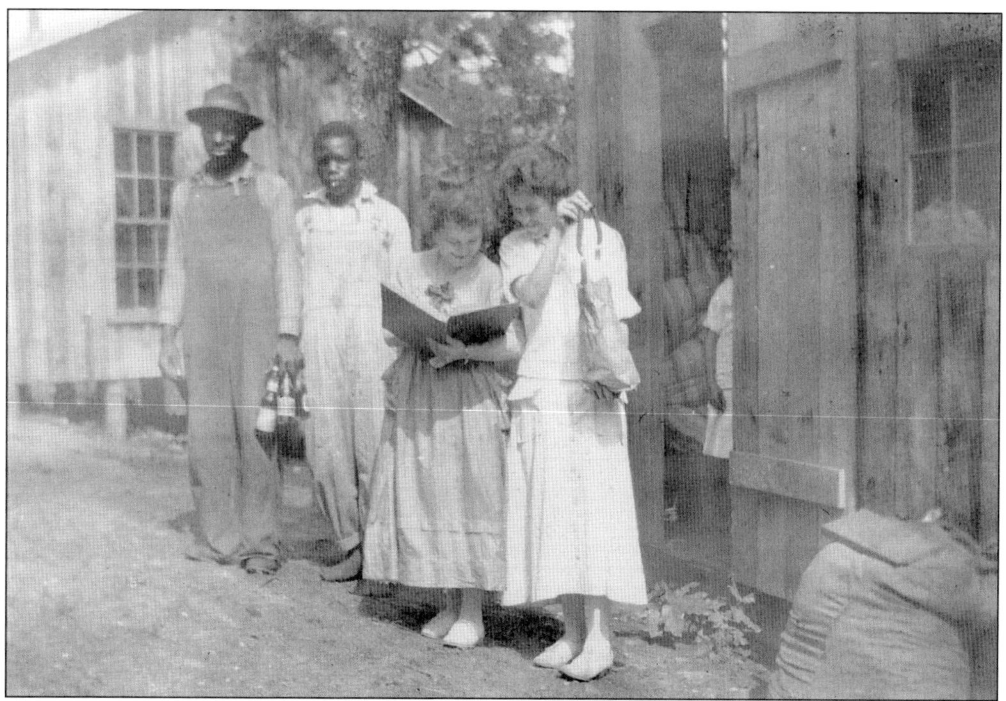

A commissary built for those employed by the power company at Tallulah Falls provided at-hand shopping. Support stores, such as this, were built as a result of the hydroelectric project. Note the sausage links the lady is holding. (Courtesy of Rope Roberts.)

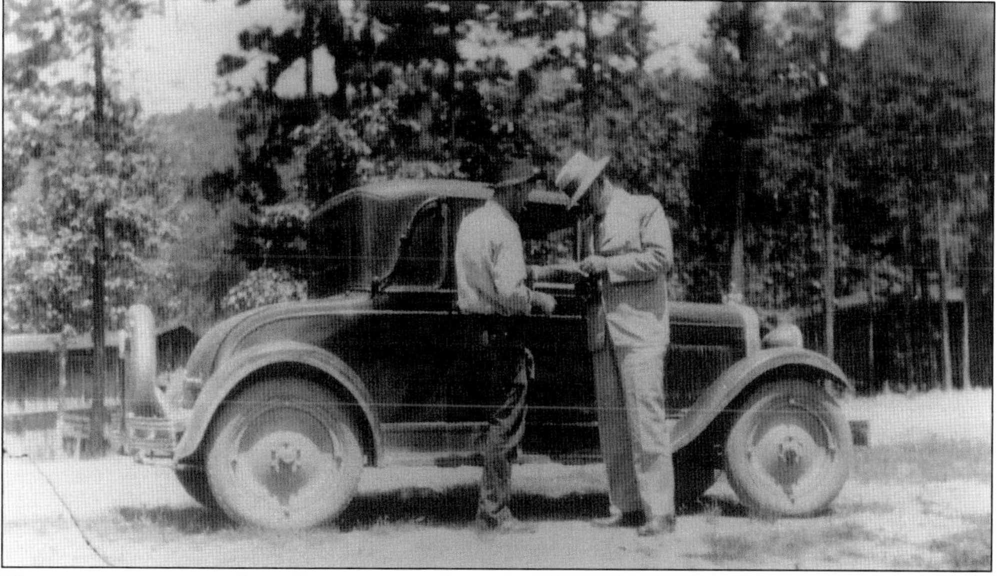

The power company brought its own physician, Dr. Charles Hardman, to Tallulah Falls during power plant construction. Dr. Hardman (right) checks out the injured hand of a power company employee. Hardman was the doctor for the power company throughout his career but also treated neighboring mountain residents. Many times he was paid in goods or services, and he once received a shotgun for delivering a baby. (Courtesy of Georgia Power Land Department Photo Archives.)

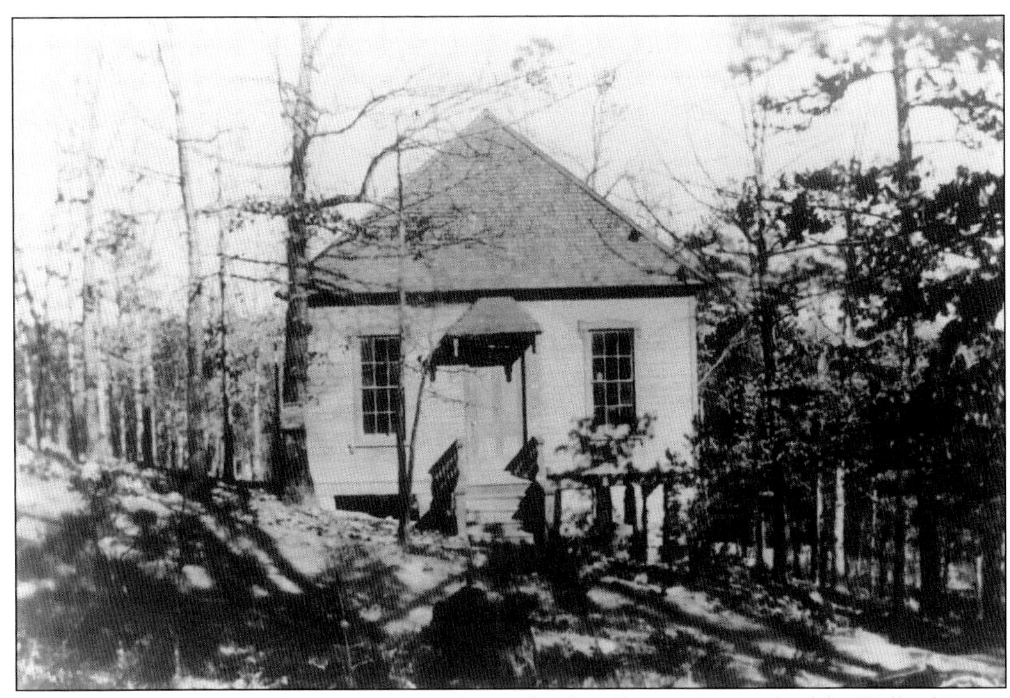

St. James Episcopal Church was constructed in Tallulah Falls, *c.* 1890, south of the Willard House Hotel above the railroad. (Courtesy of Georgia Power Land Department Photo Archives.)

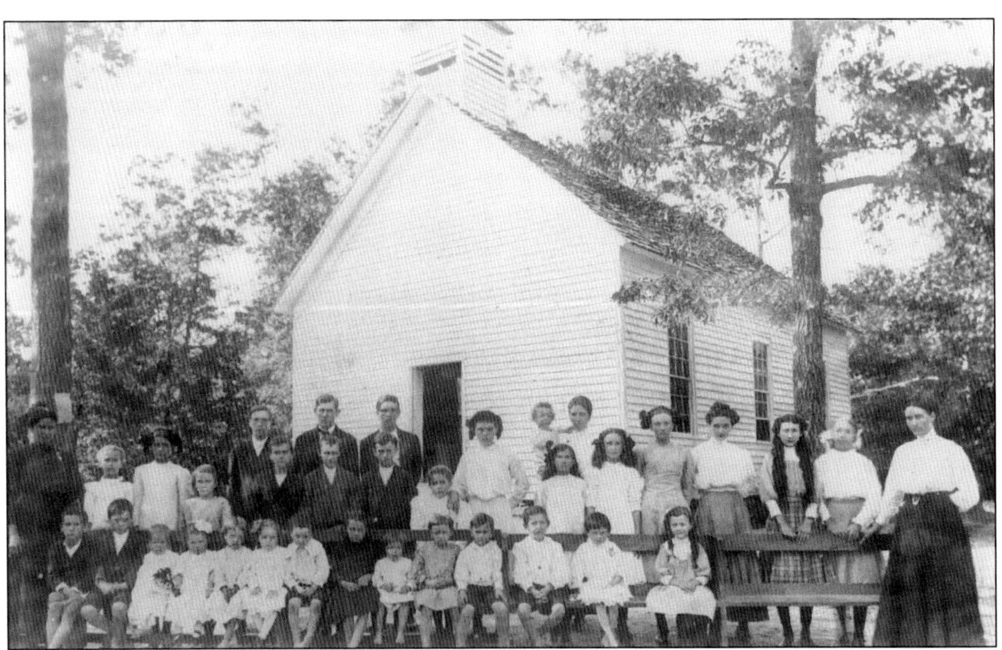

There were other churches in Tallulah Falls and in the neighboring communities. In the early 1900s this Sunday School group gathered in the Germany community near Clayton. (Courtesy of Georgia Department of Archives and History.)

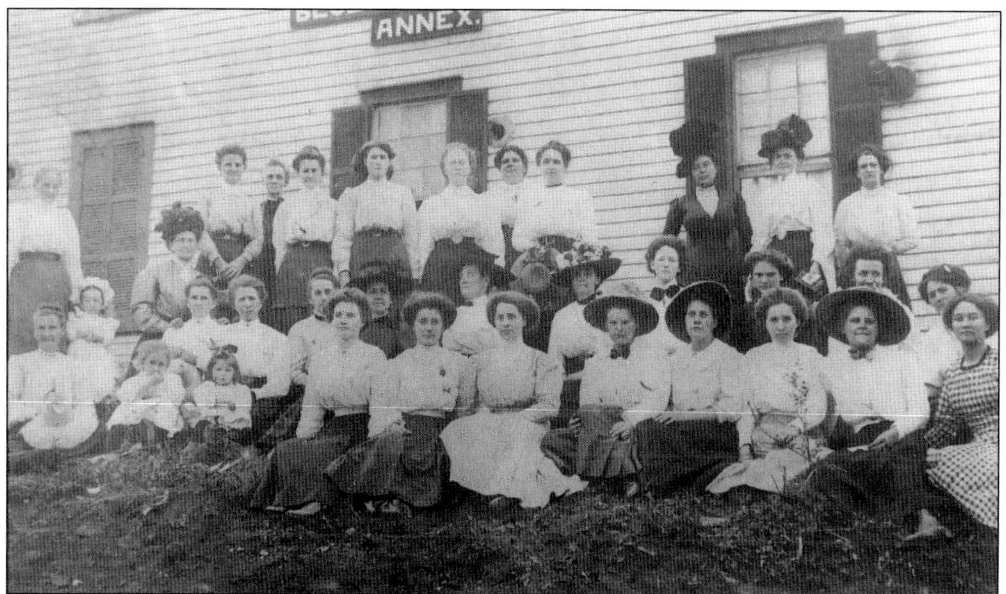

The Clayton Woman's Club was organized in 1910. The group is seen in front of the Blue Ridge Hotel Annex, *c.* 1910–1911. (Courtesy of Georgia Department of Archives and History.)

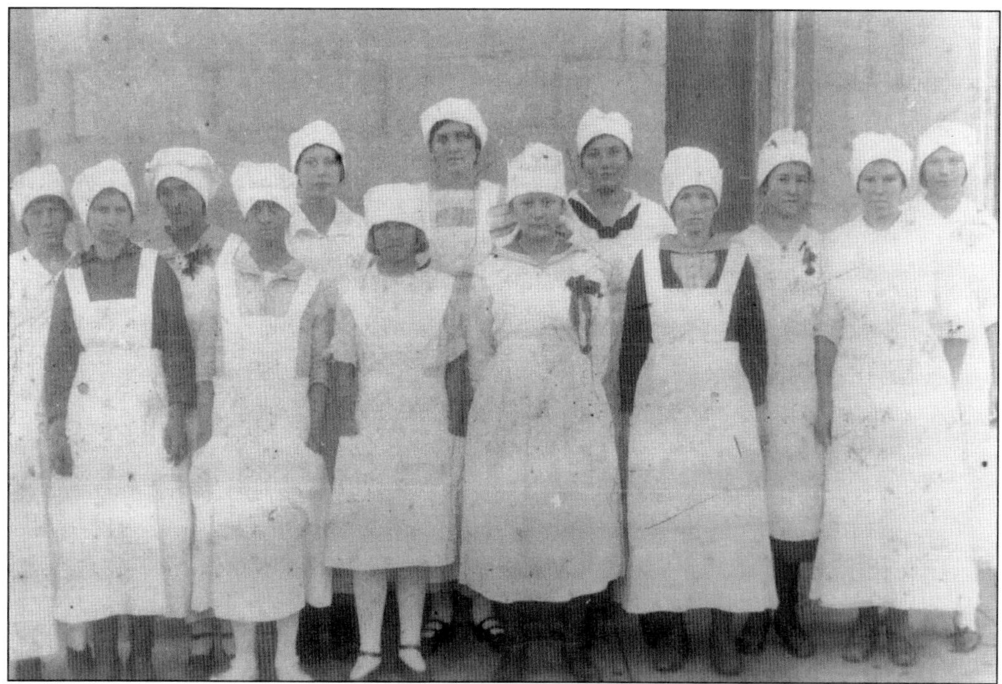

These girls from the Rabun County Canning Club are shown outfitted in their aprons and hats in 1916. The club provided a community gathering place for these young women. Before the introduction of freezers and widespread produce distribution, home canning was a necessity to utilize the bounty of the summer's garden for sustaining families over the winter months. (Courtesy of Georgia Department of Archives and History.)

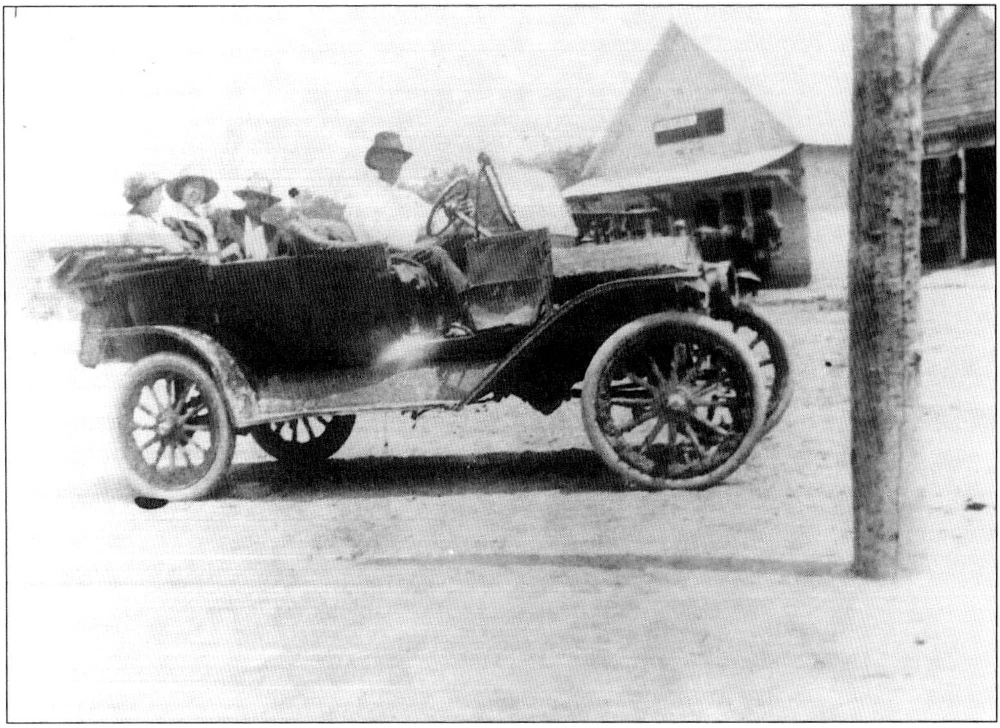

A Model-T Ford is being driven through the town of Tallulah Falls in this *c.* 1911 image . Note the frame storefront buildings in the background. The first car ever to appear in Rabun County was brought in by the power company and driven by company employees. (Courtesy of Rope Roberts.)

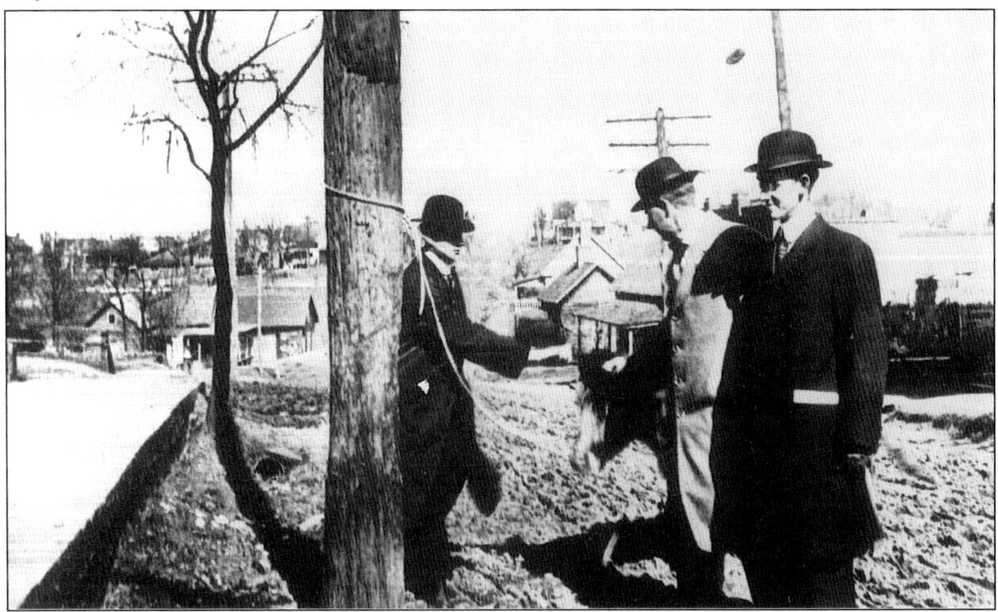

This photograph provides one of the few wide views of the town of Tallulah Falls, c. 1911. The town was incorporated in 1885. Note the dirt roads, as well as the cow tied to the tree. (Courtesy of Georgia Power Land Department Photo Archives.)

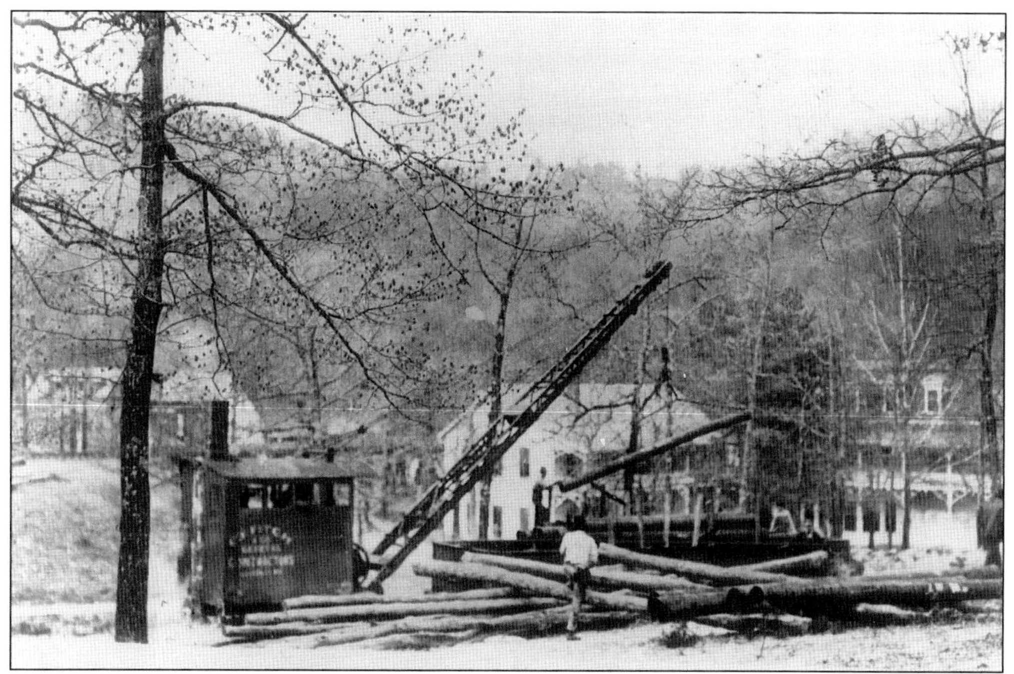

Materials are being delivered for the power plant in this *c.* 1911 photograph. The natural abundance of wood provided construction material for new company buildings, as well as for homes in Tallulah Falls, as seen in this photograph. (Courtesy of Georgia Power Land Department Photo Archives.)

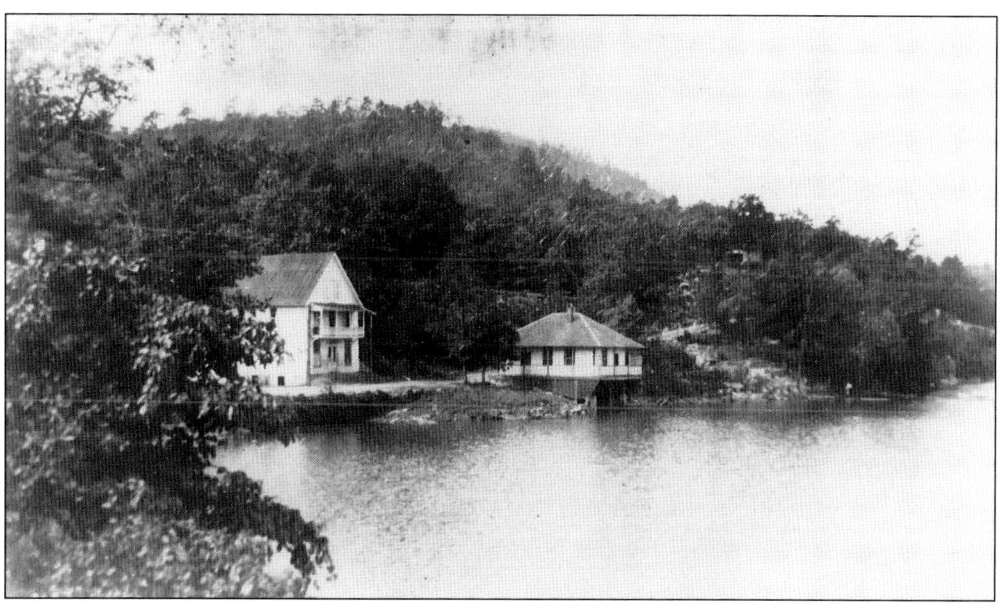

The building on the right is the Tallulah Falls Jail. When the lake was filled in 1913, the power company rebuilt the jail, which also contained city hall. Inmates must have been uncomfortable in the wintertime because there was no glass in the open, barred windows. In 1991 the jail was restored by Georgia Power Company and moved to the north side of the lake. (Courtesy of Rope Roberts.)

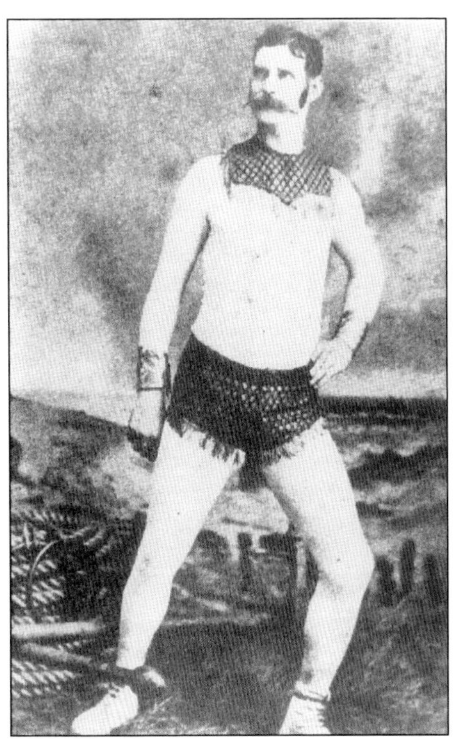

On July 24, 1886, J.A. St. John, alias Professor Leon, walked across Tallulah Gorge on a tightrope for $250. Using 1,440 feet of rope and balancing himself with a 46-pound, 30-foot-long pole, Leon attempted "the greatest feat of rope walking on record." Halfway across, a guy wire broke. With the ropes swaying, he managed to steady himself and finish the walk, landing at Lover's Leap several minutes later. (Courtesy of Tallulah Falls School.)

Almost a century later, the high-wire artist Karl Wallenda walked across the gorge on July 18, 1970 on a 2-inch-diameter steel cable. In 18 minutes, Wallenda crossed the 750-foot span above the gorge, pausing twice to perform headstands. Guy wire anchors in the bottom of the gorge and the steel towers on both rims remain today as evidence of this feat. (Courtesy of Rope Roberts.)

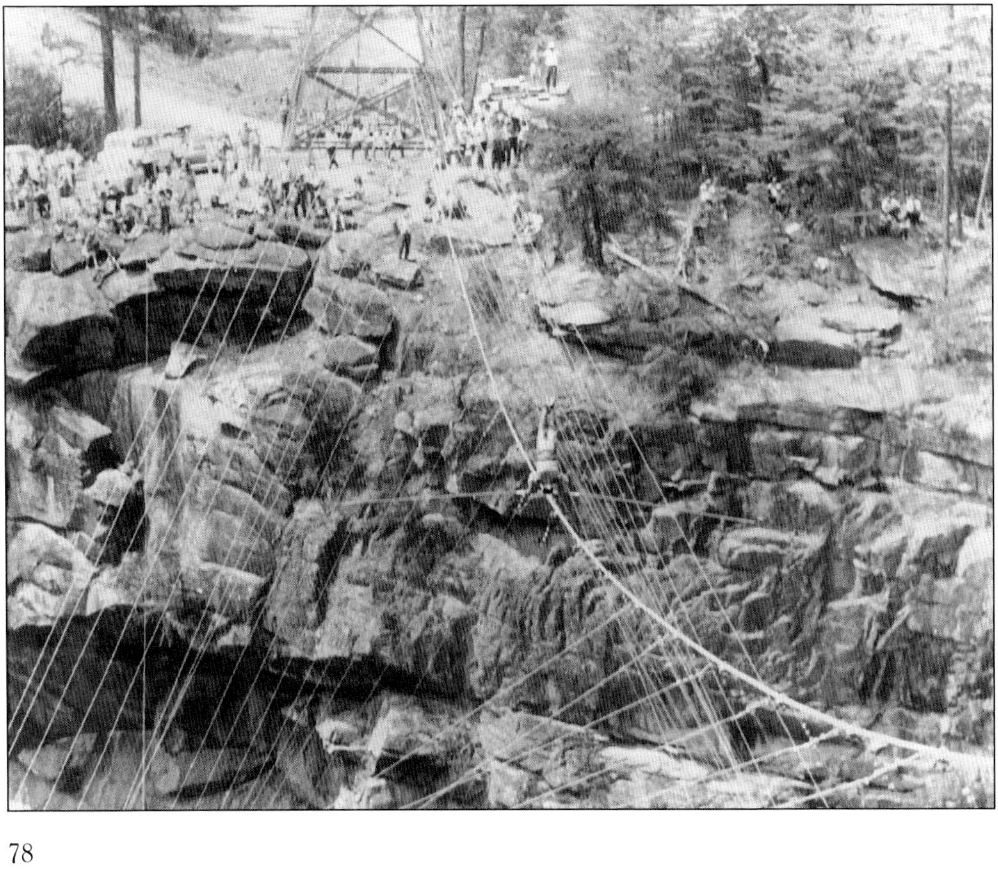

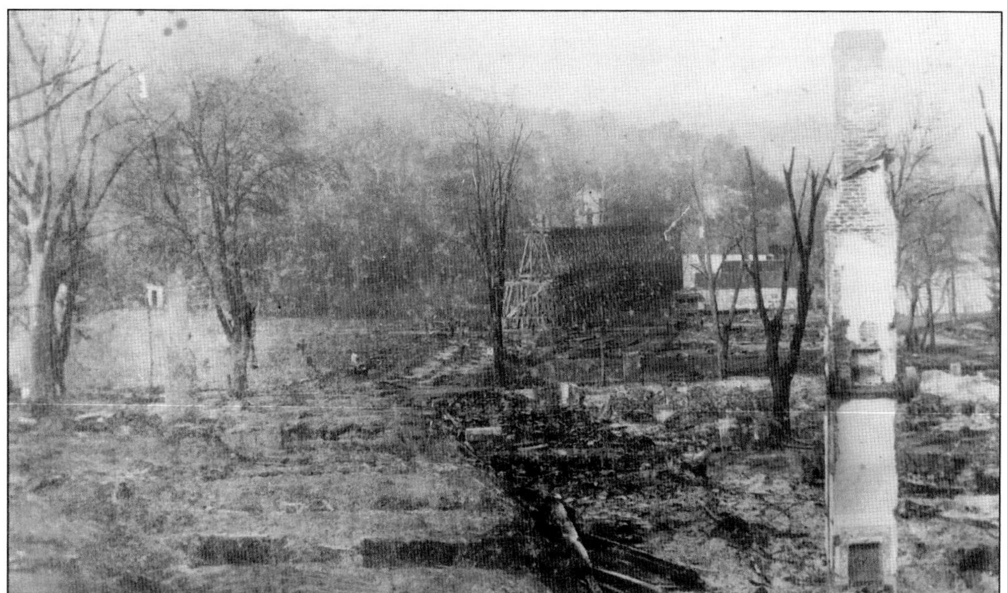

In 1921, just two weeks before Christmas, a blustery wind spread fire from an undetermined cause throughout Tallulah Falls. It burned for days, destroying homes, stores, and hotels. The railroad trestle crashed to the ground. Livestock ran up and down the street until they collapsed. (Courtesy of Mrs. M.M. Fincher.)

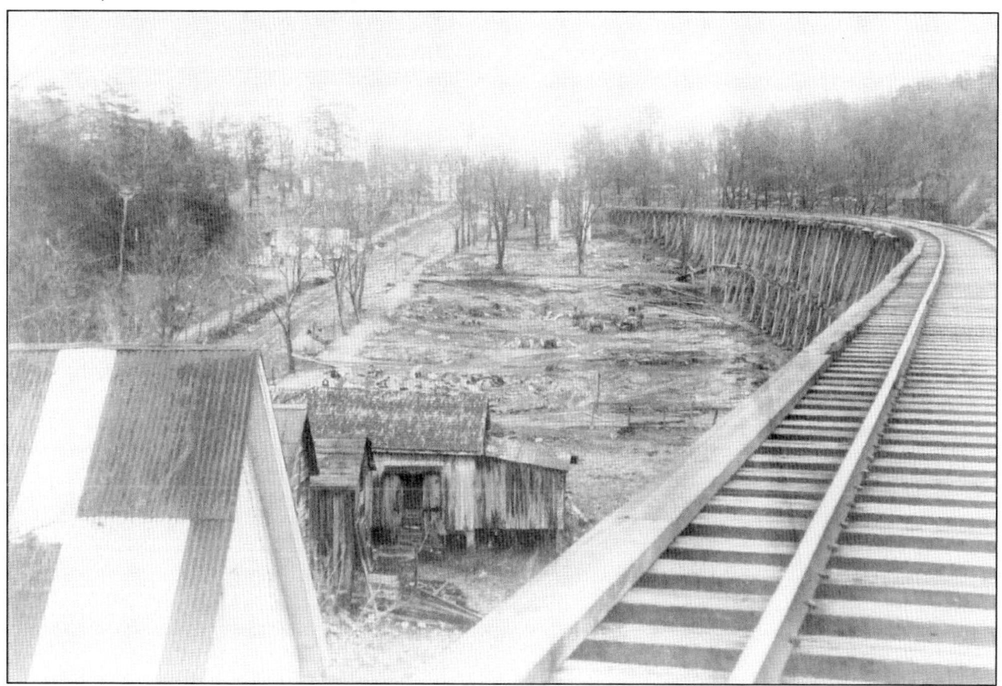

Lack of a fire department proved devastating. Little of the town that was destroyed was ever rebuilt, except for the railroad trestle. "I have never seen nor heard the wind blow so hard as it did that night. The wind carried burning bark and shingles as far away as Tugalo . . . I remember the screaming, mooing and braying of those poor animals."—Bertha Burrell, Tallulah Falls resident. (Courtesy of Georgia Power Land Department Photo Archives.)

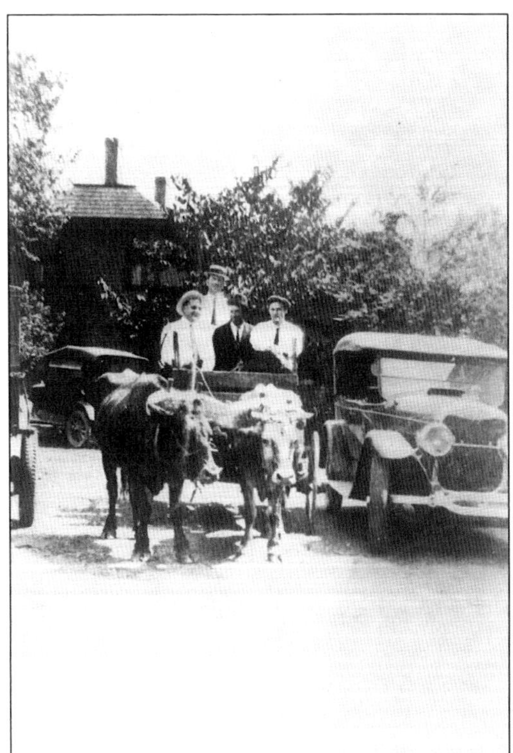

Sure-footed means of transportation on the muddy, hilly terrain endured for a long time in the mountains. This photograph shows a team of oxen and a Ford Model A in Clayton in the 1920s. (Courtesy of Georgia Department of Archives and History.)

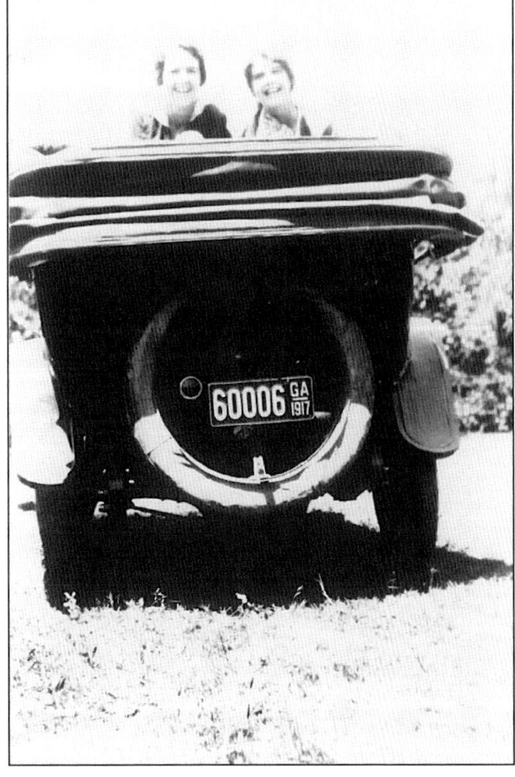

These girls appear delighted to be on a drive in Tallulah Falls in 1917. The arrival of the automobile and better roads would help bring about the decline of the town of Tallulah Falls. Route 441 bypassed the town in 1924, opening up areas once thought isolated. (Courtesy of Rope Roberts.)

Seven

Tallulah Falls School "Romance of a Hill in Habersham"

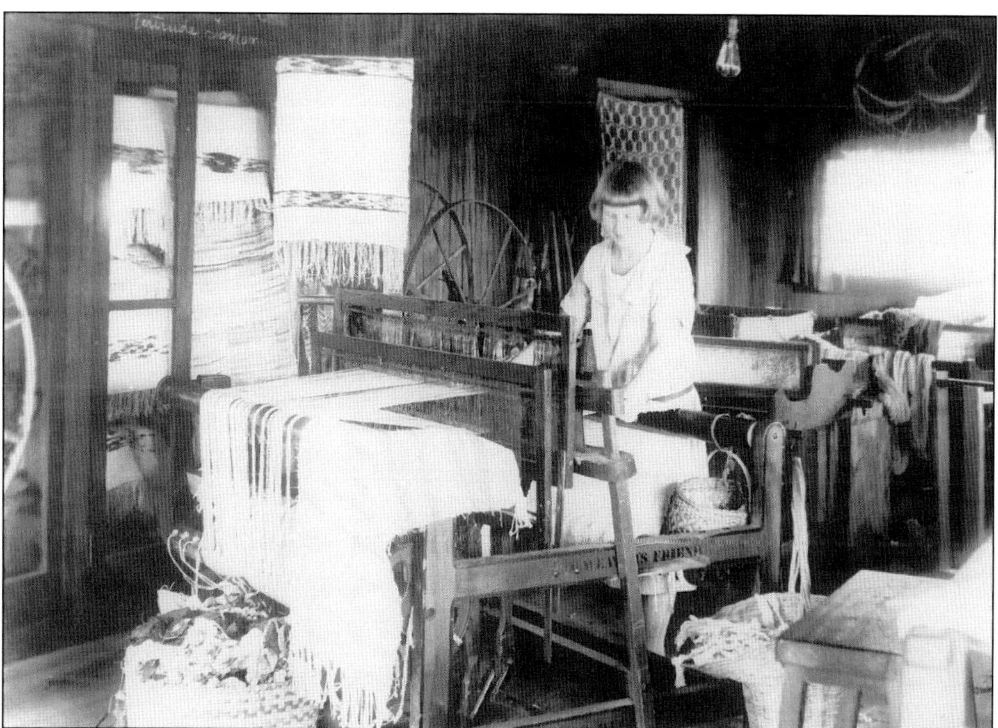

Here Gertrude Taylor, one of four motherless sisters, receives training in weaving while in her fifth year at Tallulah Falls School. In the belief that education was three-fold, Tallulah Falls School (originally founded as the Tallulah Falls Industrial School) provided training for children of the mountains for the head, the hands, and the heart. It was this mental, physical, and spiritual training that opened new doors for the students. (Courtesy of Tallulah Falls School.)

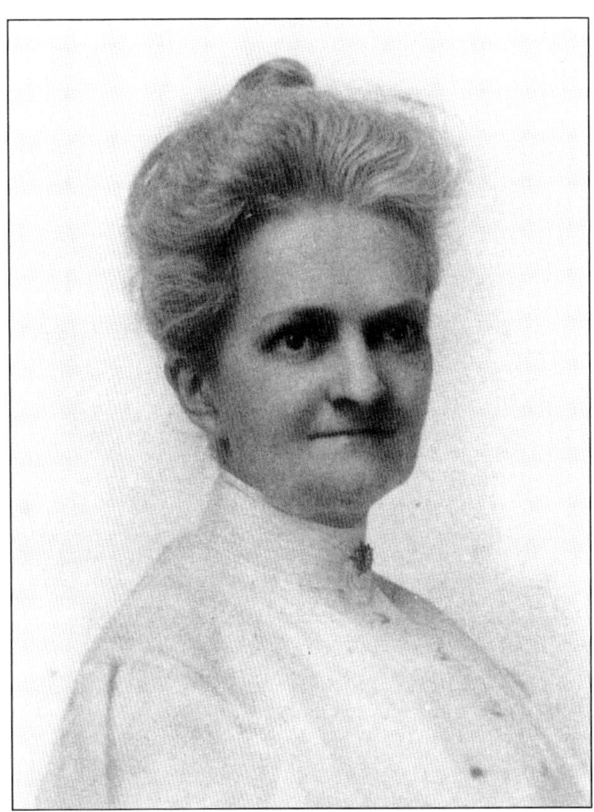

The idea of Tallulah Falls School was conceived in 1904 by Mary Ann Lipscomb, the director of the Lucy Cobb Institute in Athens, as a means to educate the children of Tallulah Falls who had little opportunity to acquire formal learning. It was in 1906 that she proposed a resolution to the Georgia Federation of Women's Clubs to initiate the founding of the school. (Courtesy of Tallulah Falls School.)

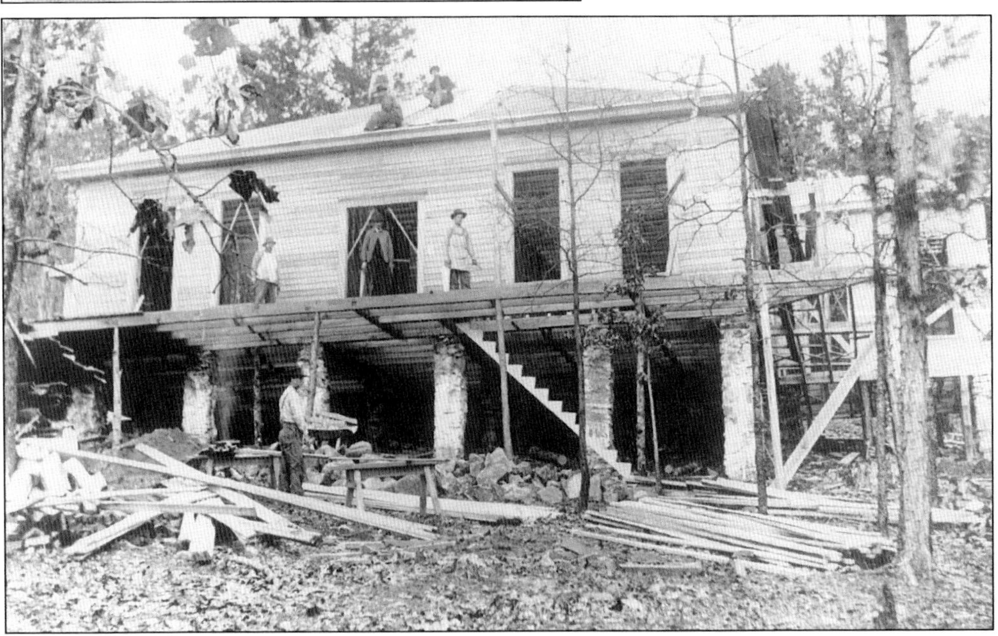

Miss Sarah White of Tallulah Falls donated a 5-acre tract of land for the school and construction began. The original one-story structure contained an assembly room, two recitation rooms, a cook room, a workshop, and large porches. (Courtesy of Georgia Department of Archives and History.)

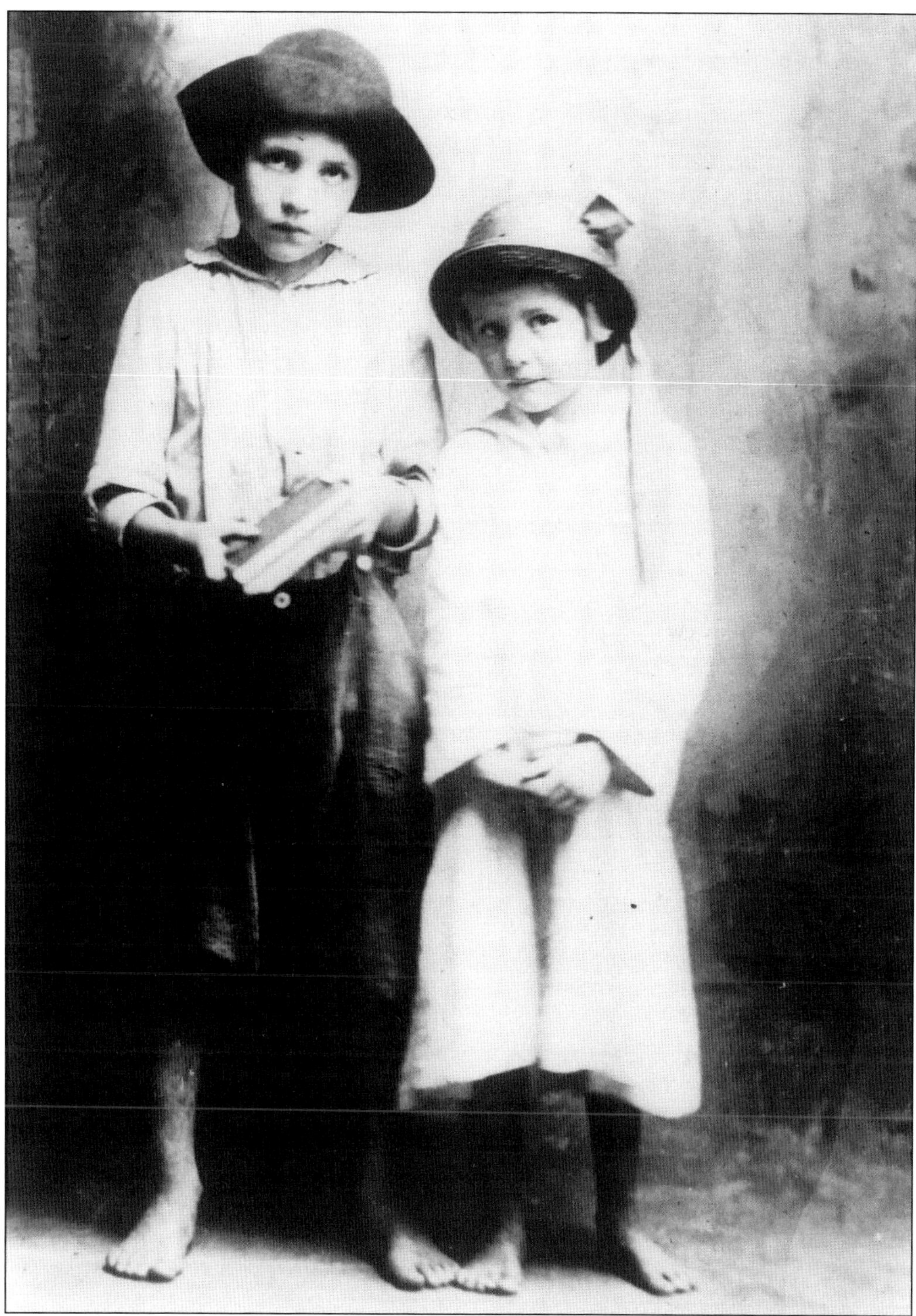

Before the school's completion in 1909, the children in Tallulah Falls went to school only three months out of the year in a single room located over the jail. There were no other schools nearby. These beautifully dressed but barefoot children appear ready for their first day of school. (Courtesy of Tallulah Falls School.)

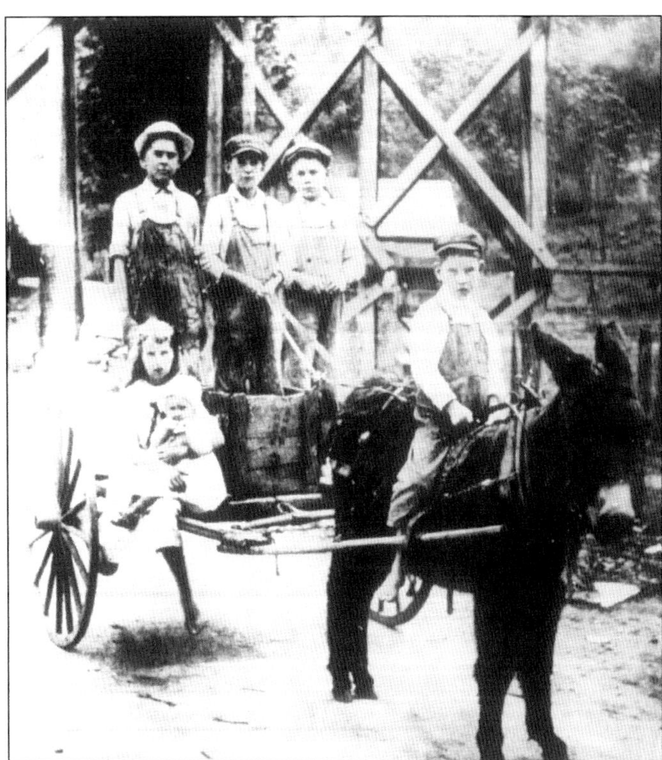

Children walked or depended upon mules and horses to get to school. Pictured are five of the 21 children attending the Tallulah Falls Industrial School when it opened on July 12, 1909. (Courtesy of Tallulah Falls School.)

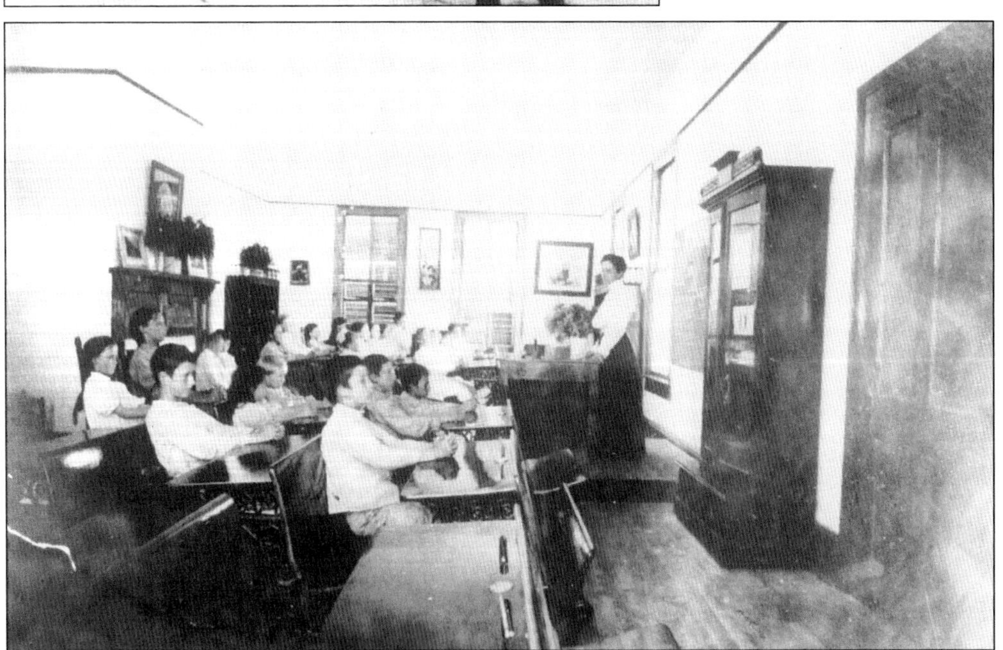

Notice the well-furnished and equipped schoolroom as Miss Annie Thrasher and her 21 pupils began classes that first summer of 1909. By the end of the year, 66 children from Rabun and Habersham Counties were enrolled. The school grew rapidly, and by 1912 there were two buildings on the campus, housing 86 students and three teachers. Some of the students boarded at Lipscomb Cottage, the second structure built. (Courtesy of Tallulah Falls School.)

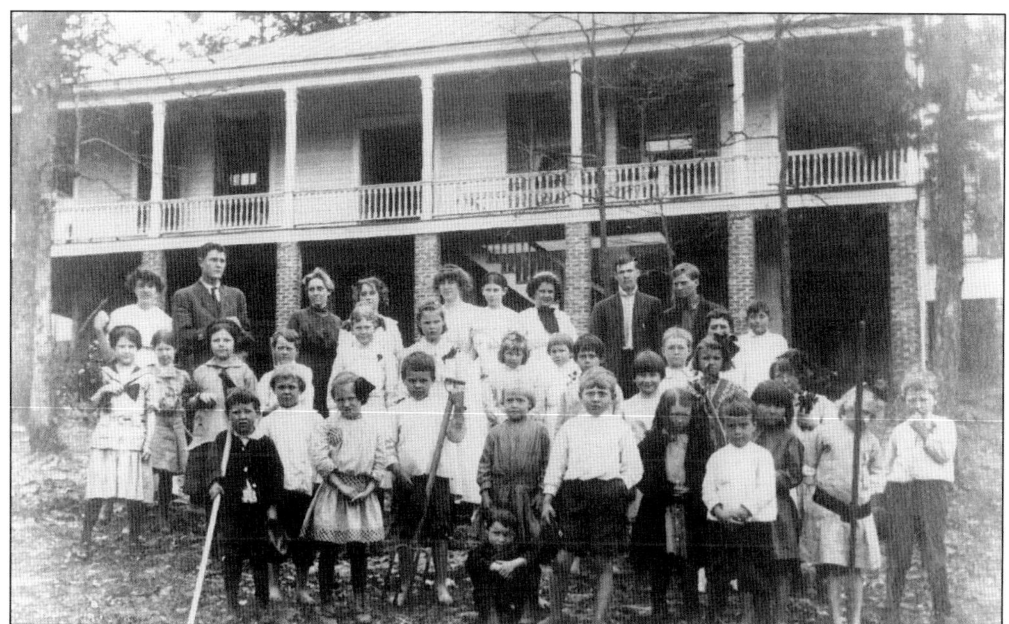

These are children and faculty from Tallulah Falls School who were recruited to serve as part of the Junior Civic League for town and neighborhood cleanup established by Laura Blackshear. They are pictured c. 1915 standing in front of the school. One student, all ready for work, holds a pitchfork. (Courtesy of Georgia Department of Archives and History.)

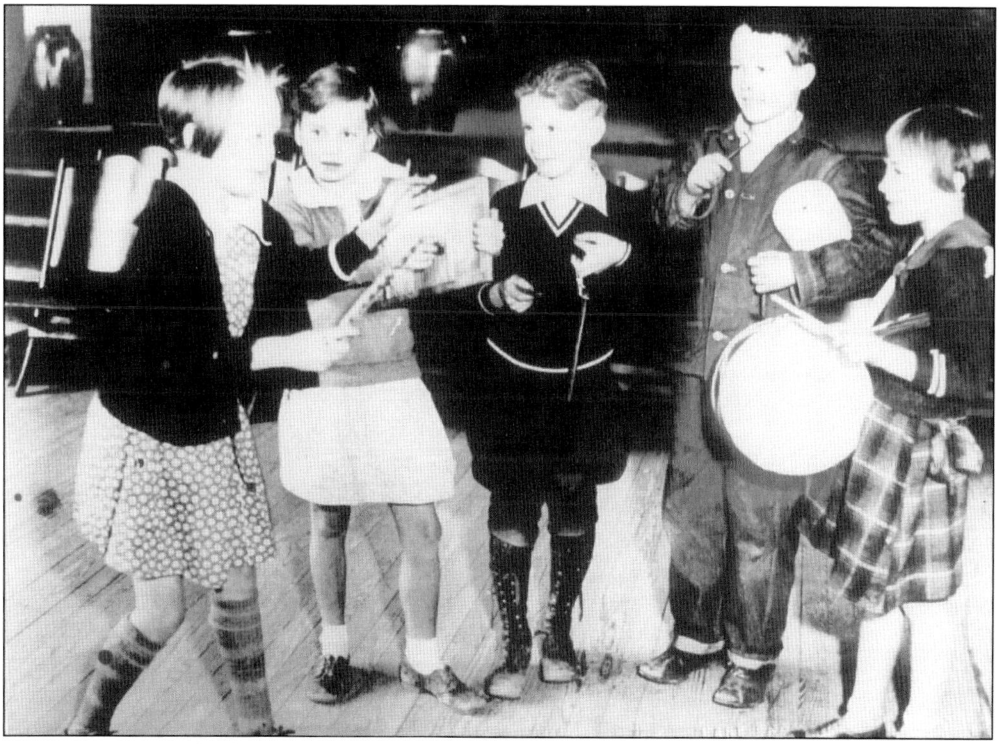

Instruments provided both fun and education for these five Tallulah Falls students. Music played an important part in the daily lives of the children. (Courtesy of Tallulah Falls School.)

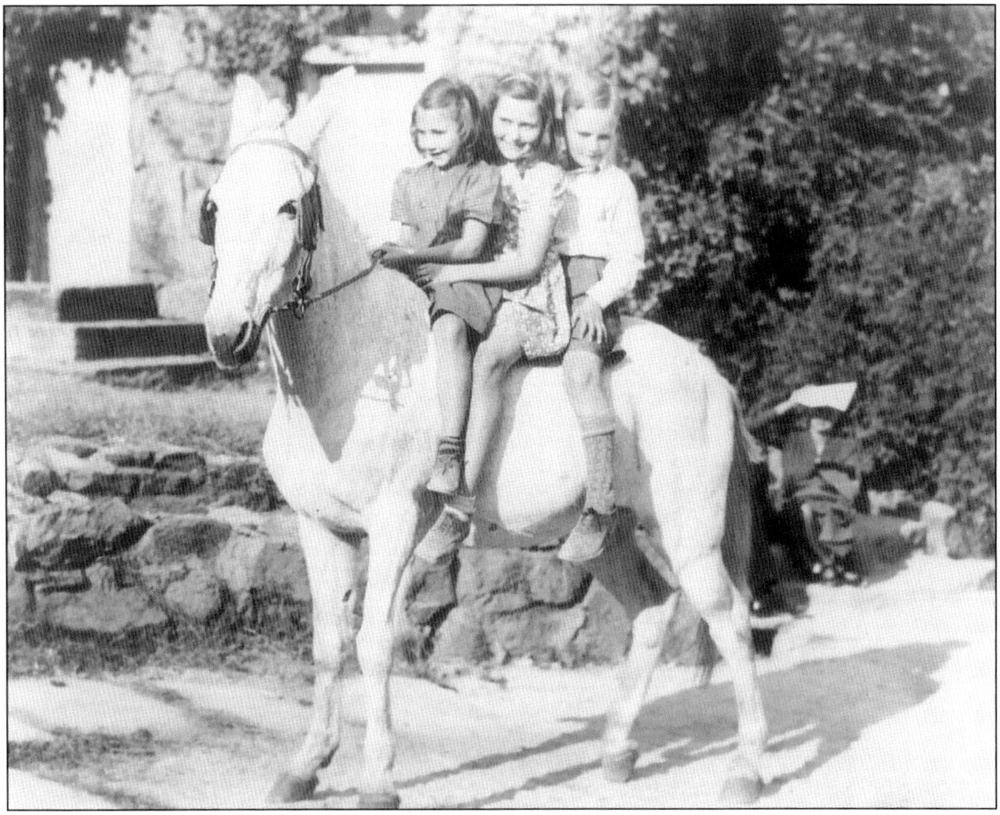

In 1924, when two boys rode up to the school on their mule, offering to trade him for an education, the offer was accepted. "Old Frank" became "Frank Tallulah," and provided 27 years of service to the school and its children. Seated aboard "Frank Tallulah," from left to right are: Bessie Gregg, Mary Anne Martin, and Jess Rickman, c. 1927. (Courtesy of Tallulah Falls School.)

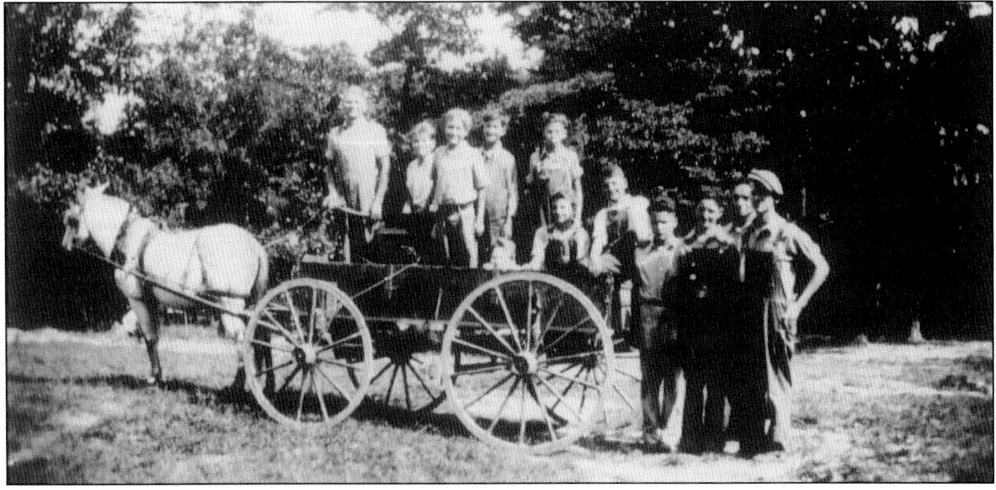

Here "Frank Tallulah" pulls a cartload of boys. All of the work at the school, including farming, was done by the students. "Frank Tallulah" helped in hauling rocks for building, pulling carts, and gardening work for many years before he died in 1951. (Courtesy of Tallulah Falls School.)

The agricultural program of the school began in 1910. Gardening, woodworking, and stone masonry were taught to the boys, along with math and English. Mr. Thomas Early, a professor at the State Agricultural School, helped in establishing this program. Mr. John Fort of Mt. Airy donated apple trees. These trees supplied ample harvests for years to come, as evidenced in this photograph of Robert Williams and students. (Courtesy of Tallulah Falls School.)

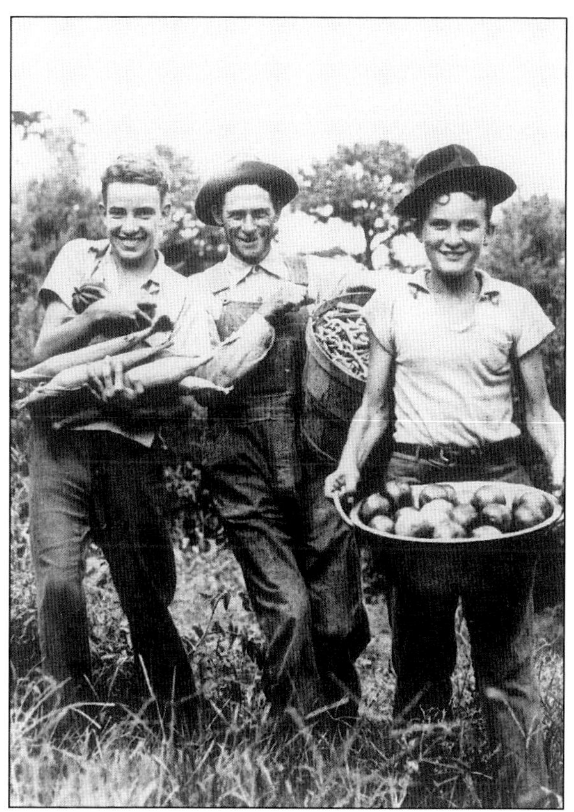

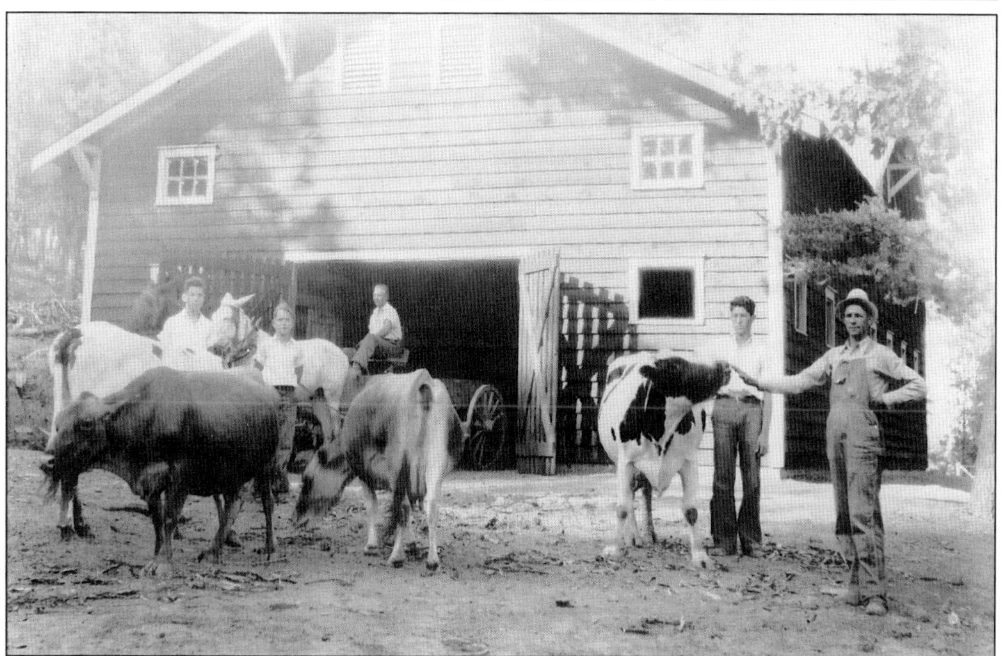

Courses in animal husbandry supplied valuable knowledge that the children shared with their families. "Fitzy," named for Mrs. Z.I. Fitzpatrick, director of the school in the 1930s, provided an astonishing nine gallons of milk a day. (Courtesy of Tallulah Falls School.)

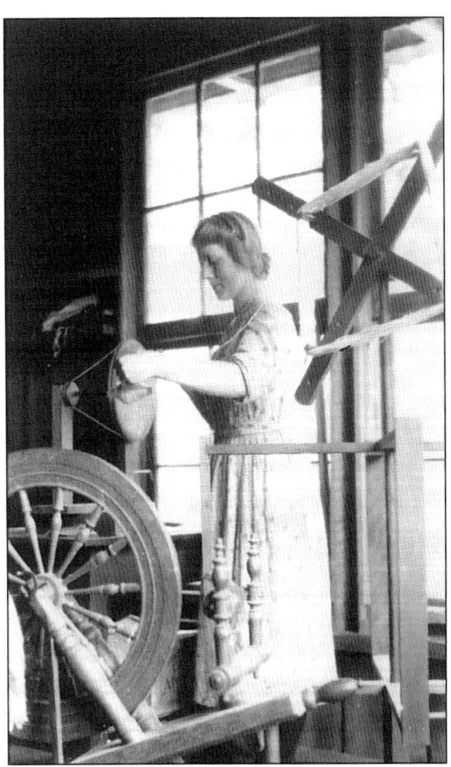

Eliza Shirley, a former student who became a teacher in 1919, provided instruction in spinning by demonstrating the wheel. The girls were also taught weaving, sewing, and basketry, in addition to their studies in math and English. (Courtesy of Tallulah Falls School.)

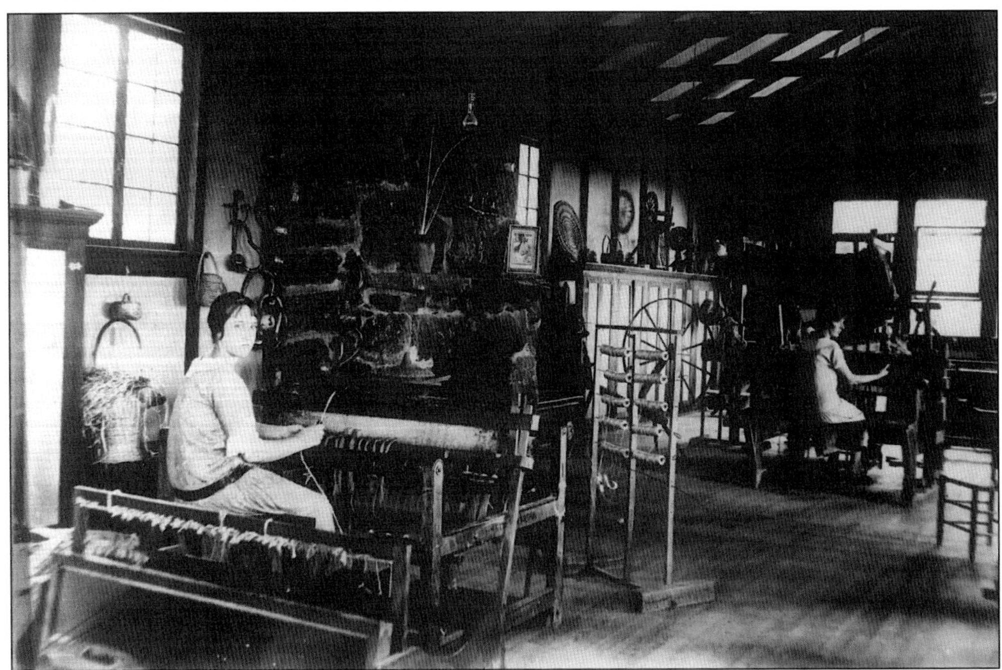

Students are weaving at the loom; note the large spinning wheel, center background, that was used to spin cotton or wool. Natural vegetable dyes were made by the girls to use in their work. They became proficient at weaving patterns handed down for generations, including Orange Peel, Snail Trail, Pine Bloom, and Lover's Knot. (Courtesy of Tallulah Falls School.)

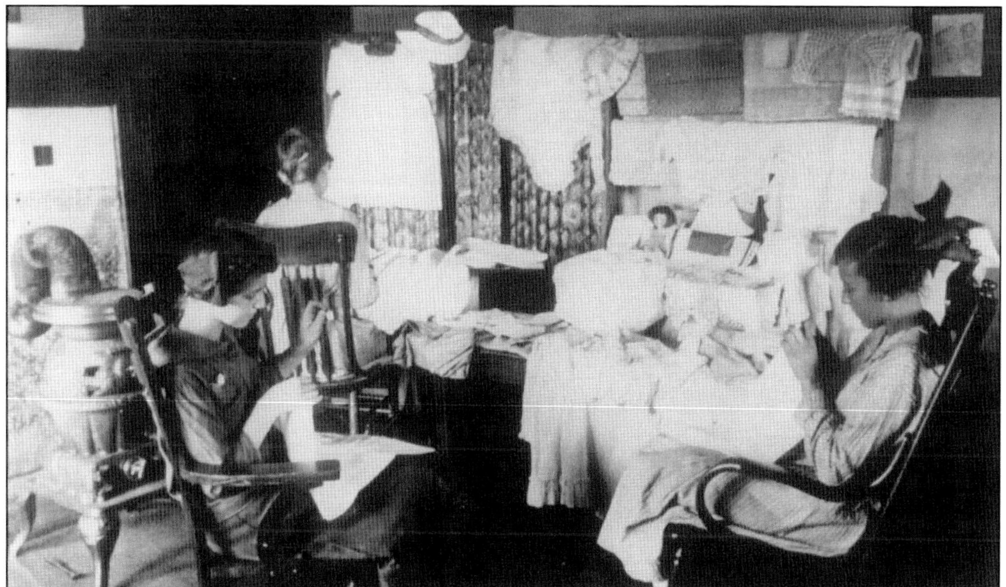

Seated near their handwork display, these students continue their sewing. With the addition of Eliza Shirley to the staff, handwork and crocheting were taught to the female students. Their finished goods were exhibited in cities as far away as Washington, D.C. This exposure resulted in monetary gifts to the school, as well as increasing the number of visitors to the campus. (Courtesy of Tallulah Falls School.)

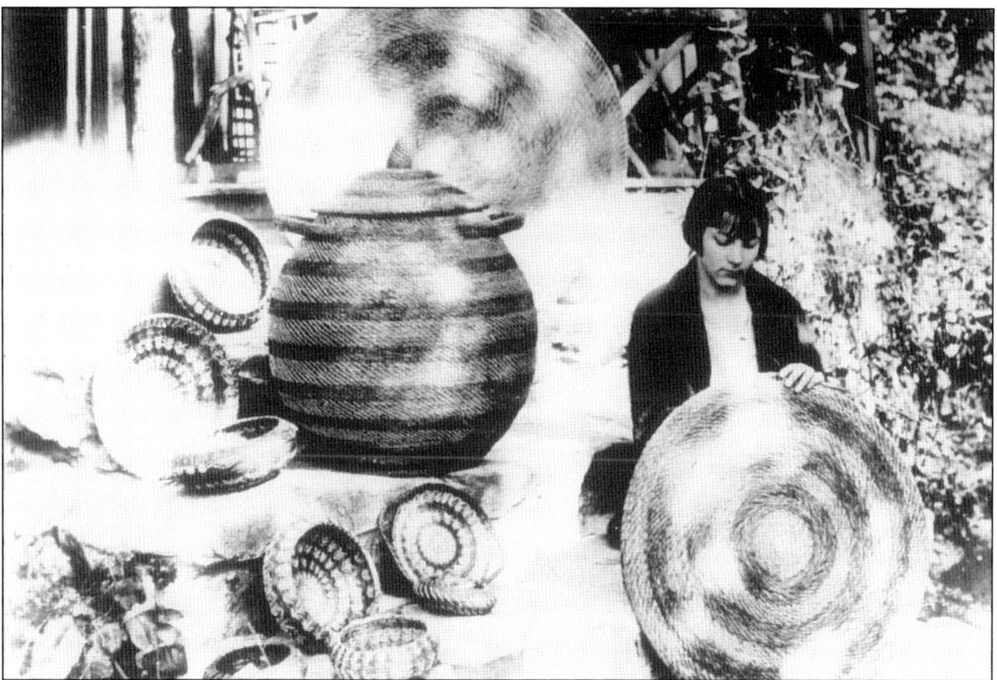

Baskets, a hand-crafted staple in the mountains, were usually made from unseasoned white oak in time-honored patterns. "Coiled baskets" are shown here. By 1924 a crafts shop was built at the school, and basketry, weaving, and rug making, indigenous crafts of the local mountain people, were promoted. (Courtesy of Tallulah Falls School.)

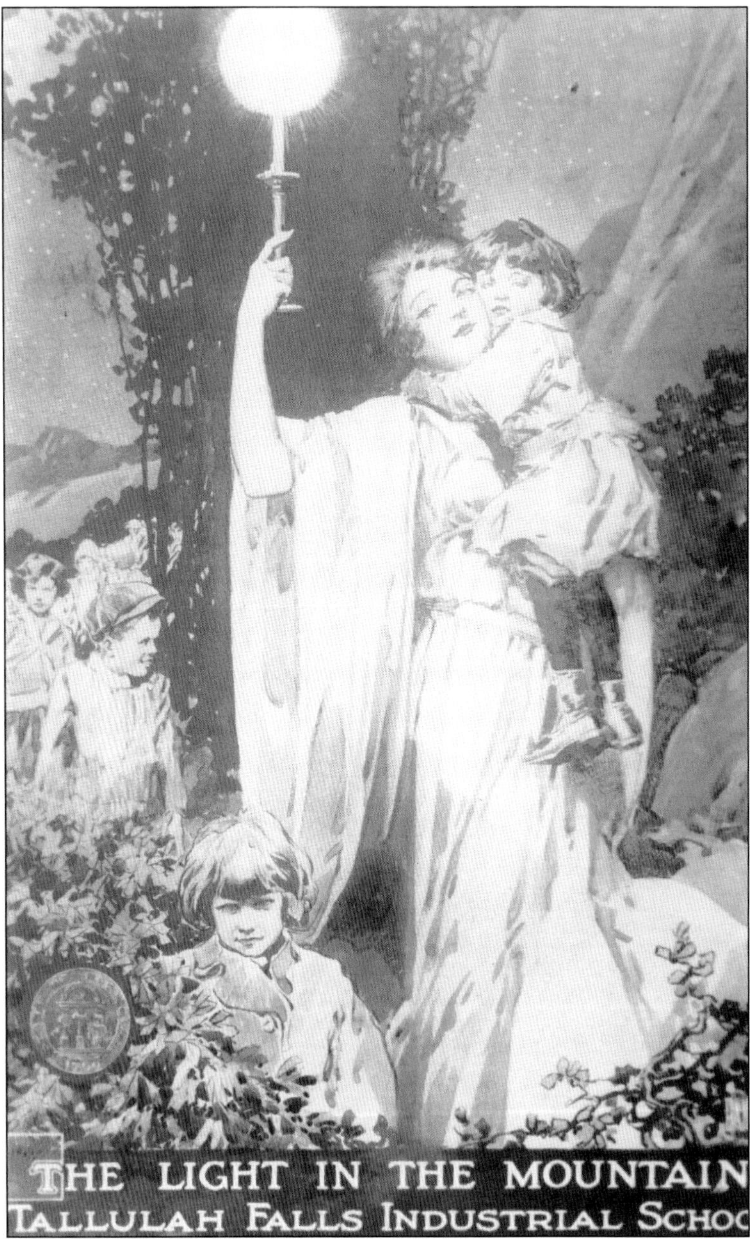

Originally dubbed the "Romance of a Hill in Habersham," the name "Light in the Mountains" was given to the school by Lamar Trotti, editor of *The Georgian*. This drawing was produced by Don Smith of New York, a well-known design artist. (Courtesy of Tallulah Falls School.)

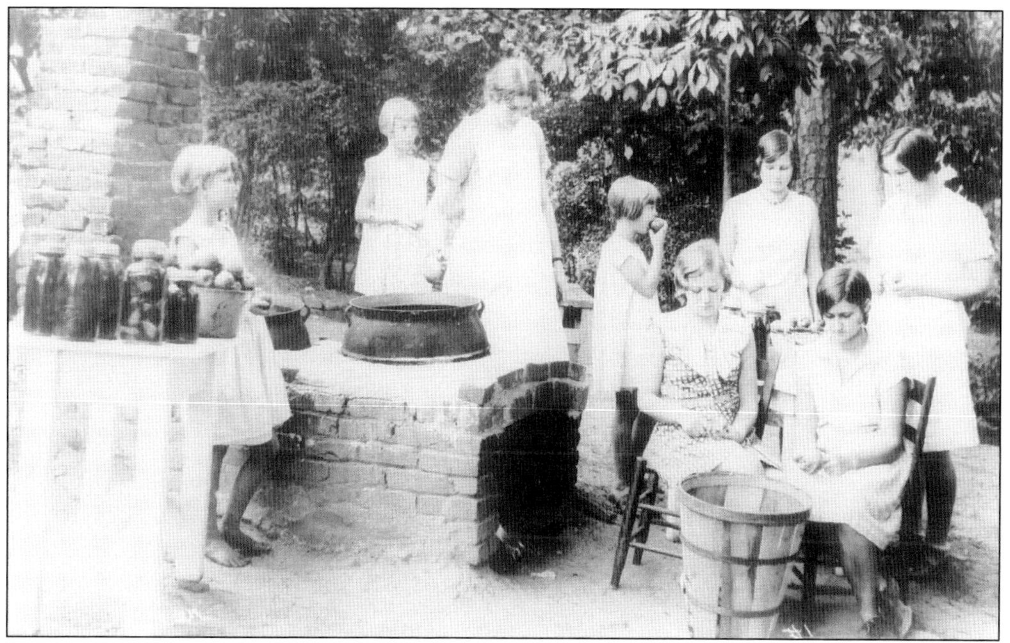

Here a group of summer students at the school on August 31, 1930 prepare apples for butter or sauce. All of the farm products were utilized in feeding the students and staff. Note the jars of canned vegetables. (Courtesy of Tallulah Falls School.)

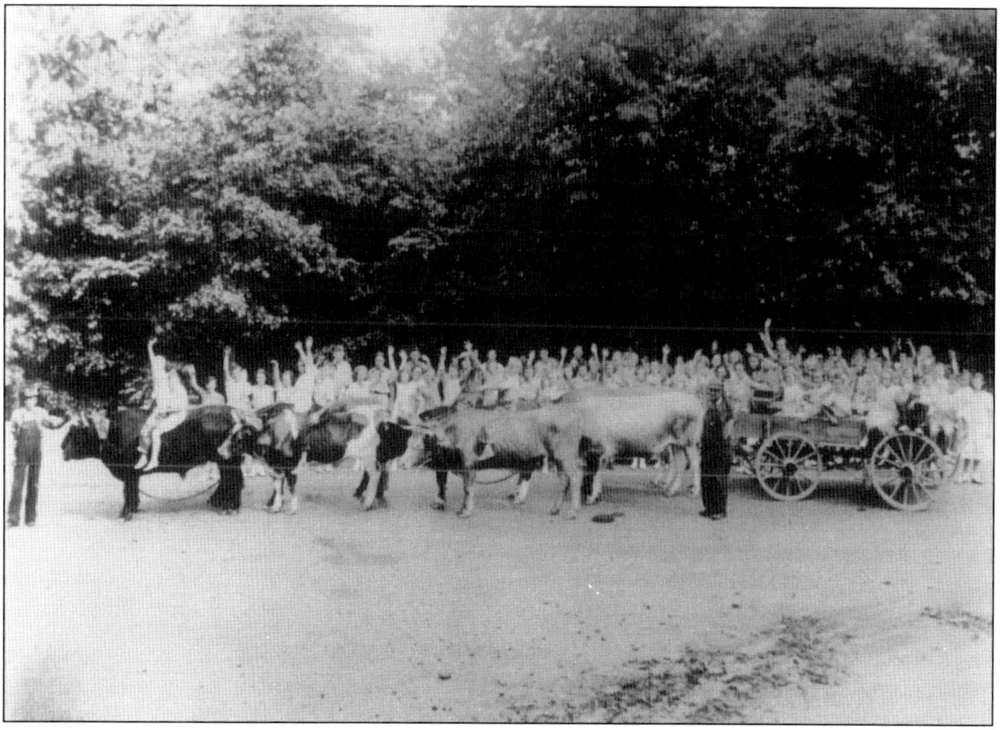

Along with cart and livestock, the student body greets visitors. This was very likely a publicity photograph taken to promote the school in hopes of increasing contributions. (Courtesy of Tallulah Falls School.)

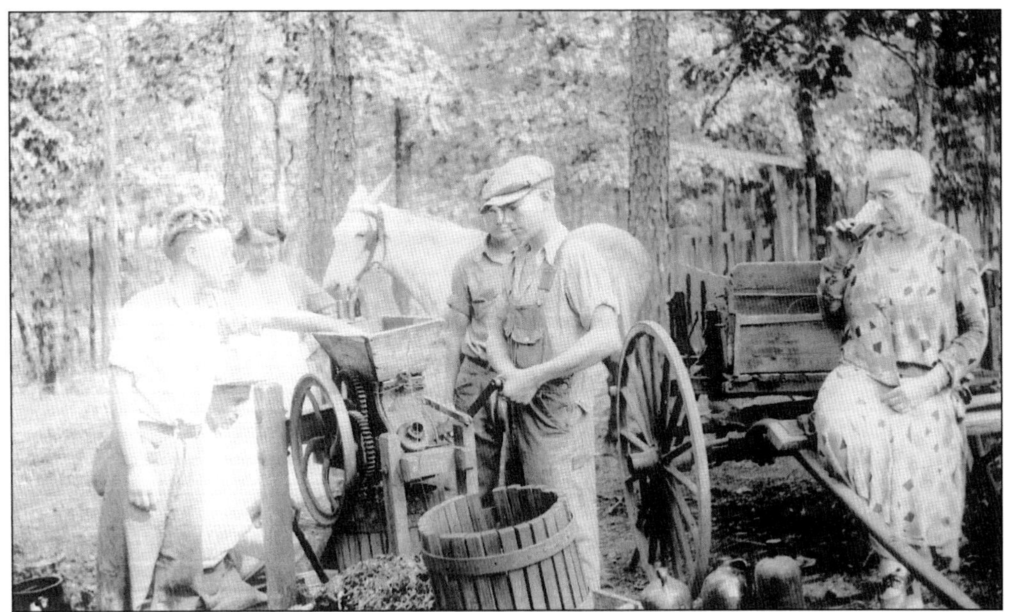

In this image, "Frank Tallulah" and company enjoy the fruits of a day harvesting and pressing apples. (Courtesy of Tallulah Falls School.)

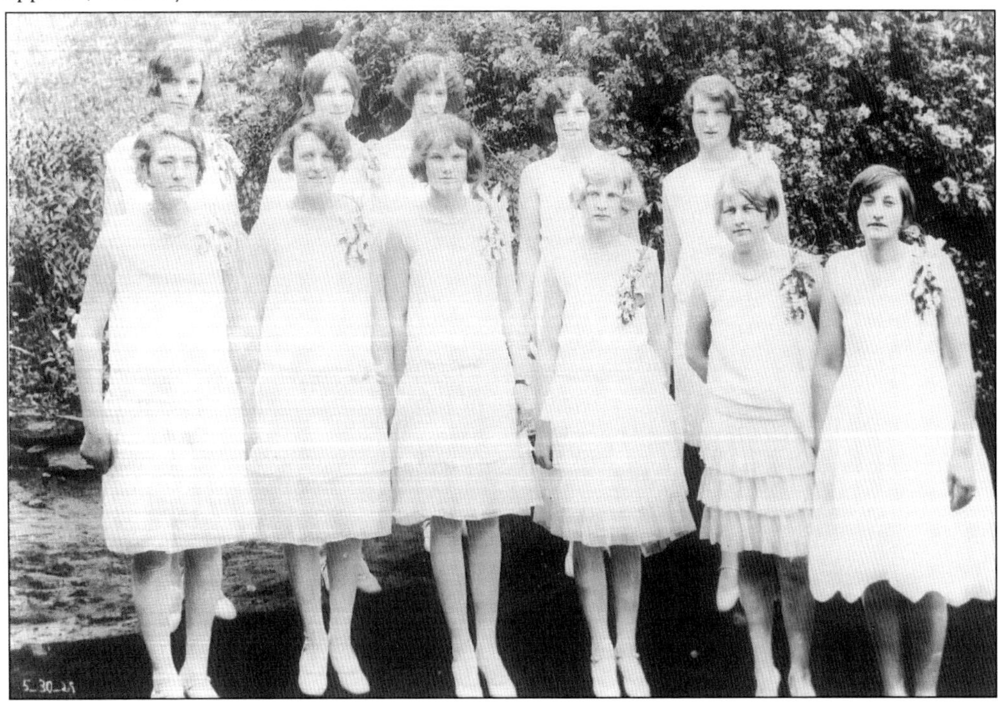

The year 1928 marked the first graduating class at Tallulah Falls School. This group of girls is from the Class of 1929. Today the school is still operated by the Georgia Federation of Women's Clubs. Over time, the focus of the school changed, and academic excellence became its top priority. The original campus has grown in size to its current 500 acres, and provides an excellent coeducational experience for students from all over the United States. (Courtesy of Tallulah Falls School.)

Eight

Harnessing the Tallulah

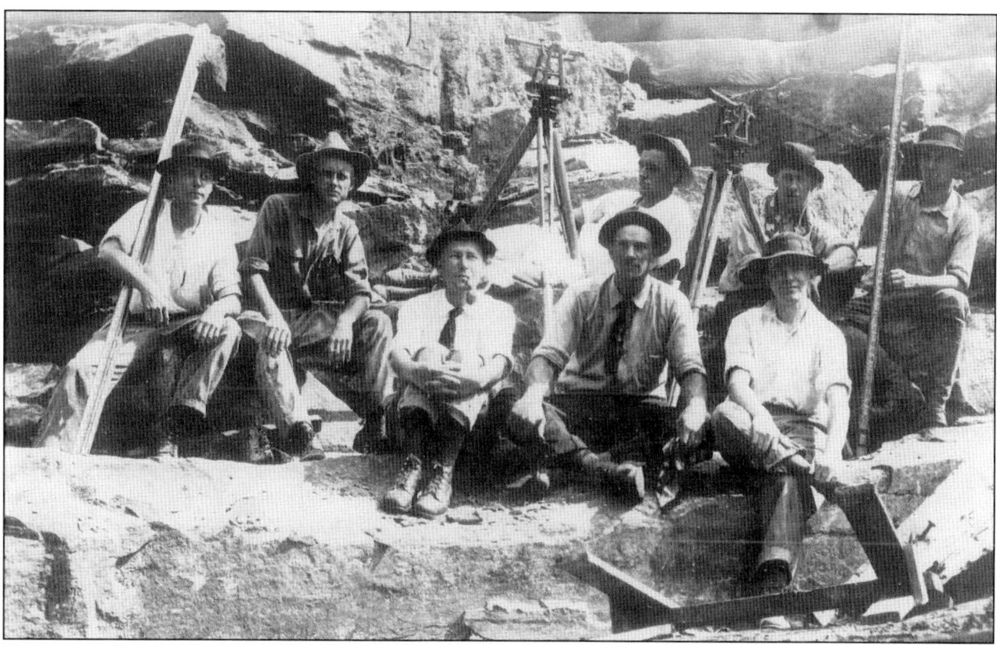

Surveyors for the Tallulah Falls hydroelectric construction project sit on the rocky terrain of the gorge with their equipment, *c.* 1911. An attempt was initiated in 1910 to harness the mighty force of the Tallulah River for hydroelectric power. The company soon ran into financial difficulties and construction halted. Henry M. Atkinson saw the Tallulah Falls project as a reliable power source for his Atlanta street railway system. He began negotiations to purchase and implement the project. Under his leadership, the Georgia Railway and Power Company (later Georgia Power Company) was formed to complete the power project. (Courtesy of Georgia Power Land Department Photo Archives.)

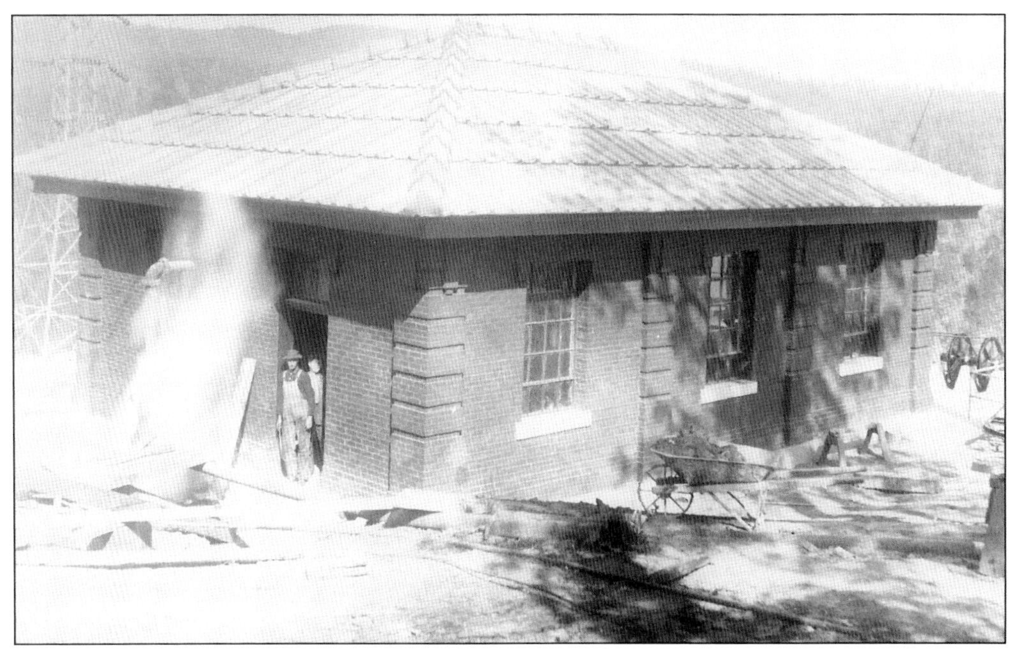

To gain access from the rim of the gorge to the power plant construction site at the bottom of the gorge, the power company built an incline railway. Machinery to operate the incline was located in the hoist house, shown here in 1913. (Courtesy of Georgia Power Land Department Photo Archives.)

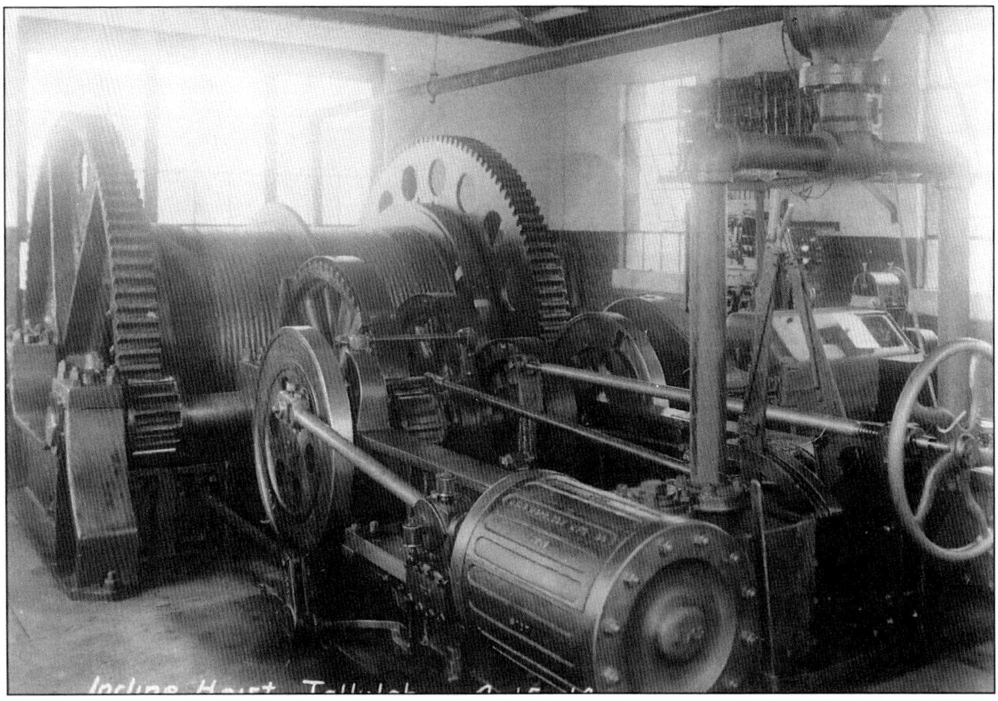

The interior of the hoist house, including the steam engine and large gears to wind the cable that raised and lowered the incline car, is shown in this April 1914 photograph. (Courtesy of Georgia Power Land Department Photo Archives.)

The incline railway carried equipment, material, and laborers to the bottom of the gorge where the switchhouse and powerhouse were under construction. It was the steepest incline in the country without being perfectly vertical. (Courtesy of Georgia Power Land Department Photo Archives.)

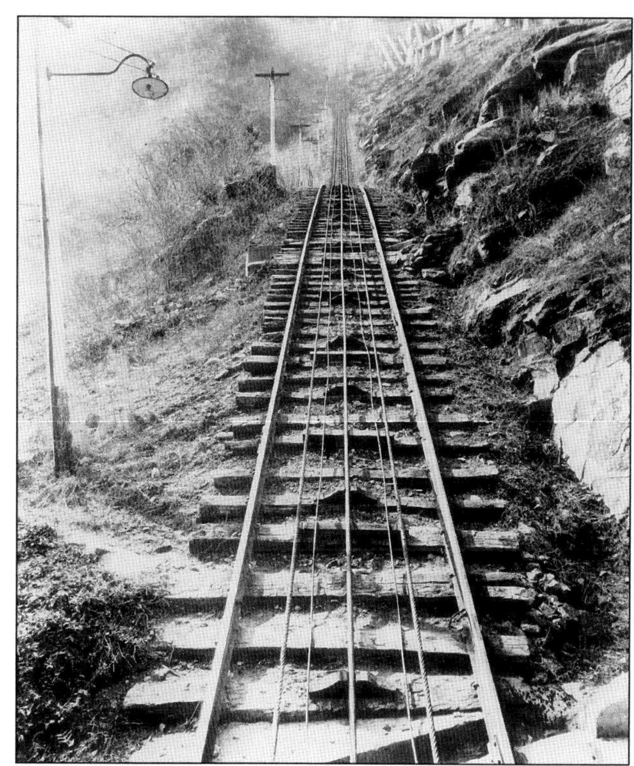

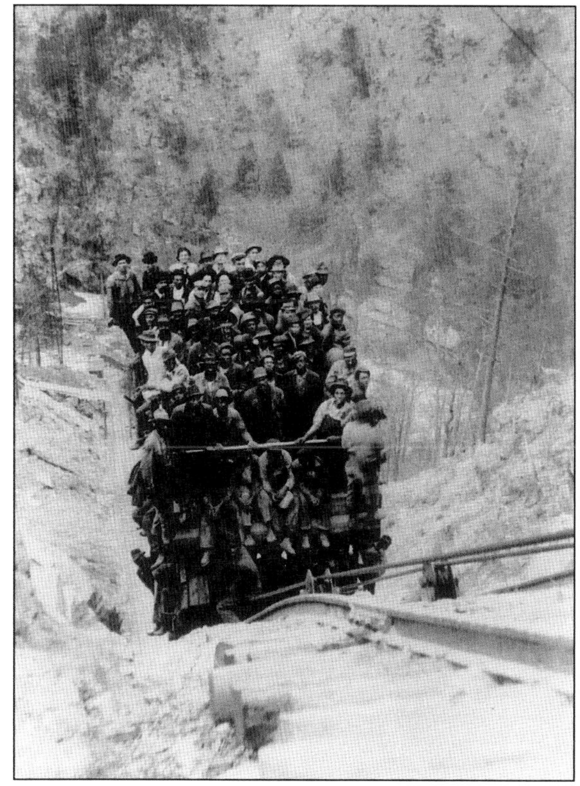

One hundred thirty-five workmen ascend on the incline railway from the construction site below. This 1,200-foot incline transported 30,000 tons of material and 400,000 workers and passengers without an accident during construction of the power plant. Today it is still the only means of transportation between the power plant and the top of the gorge. (Courtesy of Georgia Power Land Department Photo Archives.)

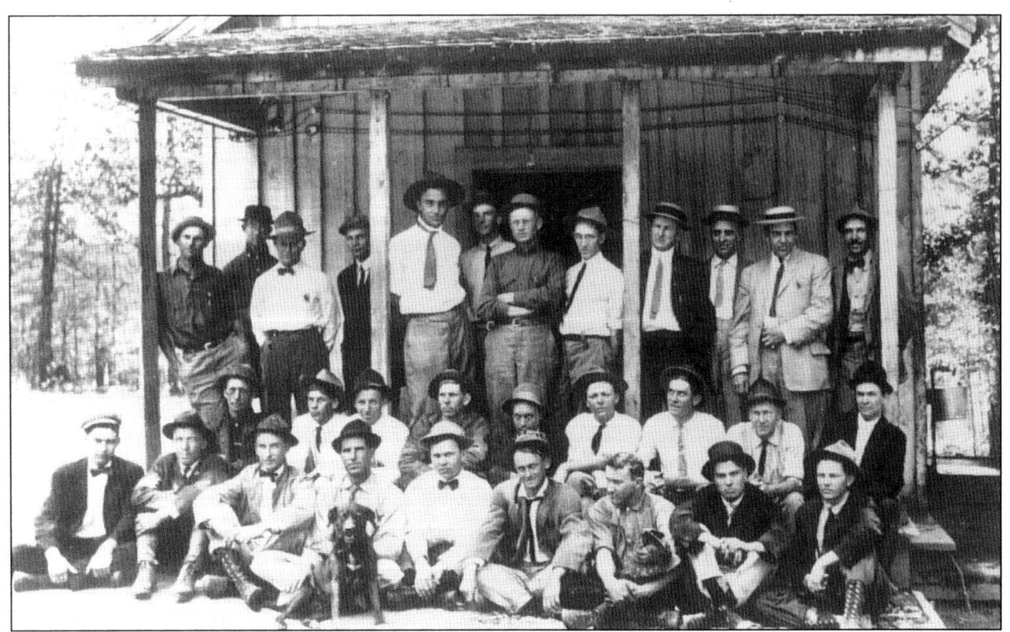

The engineering corps and a dog posed in front of the construction office, c. 1912. This hydroelectric project was a notable engineering achievement which overcame the challenges presented by the steep gorge walls and rocky terrain. At the time it was built, its 608-foot head, from lake level to turbines, was the highest east of the Rocky Mountains. (Courtesy of Georgia Power Land Department Photo Archives.)

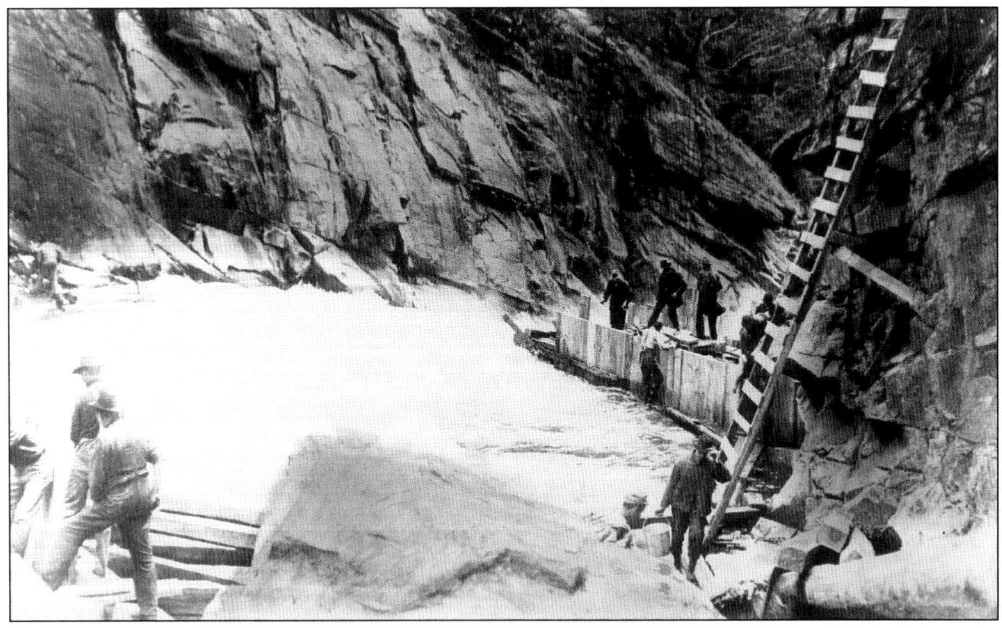

Laborers building the coffer dam are shown here. The coffer dam was a temporary dam constructed to clear water from the permanent dam construction site so the area would be dry enough to build upon. (Courtesy of Georgia Power Land Department Photo Archives.)

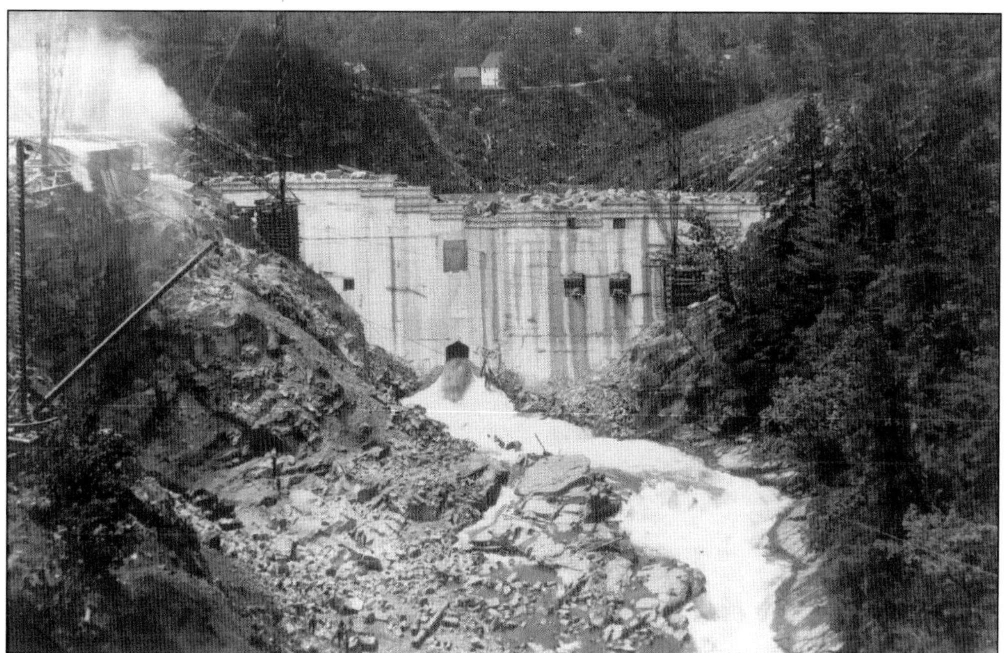

The dam was built using the solid rock walls of the gorge for stability. As seen here, the dam is nearing completion. Hoisting equipment and vapor from the machinery is visible on the left. The 129-foot-tall dam is 426 feet long. (Courtesy of Rope Roberts.)

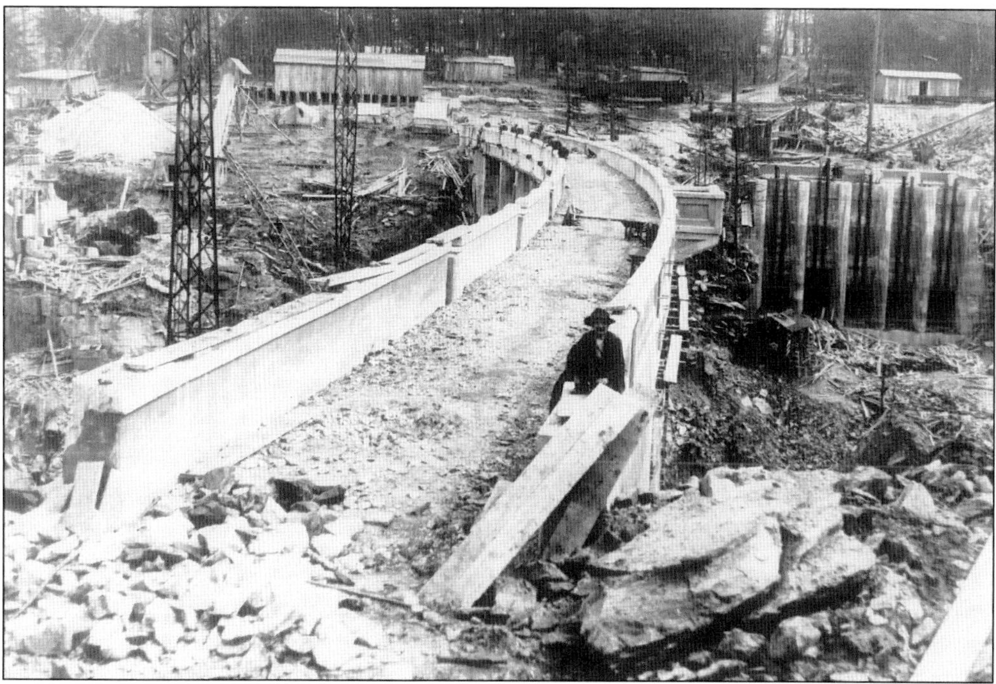

A construction view of the dam from above shows a road under construction. This one-lane road was built across the top of the dam to replace the bridge and road that was removed for the work. An unknown lady is standing in the midst of construction debris. (Courtesy of Georgia Power Land Department Photo Archives.)

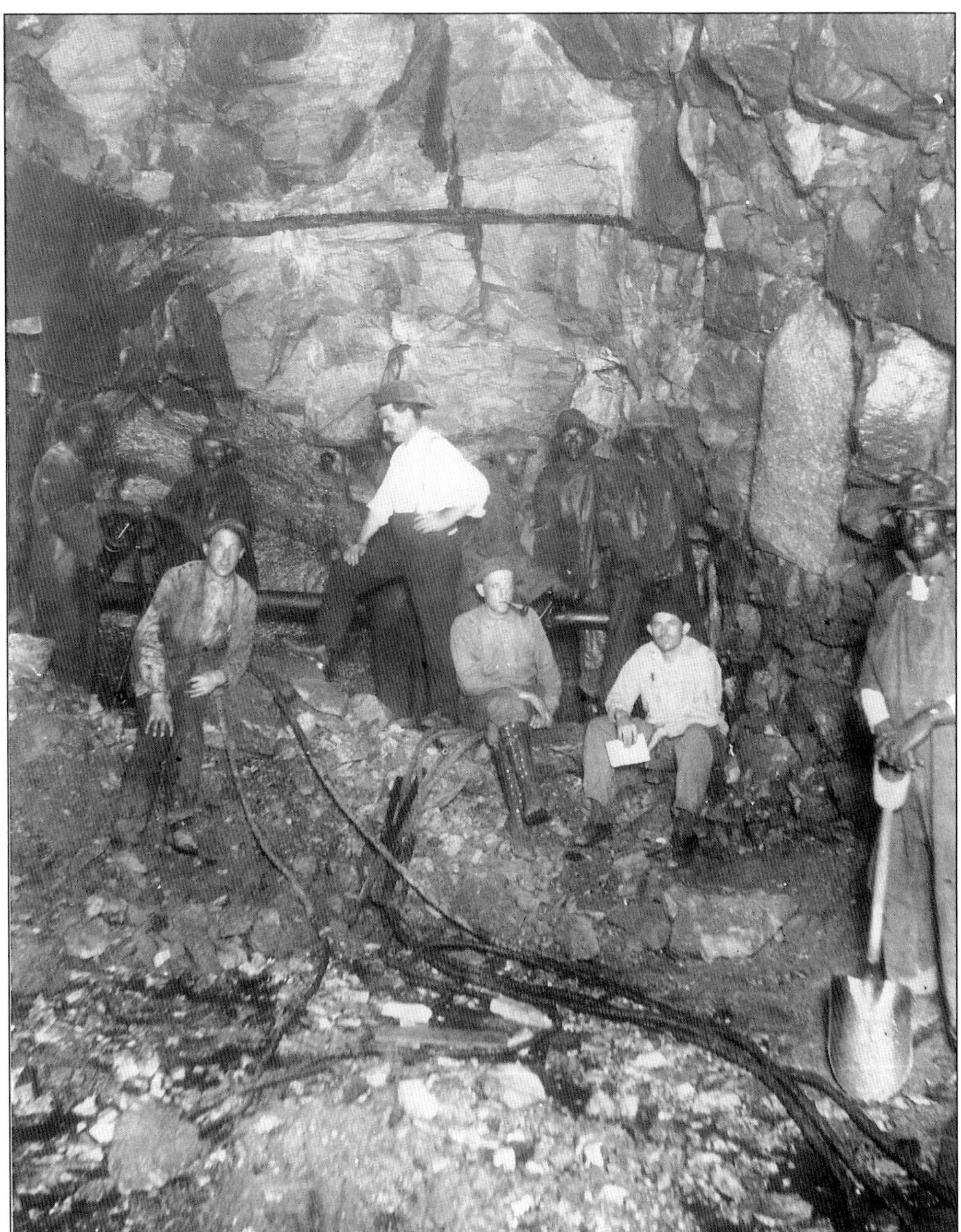

Here, men are preparing to blast out the tunnel through solid rock 100 feet below the surface of the ground, c. 1912. Today water flows, by means of gravity, from the lake through this 6,666-foot horseshoe-shaped tunnel to the surge tank at the top of the gorge above the power plant before entering the penstocks. (Courtesy of Georgia Power Land Department Photo Archives.)

Men install steel forms in the 12-foot-wide tunnel. It is 14 feet high and lined with 18 inches of concrete. The slow and tedious work of blasting out the tunnel took two work shifts of 17 men each, working for 15 months, to complete the tunnel. Some of the stone removed from the tunnel was crushed and used in concrete mix for the dam. (Courtesy of Georgia Power Land Department Photo Archives.)

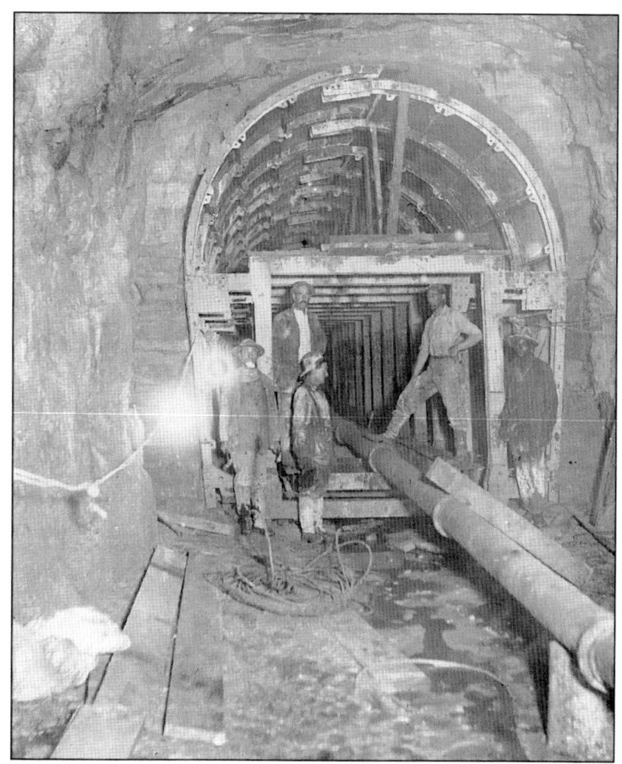

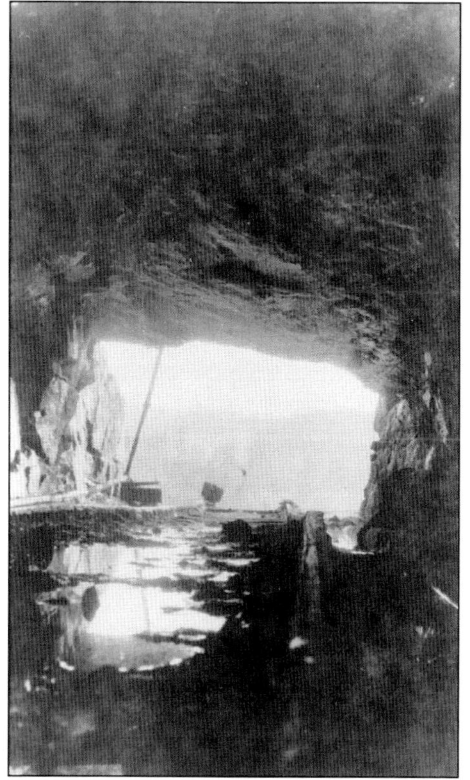

There were three adits, or horizontal exits in the tunnel. This image shows adit number one from inside the tunnel looking out. Adits allowed air to come in, as well as serving as an exit to dispose of stone hollowed from the tunnel. (Courtesy of Georgia Power Land Department Photo Archives.)

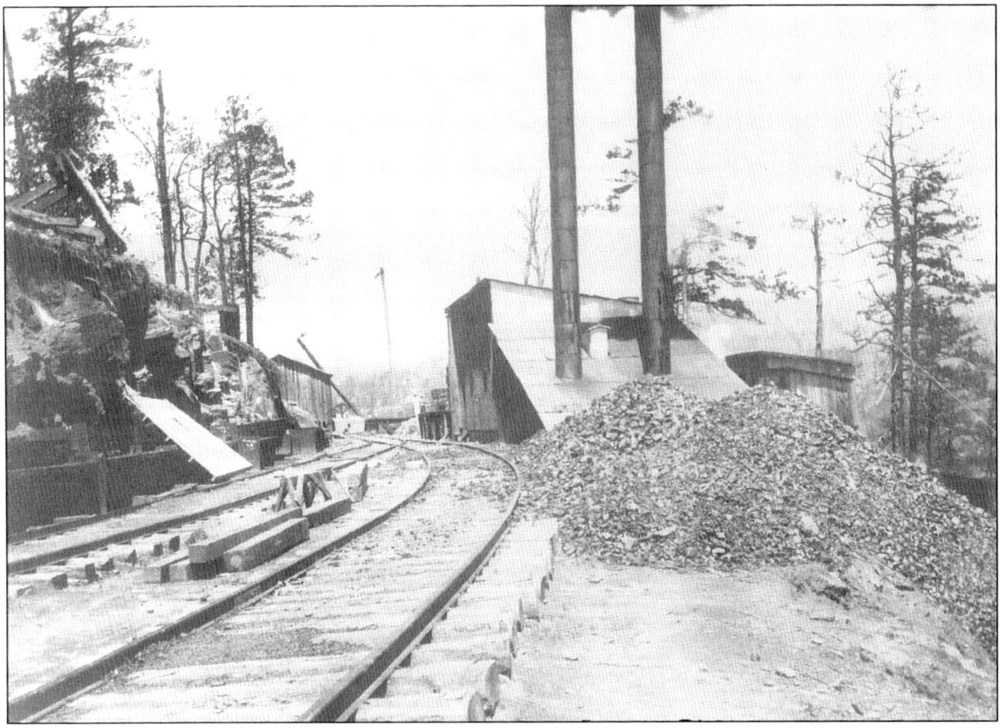

The steam compressor plant produced steam to operate drills used to make holes in the rock in which explosive powder was placed to blast out the tunnel. (Courtesy of Georgia Power Land Department Photo Archives.)

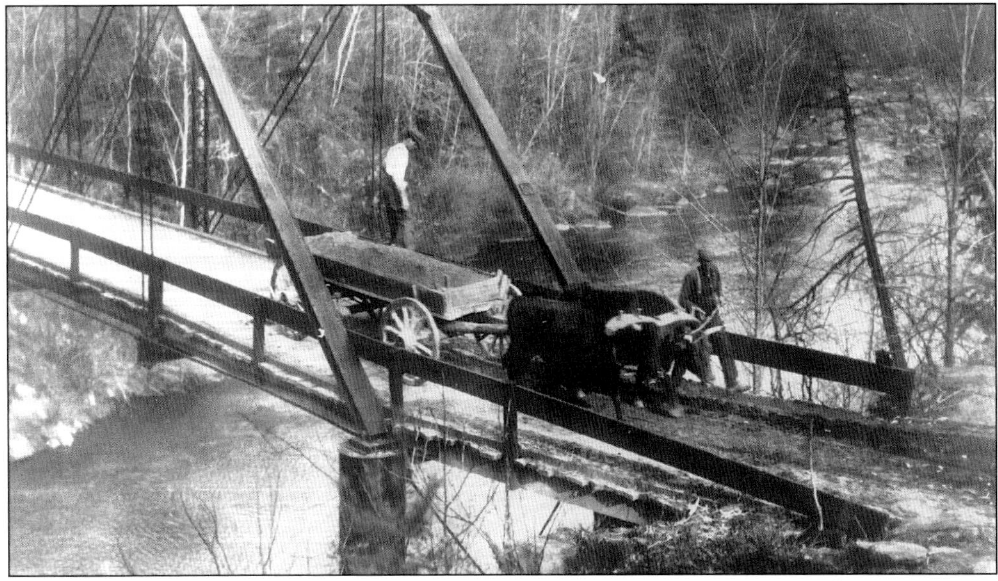

Here, a pair of oxen haul a wagon of sand, dug near the falls, across the river to the construction site. Because there was no heavy mechanized equipment in 1911, many animals were used in the construction of the project. Horses provided transportation, whereas mules and oxen were used for hauling equipment and materials. (Courtesy of Georgia Power Land Department Photo Archives.)

Tallulah Falls law enforcement was overwhelmed with the population increase from construction workers. "Shackrousters" were hired by the power company to act as police and foremen on the construction site and in the construction village to maintain order. Often wearing guns and carrying big sticks, they rousted men from their bunks and swept through town looking for workers who stayed to gamble and drink with the few women they could find. (Courtesy of Ronald Vandiver.)

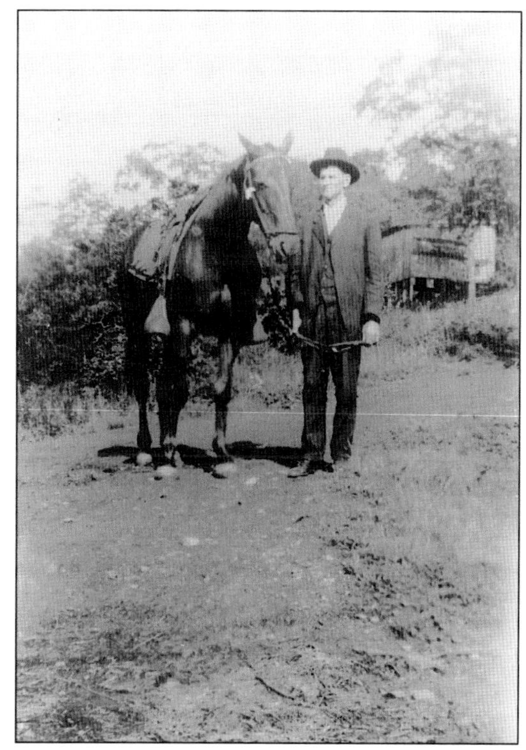

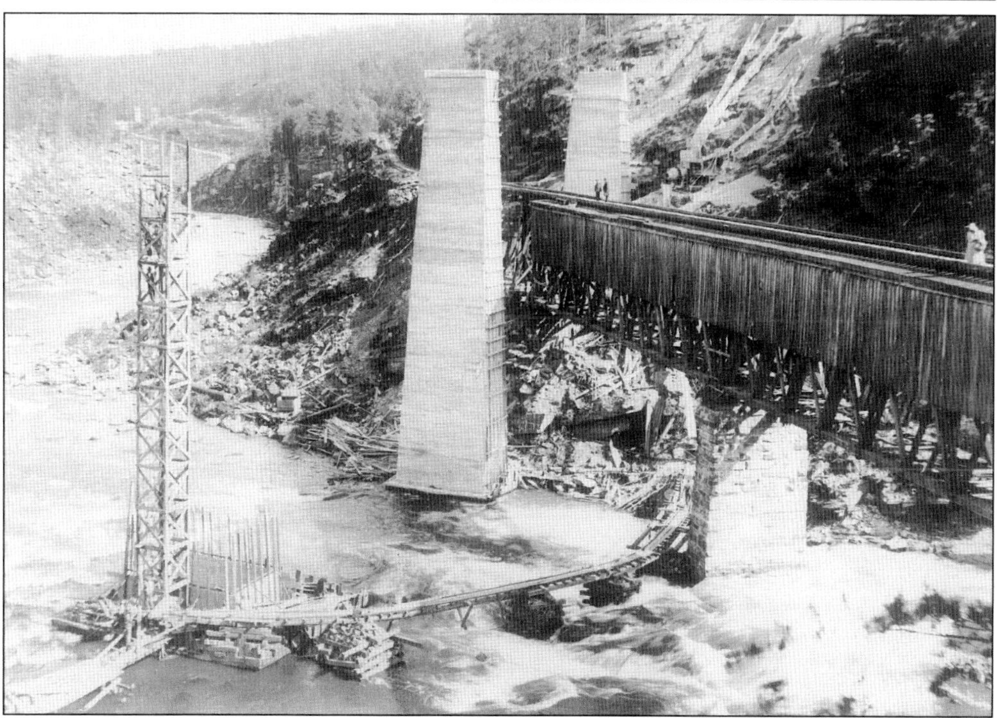

The old Tallulah Falls Railroad bed is pictured on the right. Before the lake was filled, new pillars, seen in this c. 1912 photograph, had to be constructed to raise the level of the railroad tracks. (Courtesy of Georgia Power Land Department Photo Archives.)

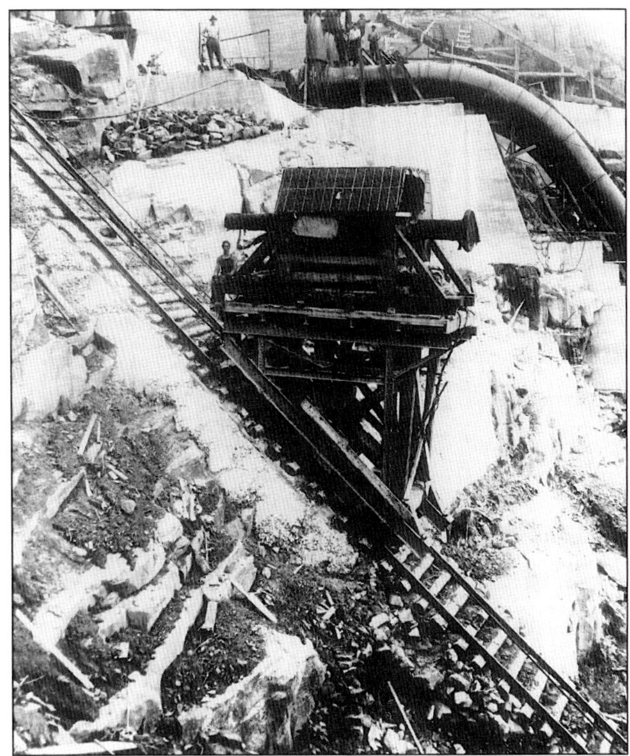

The generator rotor, weighing 60 tons, was the heaviest piece of equipment hauled on the incline to the powerhouse during construction. The power plant consists of the switchhouse and powerhouse. The turbines are located in the powerhouse and the transformers and switching equipment are located in the switchhouse. (Courtesy of Georgia Power Land Department Photo Archives.)

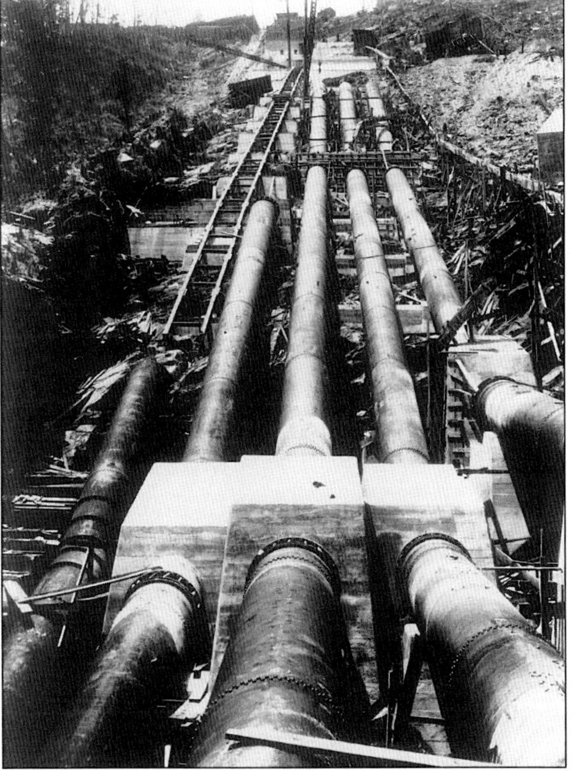

The penstocks carry water from the surge tank at the top of the hill, down the slope to turn the turbines in the powerhouse. Construction of the penstocks started at the bottom. Riveting of the joints had to be done from inside the pipes. During the summer, daytime temperatures could reach 170 degrees inside the penstocks, so riveting was done at night or early morning. (Courtesy of Georgia Power Land Department Photo Archives.)

Workers paused for the camera during the construction of the powerhouse. (Courtesy of Georgia Power Land Department Photo Archives.)

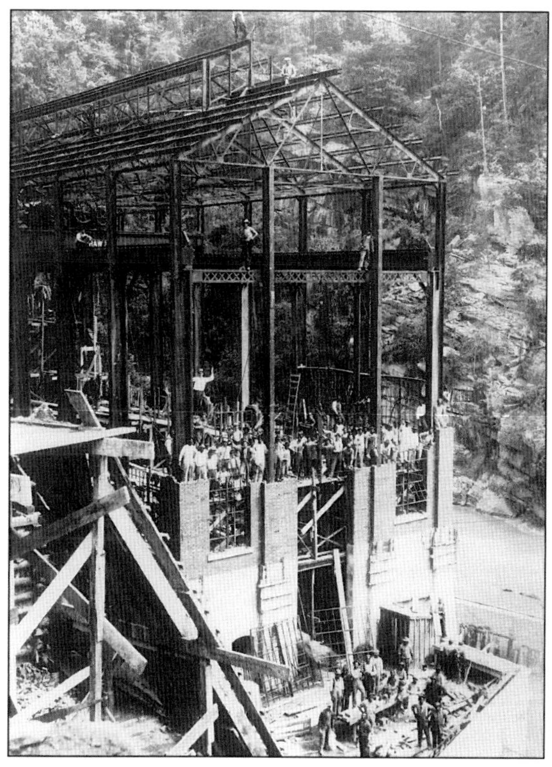

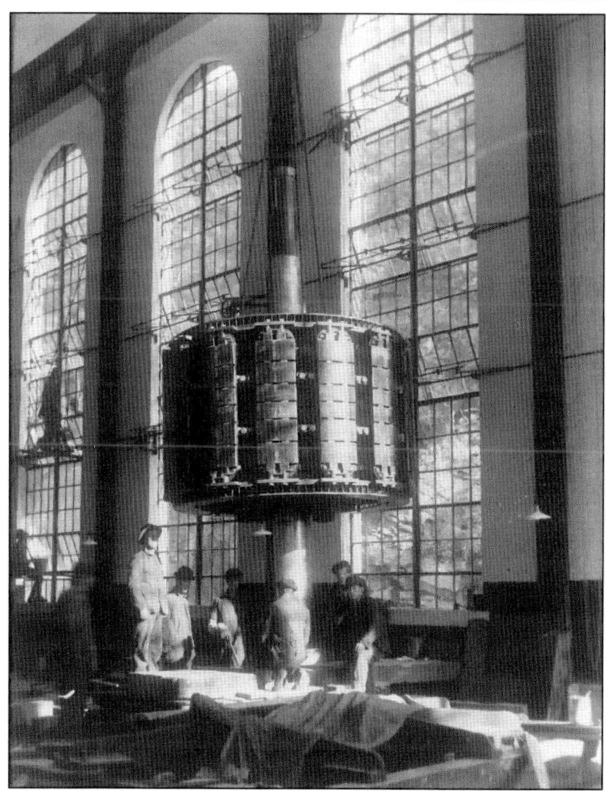

Rotor number five is being installed in the powerhouse. Note the tall, arched windows that emphasize the verticality of the structure. (Courtesy of Georgia Power Land Department Photo Archives.)

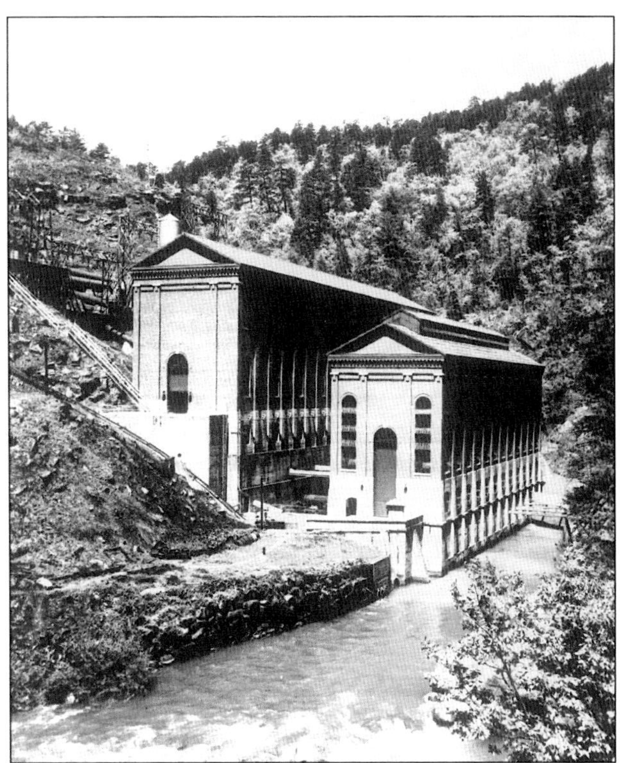

This view of the downstream face of the Tallulah Falls switchhouse and powerhouse, c. 1913, illustrates the ornate detailing of these Classical Revival-style buildings. No wood or flammable material was used in these steel-framed buildings, ensuring a fireproof structure. (Courtesy of Georgia Power Land Department Photo Archives.)

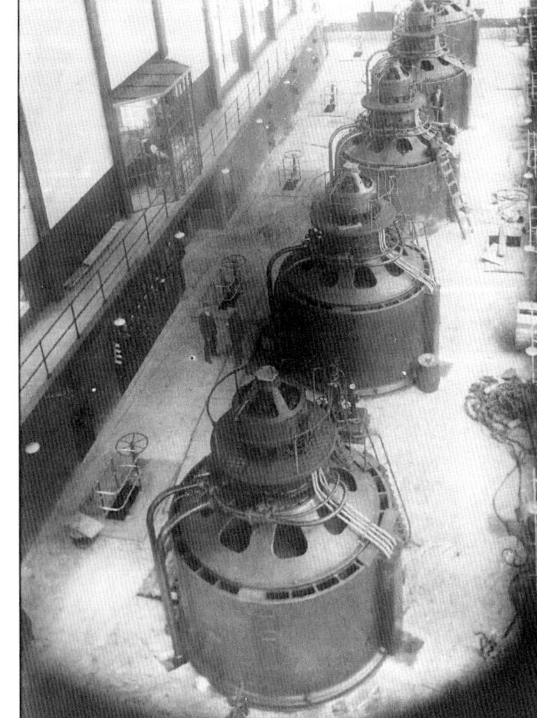

Five out of the six massive generators are shown inside the completed powerhouse. Water flows through the penstocks to turn the turbines, which then rotate these generators. (Courtesy of Georgia Power Land Department Photo Archives.)

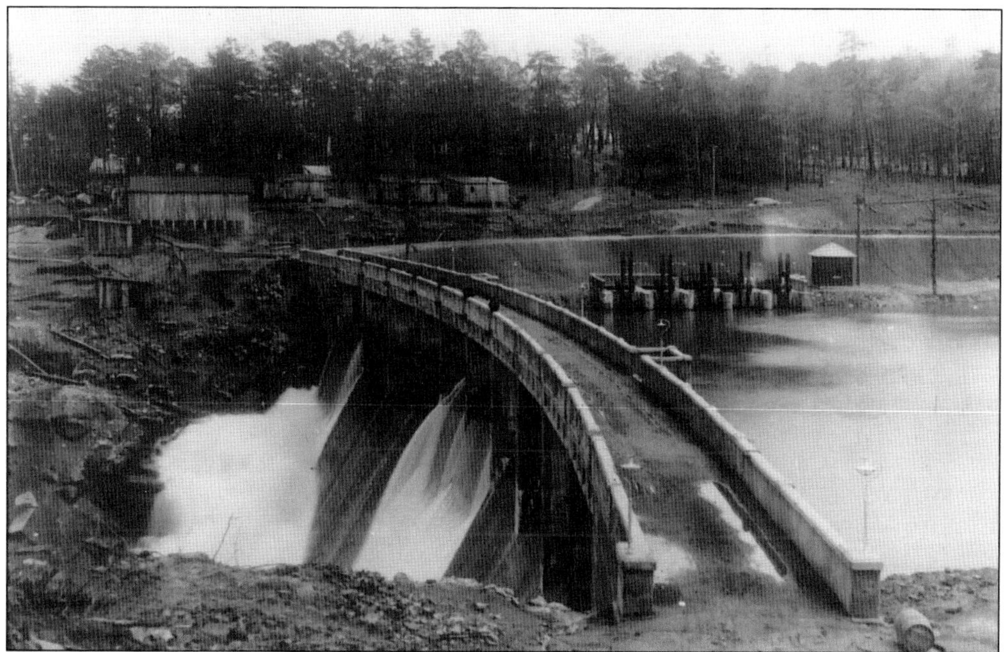

Water rushes through the gates of the dam after completion. The Stauwerke flashboards or spillway gates at the top of the dam regulate the elevation of the lake and were the first of their type to be used in this country. (Courtesy of Georgia Power Land Department Photo Archives.)

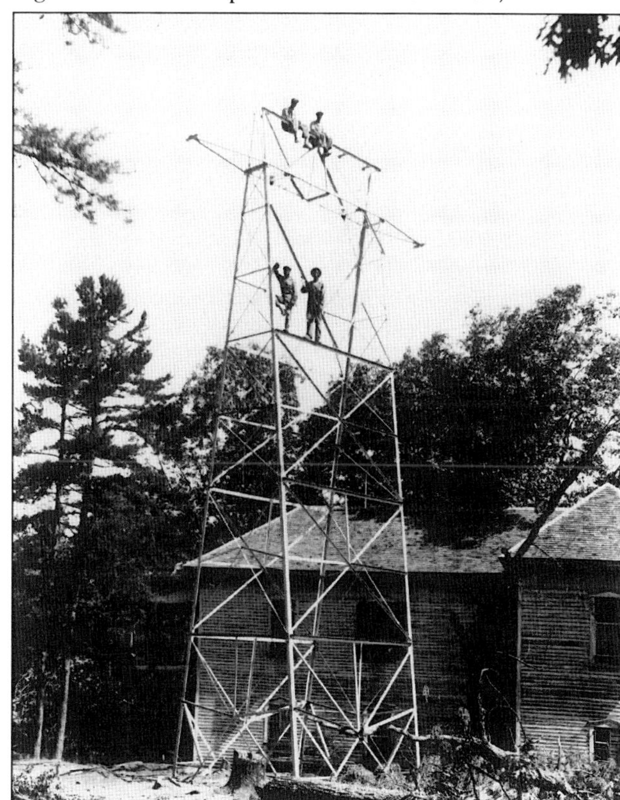

Power company workers construct an electric tower in Tallulah Falls. Power was first transmitted to Atlanta in September 1913 by way of Atlanta's Boulevard Substation, one of the earliest and largest outdoor substations in the nation at that time. (Courtesy of Rope Roberts.)

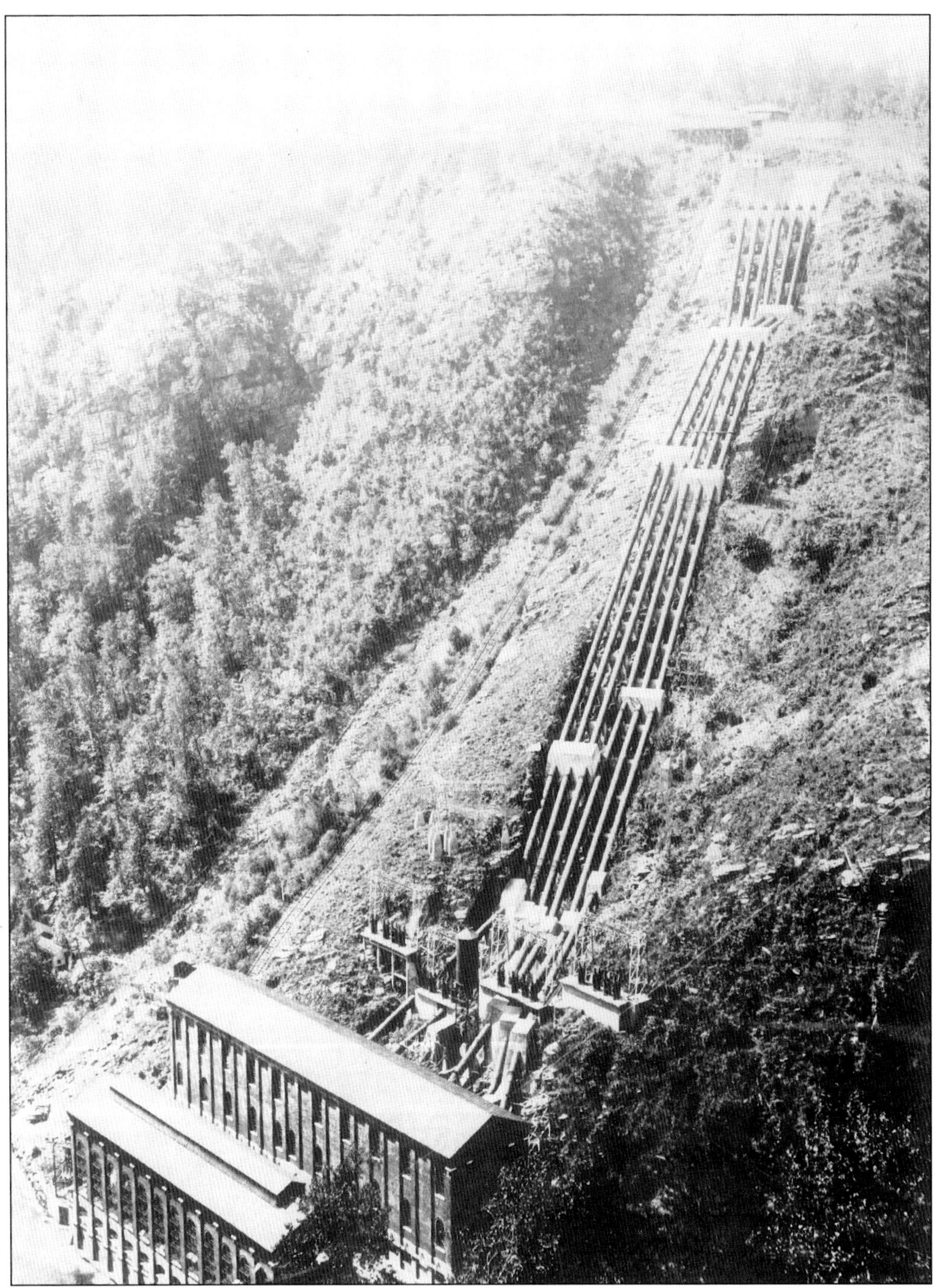

The Tallulah Falls hydroelectric project was an engineering marvel of its time. It was the third-largest hydroelectric development operating in the United States in 1913, and the largest in the South. The engineering achievements and the monumental architecture, combined with the natural beauty of the gorge, play a significant role in the history of hydroelectric development in the United States and in the Southeast. The plant is still in use after more than 80 years. (Courtesy of Georgia Power Land Department Photo Archives.)

Nine

The Camp Society

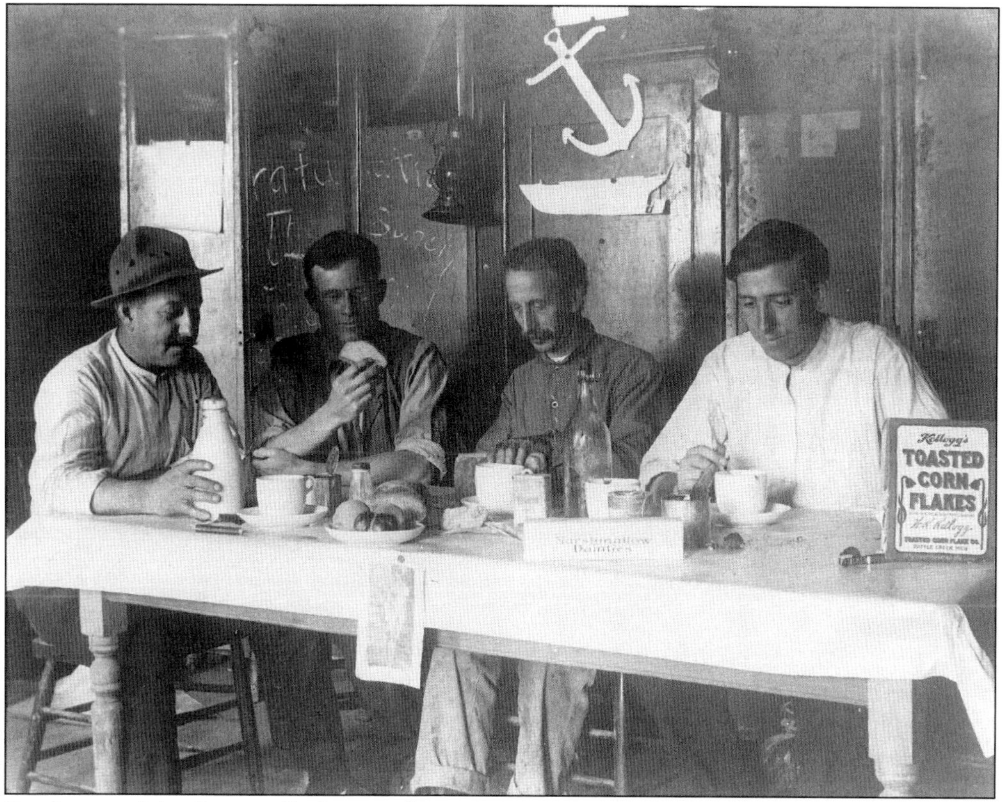

Employees of the Georgia Railway and Power Company share a meal in the bunkhouse. Note the pinup on the front of the table. Opportunity for employment during construction of the Tallulah Falls hydroelectric project brought many men to the area. They lived in construction camps or villages in rough, frontier-like conditions while on the job from 1911 to 1913. (Courtesy of Georgia Power Land Department Photo Archives.)

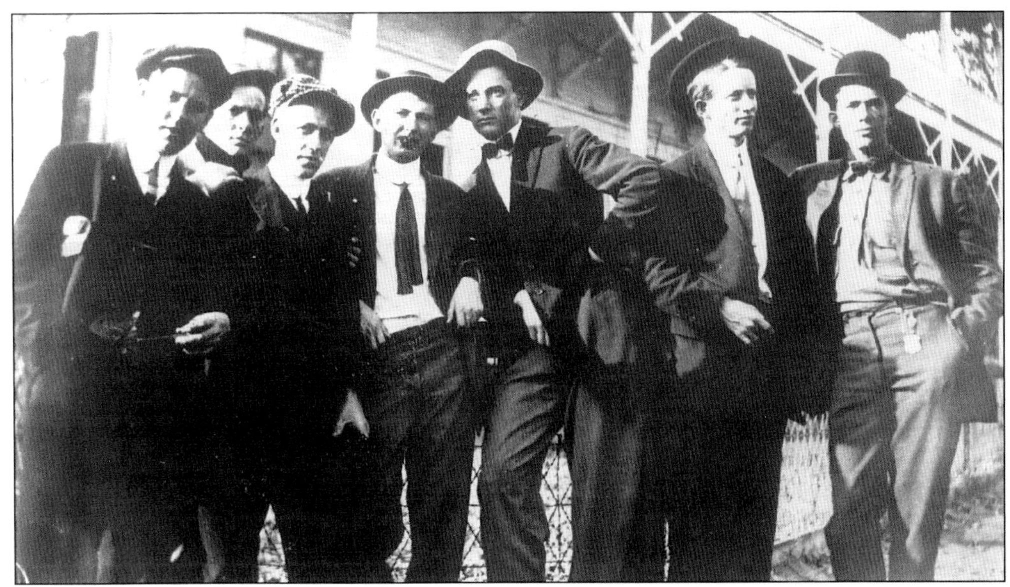

Men came from all parts of Georgia and the South to work on the project, enticed by the prospect of steady work and good pay. Due to their place of origin, this group of men, many of whom were engineers, were called the "Mississippians." Pictured from left to right are: Fuzzy, Martin, Hill, Whit, Richardson, Toots, and Meaders. (Courtesy of Georgia Power Land Department Photo Archives.)

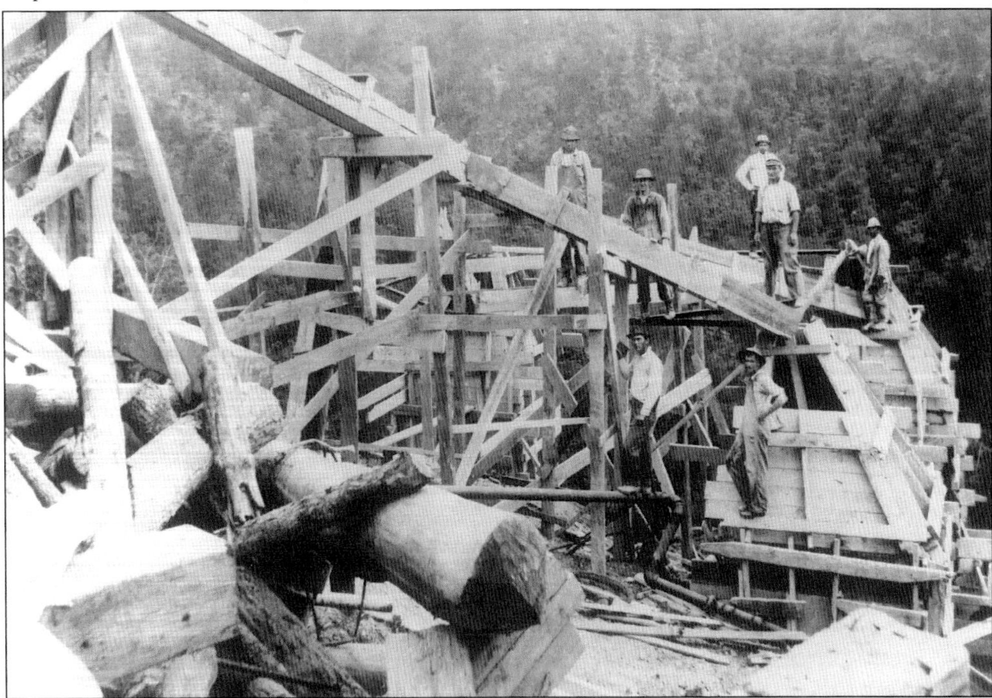

Construction laborers work on the foundation of the number 1A electrical tower. While there were over 1,000 men employed during the course of construction, it was often hard to keep them at work due to the remoteness of the job and the limited number of women available for companionship. (Courtesy of Georgia Power Land Department Photo Archives.)

There were too few of these "mountain belles" to provide companionship to the many men on the construction job. The women could be highly selective in their choice of friends. (Courtesy of Georgia Power Land Department Photo Archives.)

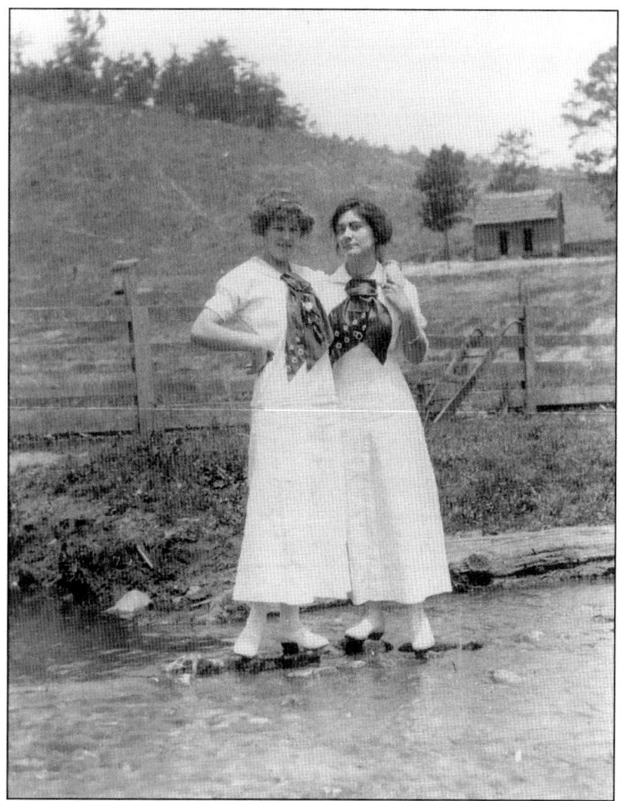

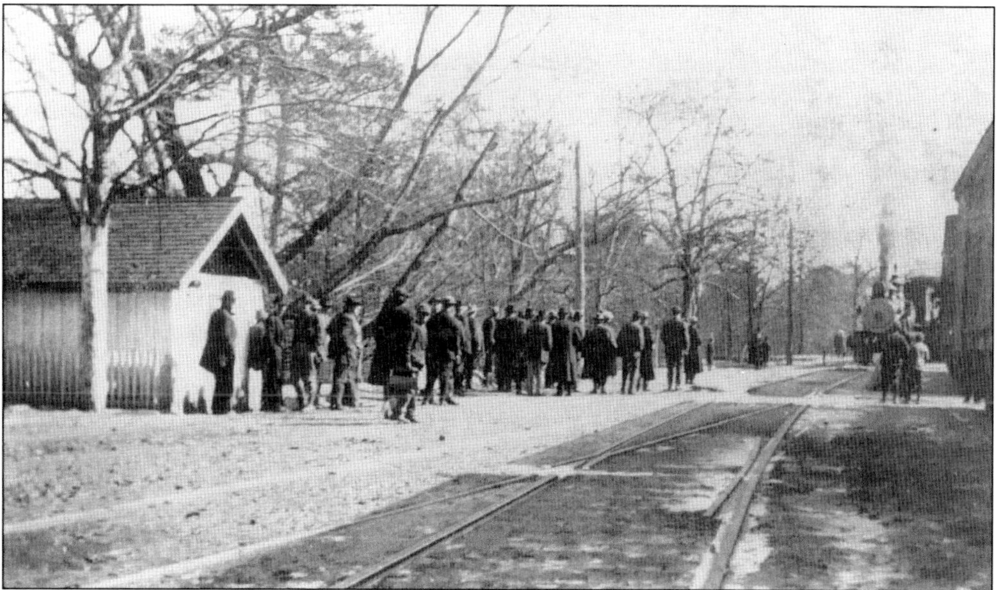

Here, construction employees wait for the train to arrive at Tallulah Falls. To keep men on the job, the power company sent word to organizations in Atlanta to advertise for brides for the workers. Benefits included an all-expense paid train trip for the women to Tallulah Falls and free housing for the couples in the construction village. (Courtesy of Georgia Power Land Department Photo Archives.)

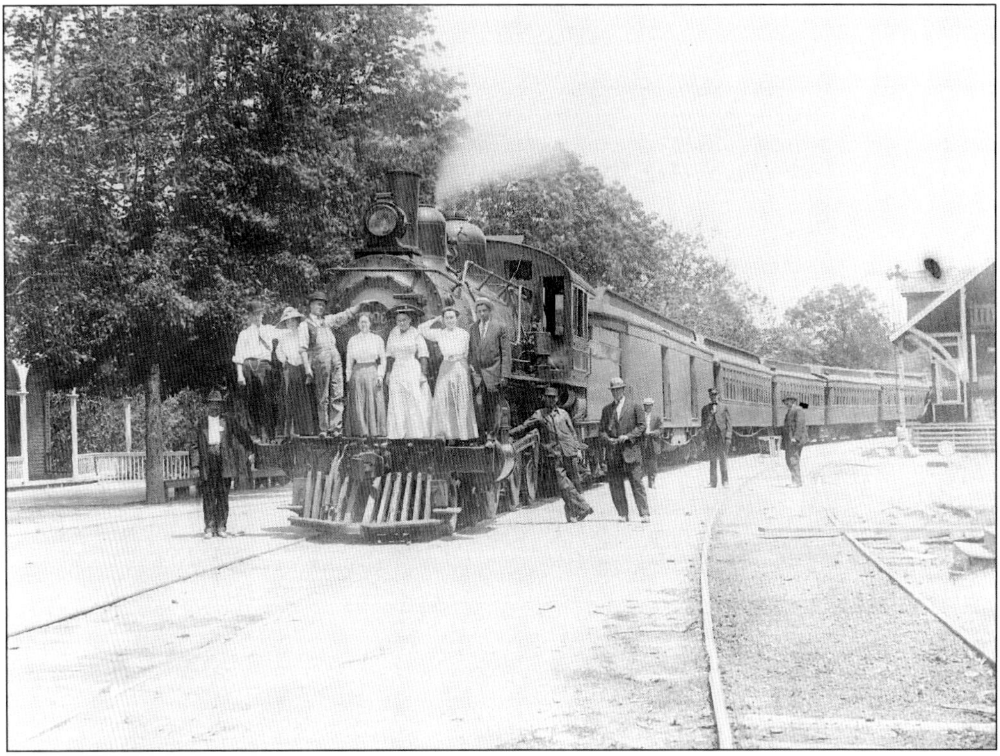

Outnumbered by gentlemen, prospective brides wait on the locomotive after their arrival in town. (Courtesy of Rope Roberts.)

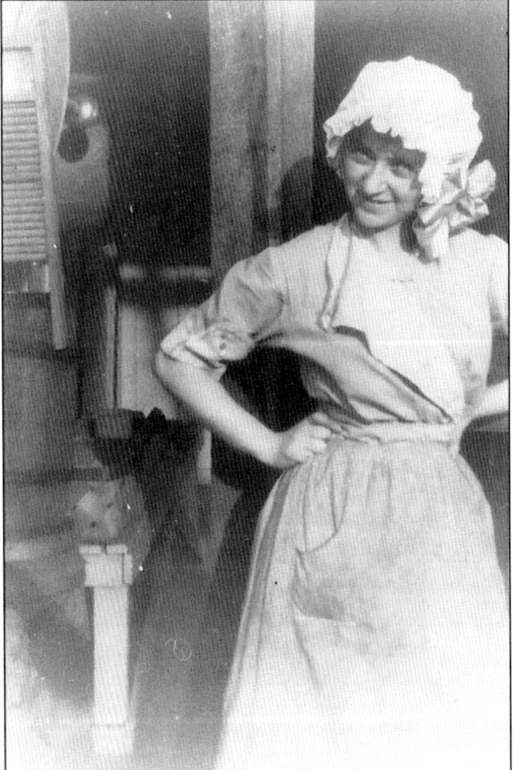

Mrs. Mac, wife of one of the workers on the construction project, posed in a rather pert fashion for the camera. (Courtesy of Georgia Power Land Department Photo Archives.)

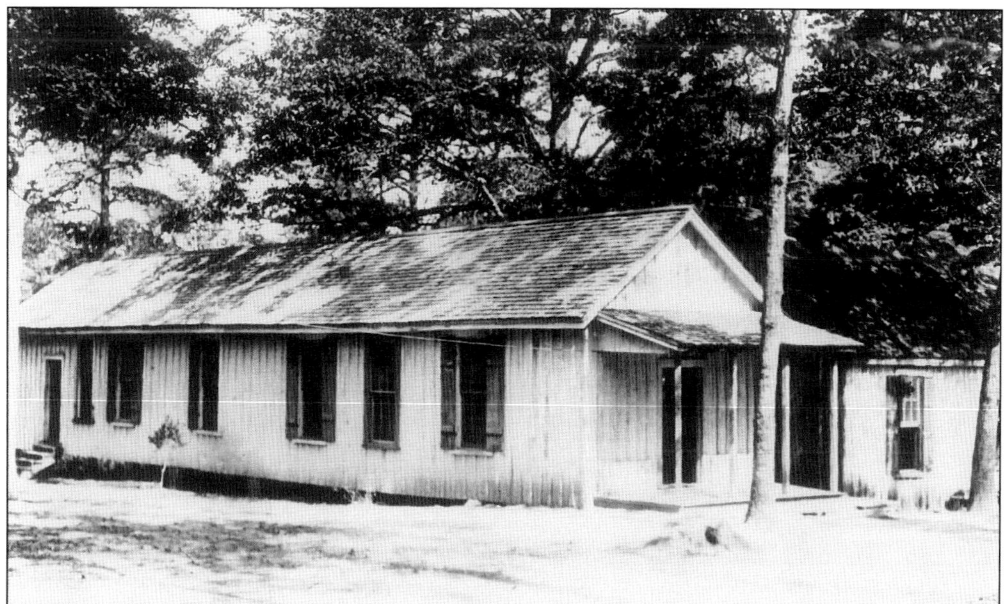

Pictured is the construction office for the Tallulah Falls project. It was of board and batten construction. The workers' homes in the construction villages, although smaller, were of the same design. (Courtesy of Georgia Power Land Department Photo Archives.)

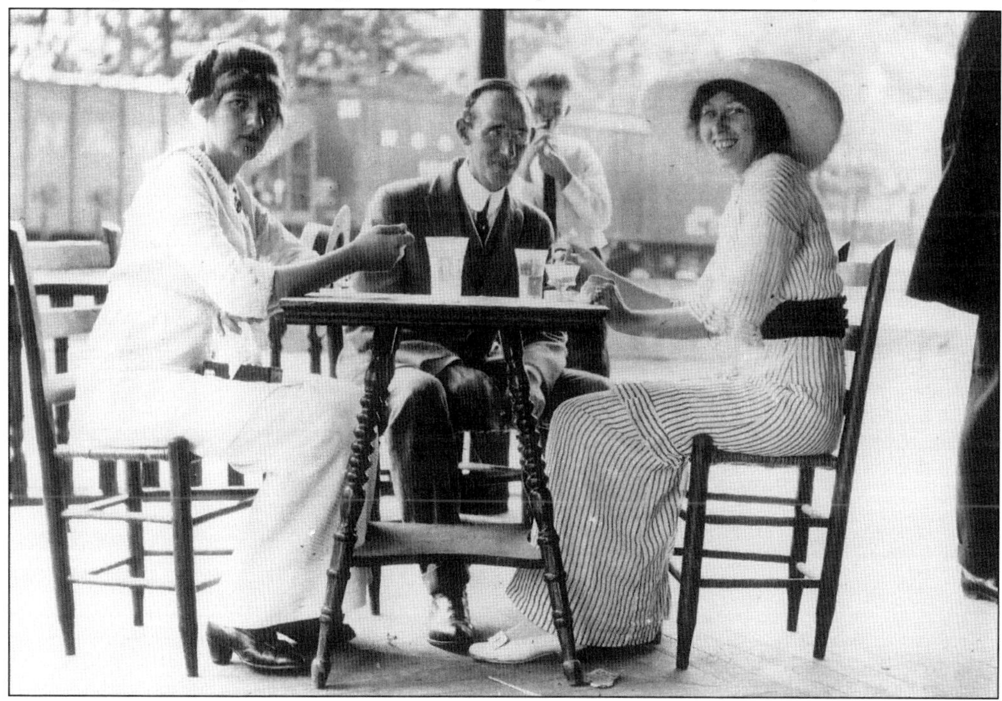

R.H. (Roby) Robson, center, was an engineer for the project contractors, the Northern Contracting Company. He was also historian of the development and was responsible for documenting the progress in photographs. Robson is breakfasting with friends on the porch of a hotel which he, with tongue-in-cheek, dubbed "The Oasis." The engineering corps lived in several of the resort hotels. (Courtesy of Georgia Power Land Department Photo Archives.)

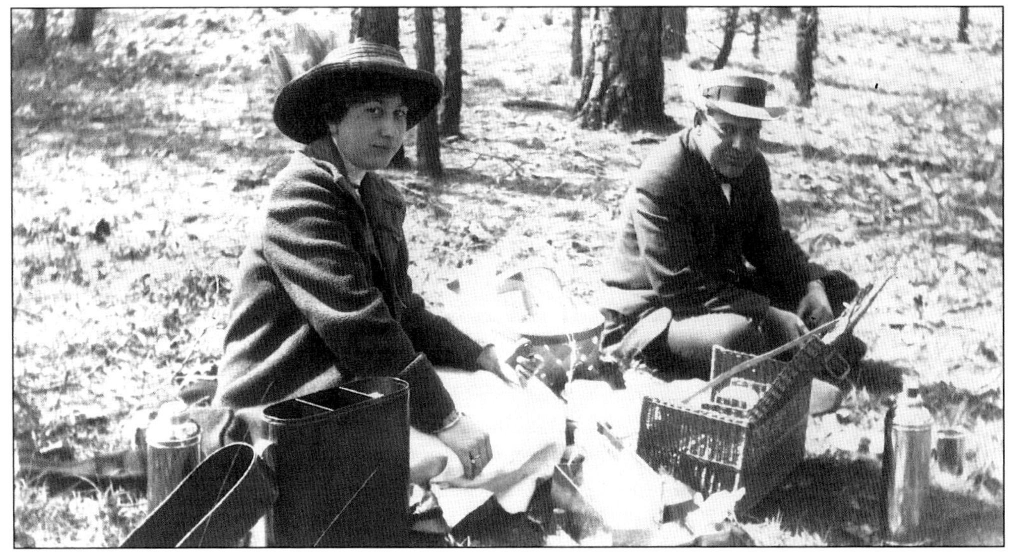

Excursions for picnics and trips to the gorge were common for couples associated with the construction project at Tallulah Falls. (Courtesy of Georgia Power Land Department Photo Archives.)

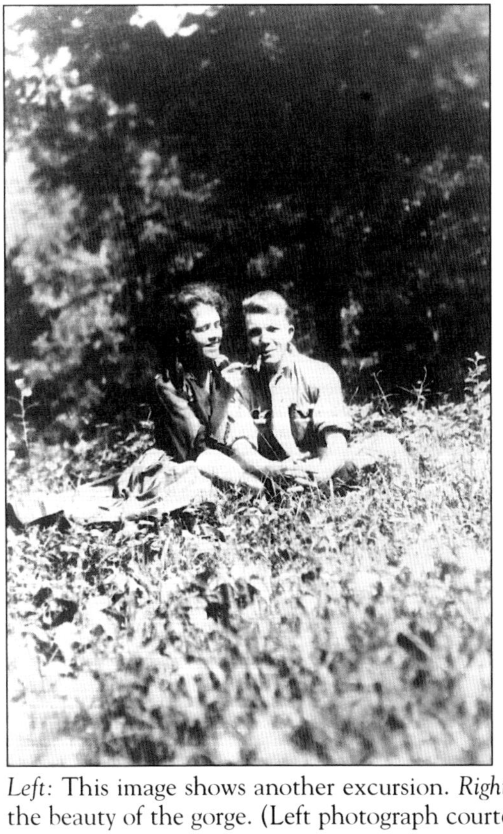

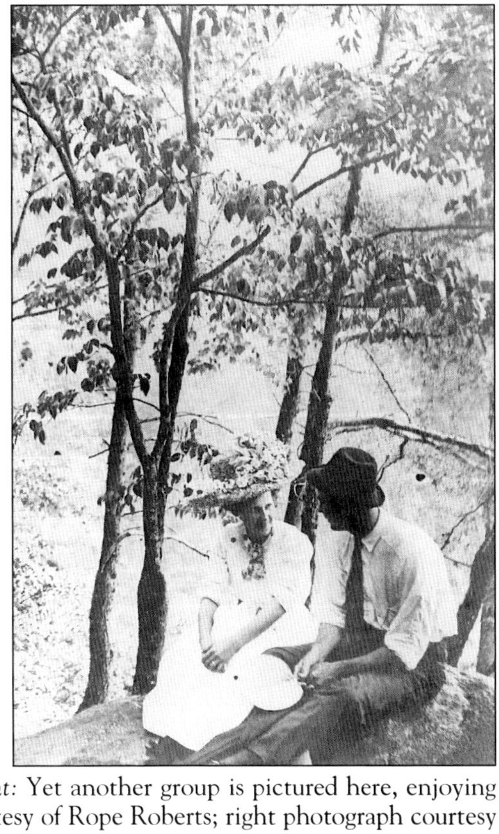

Left: This image shows another excursion. *Right:* Yet another group is pictured here, enjoying the beauty of the gorge. (Left photograph courtesy of Rope Roberts; right photograph courtesy of Gary Doster.)

While visiting the construction site, these ladies carried parasols to shade them from the sun. They are standing on the roadway across the top of the dam, overlooking the construction. Note the fashions of the ladies in their ornate and genteel apparel that was common for the Edwardian period. (Courtesy of Georgia Power Land Department Photo Archives.)

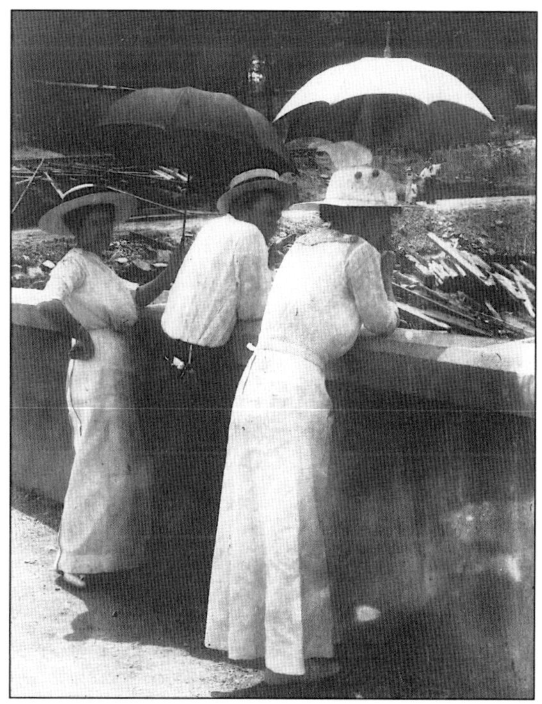

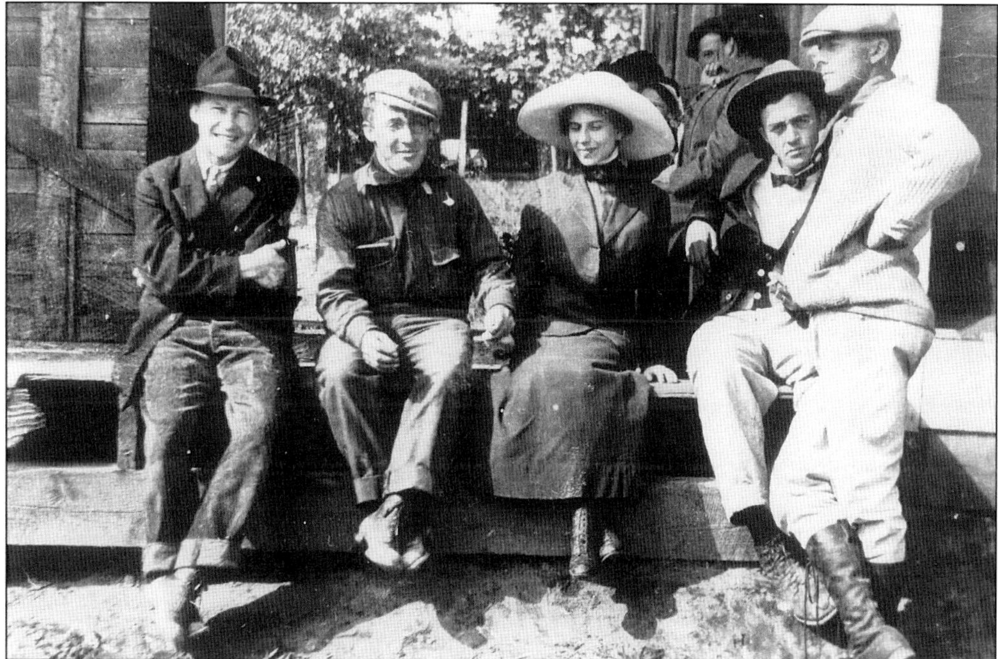

Clare Hancock (center) was nicknamed the "Belle of Tallulah Falls." Her mother operated the Willard House Hotel, which provided accommodations for many of the project engineers. Clare home-schooled some of the engineers' children. Here she attracts the attention of a group of engineers, including Benjamin Sinclair (second from right). Sinclair Dam on the Oconee River was later named for him. (Courtesy of Georgia Power Land Department Photo Archives.)

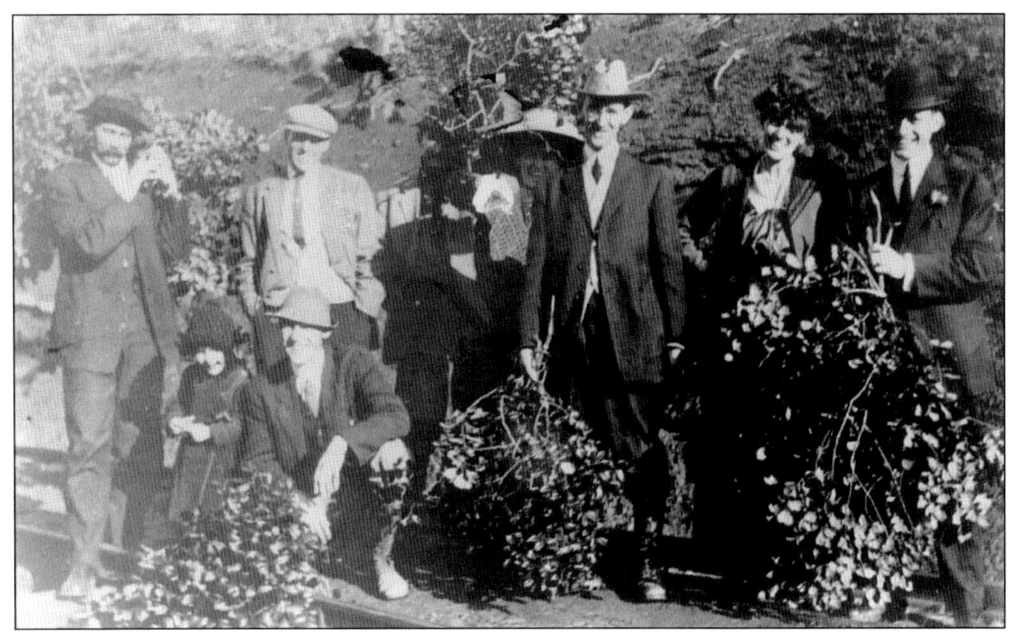

Isolated in the remote region of Tallulah Falls during Christmas, company employees made the most of it. Here, Roby Robson (third from right) with friends, a child, and other engineers collects holly and mistletoe for Christmas. (Courtesy of Georgia Power Land Department Photo Archives.)

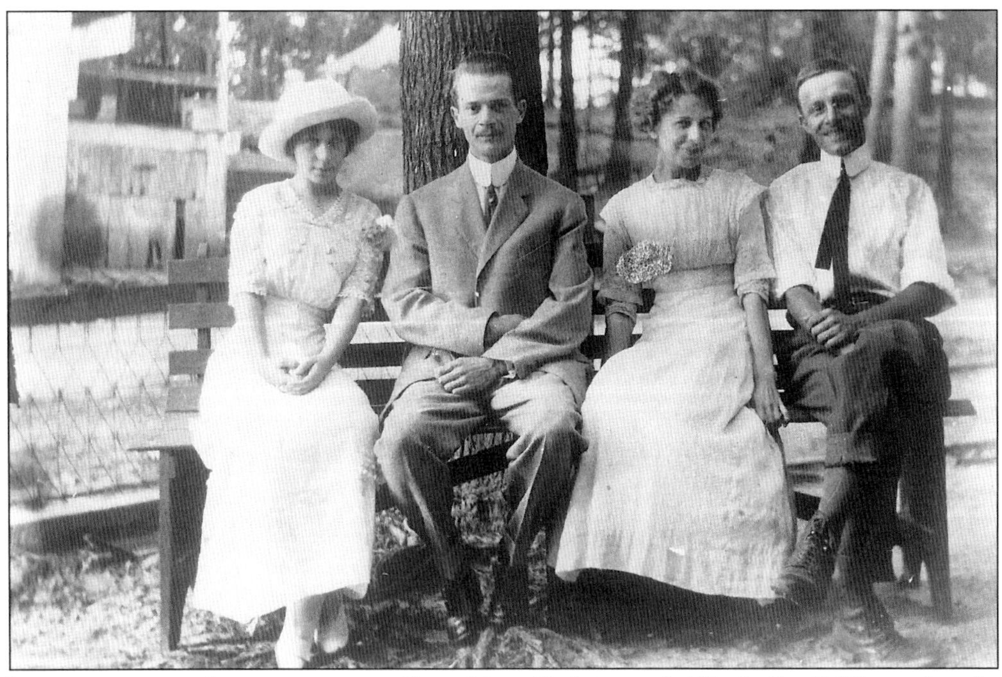

Love won out in the construction village. Mary Hudgins and Alfredo Barili III, newlyweds, are shown on their honeymoon at Tallulah Falls. Clare Hancock and Eckert Crane, right, join them. (Courtesy of Georgia Power Land Department Photo Archives.)

Son of a power company employee, little Duck Calloway is sitting on the porch of his company house in the construction village. Duck (Hubert J.) later worked for Georgia Power and retired after 44 years as foreman in the lab at Plant Arkwright. It was not unusual for several generations of a family to work for Georgia Power. (Courtesy of Georgia Power Land Department Photo Archives.)

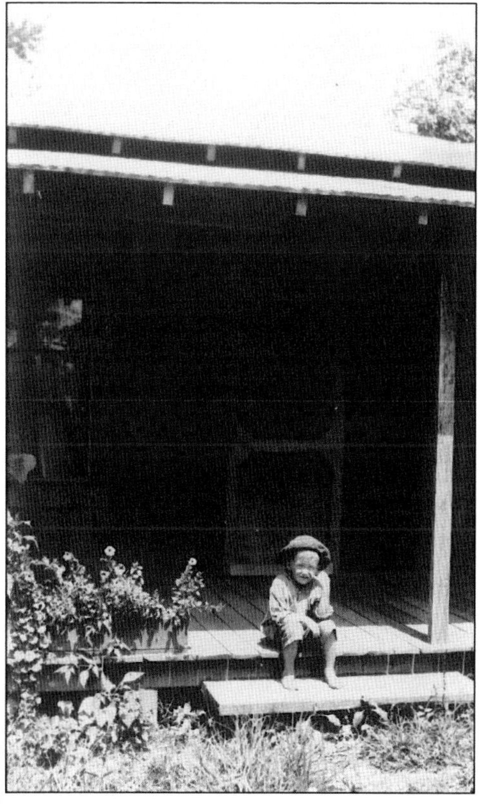

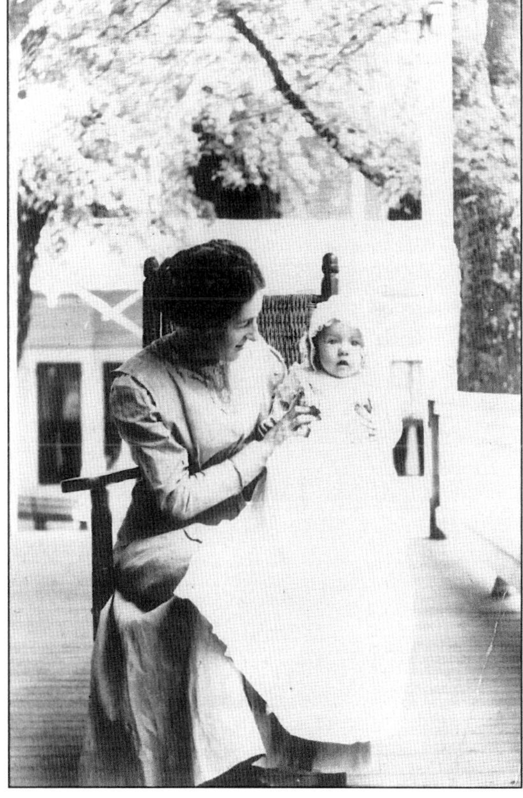

Part of the construction "family," Mrs. Margaret C. rocks on the porch and shows off tiny Ann Jo for the camera. Note the beautiful, long baby gown. (Courtesy of Georgia Power Land Department Photo Archives.).

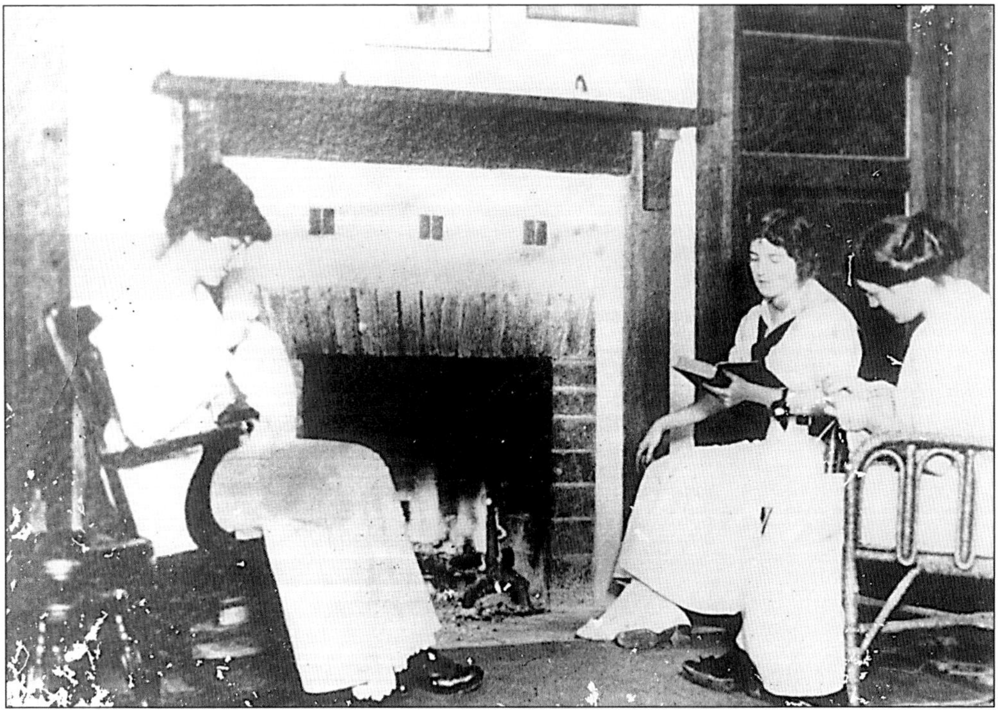

The teachers of Tallulah Falls School entertained themselves with reading and handwork around the fire. Kate Thornton is second from right. The Tallulah Falls School teachers, although few in number, were one source of single, datable women living in Tallulah Falls. (Courtesy of Georgia Power Land Department Photo Archives.)

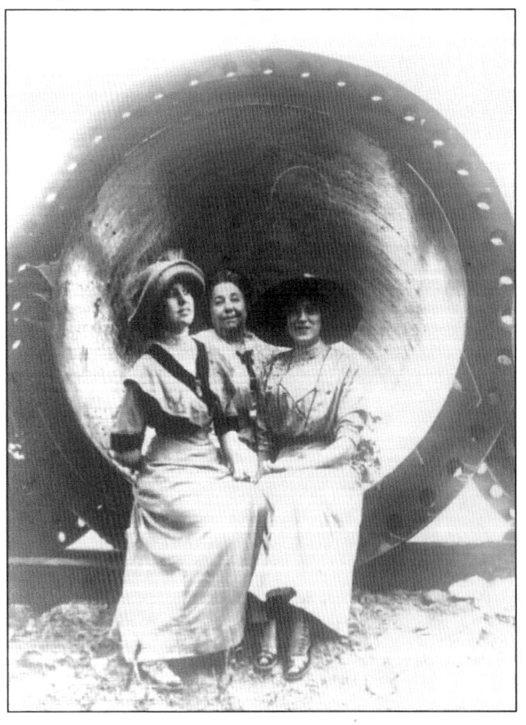

Here the teachers from Tallulah Falls School visit the construction site. The trio, with Kate Thornton on the right, sits in one of the sections of the steel penstocks. Miss Thornton met Ben Colmer, a power company employee, at work on the construction job. (Courtesy of Georgia Power Land Department Photo Archives.)

Ben Colmer arrives at Tallulah Falls School to escort Kate Thornton on an excursion. (Courtesy of Georgia Power Land Department Photo Archives.)

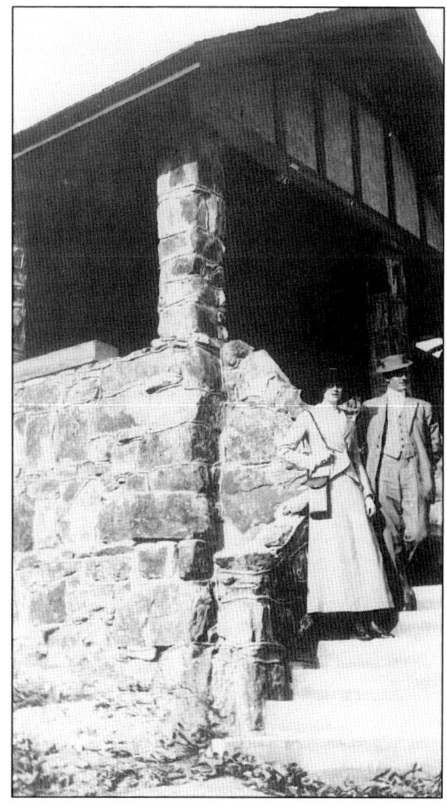

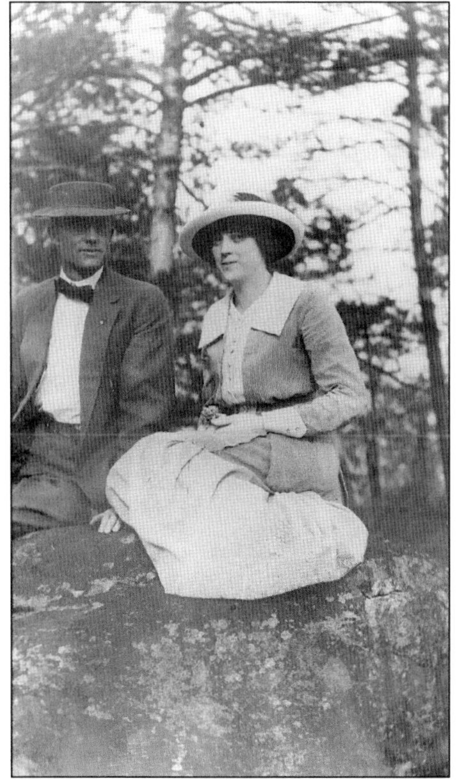

Ben Colmer and Kate Thornton continue their courtship. (Courtesy of Georgia Power Land Department Photo Archives.)

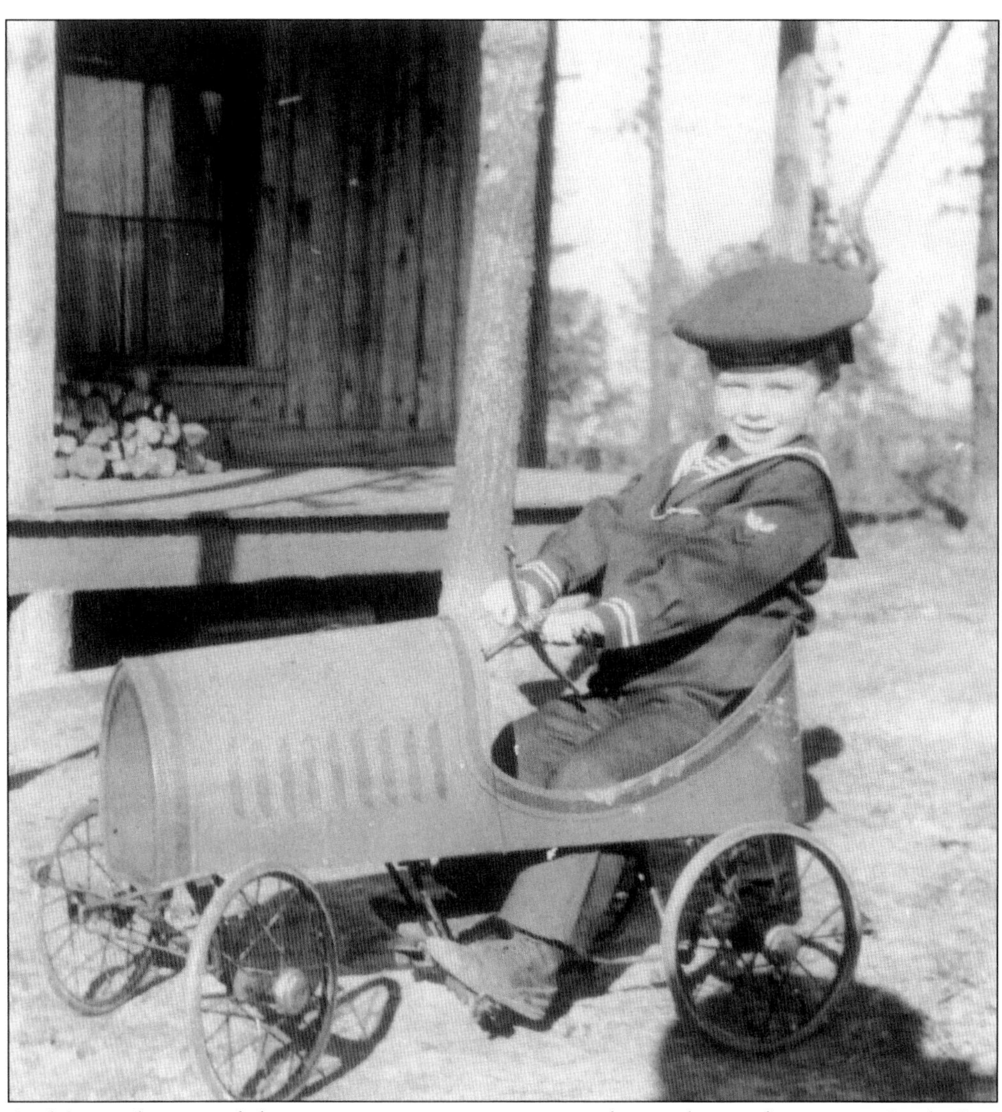

And later, the rest of the story . . . or consequences of courtship and marriage. Little Ben Colmer Jr., decked out in his sailor suit, drives his car in front of his home in the construction camp at Tugalo, 1917. Note the porch stacked with wood. The senior Colmer retired from Georgia Power in 1946. Later, Ben Jr. was also employed by Georgia Power, and retired in 1981. (Courtesy of Georgia Power Land Department Photo Archives.)

Ten

Just for Fun

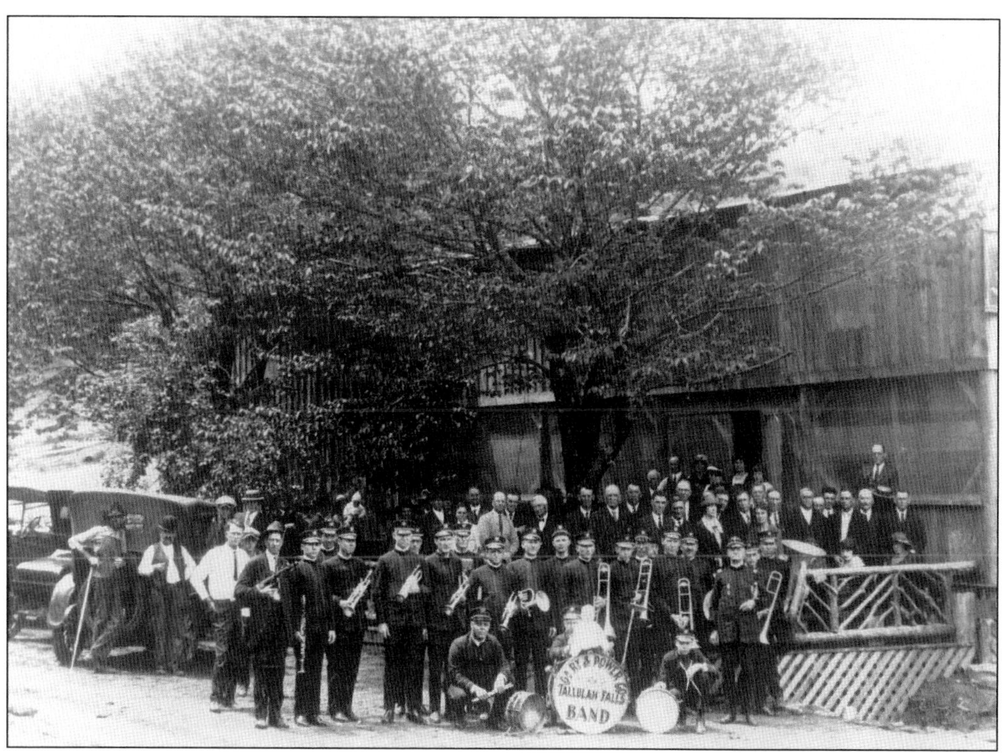

Hotel bands greeted the arriving trains carrying visitors to Tallulah Falls. The power company also formed a band to provide entertainment, as shown in this 1920 photograph taken at Lakemont on Lake Rabun, near Tallulah Falls. The band is in front of a popular local spot, the Crow's Nest, the first hotel built in the Lakemont area. (Courtesy of Georgia Power Land Department Photo Archives.)

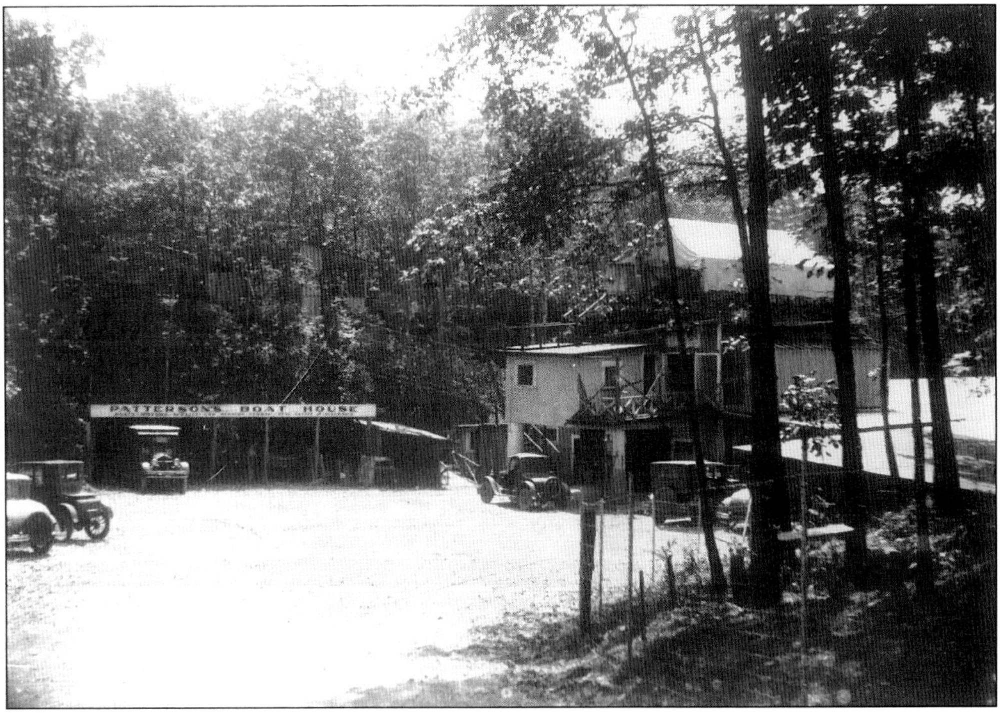

After its construction in the 1920s, Patterson's Boat House on Lake Rabun provided transportation by boat to many homes along the lake, before roads were adequately constructed. The lakes formed by the newly built hydroelectric facilities on the Tallulah and Tugaloo Rivers spawned a new generation of summer people. Lakemont was the summer place to be in the 1920s and 1930s. (Photograph by Walter Hunnicutt, courtesy of Jorene Lavender.)

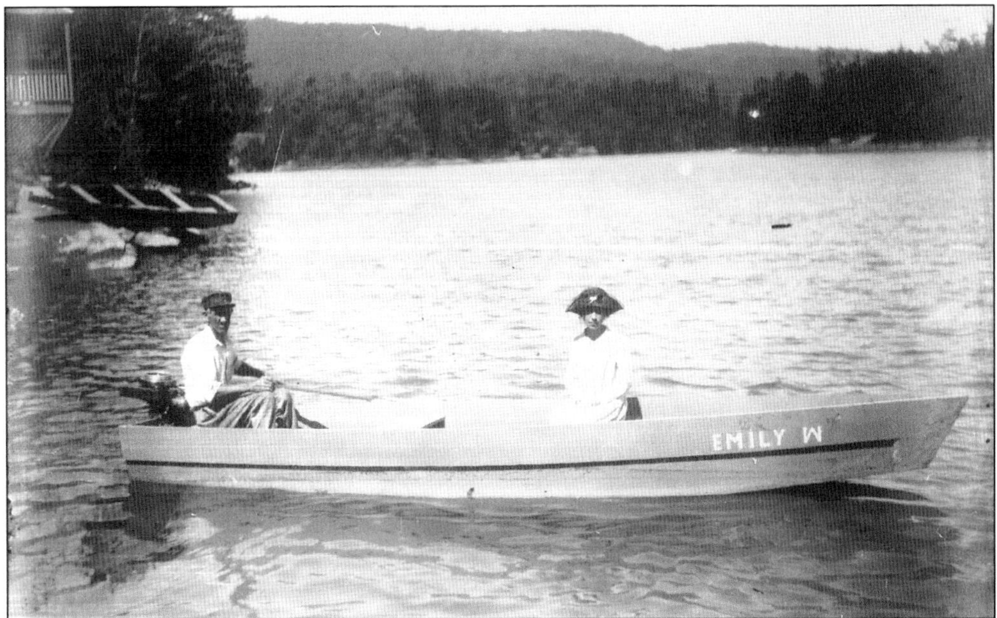

With the completion of the dam, boating, fishing, and swimming on Tallulah Falls Lake filled leisure hours. (Photograph by Walter Hunnicutt, courtesy of Jorene Lavender.)

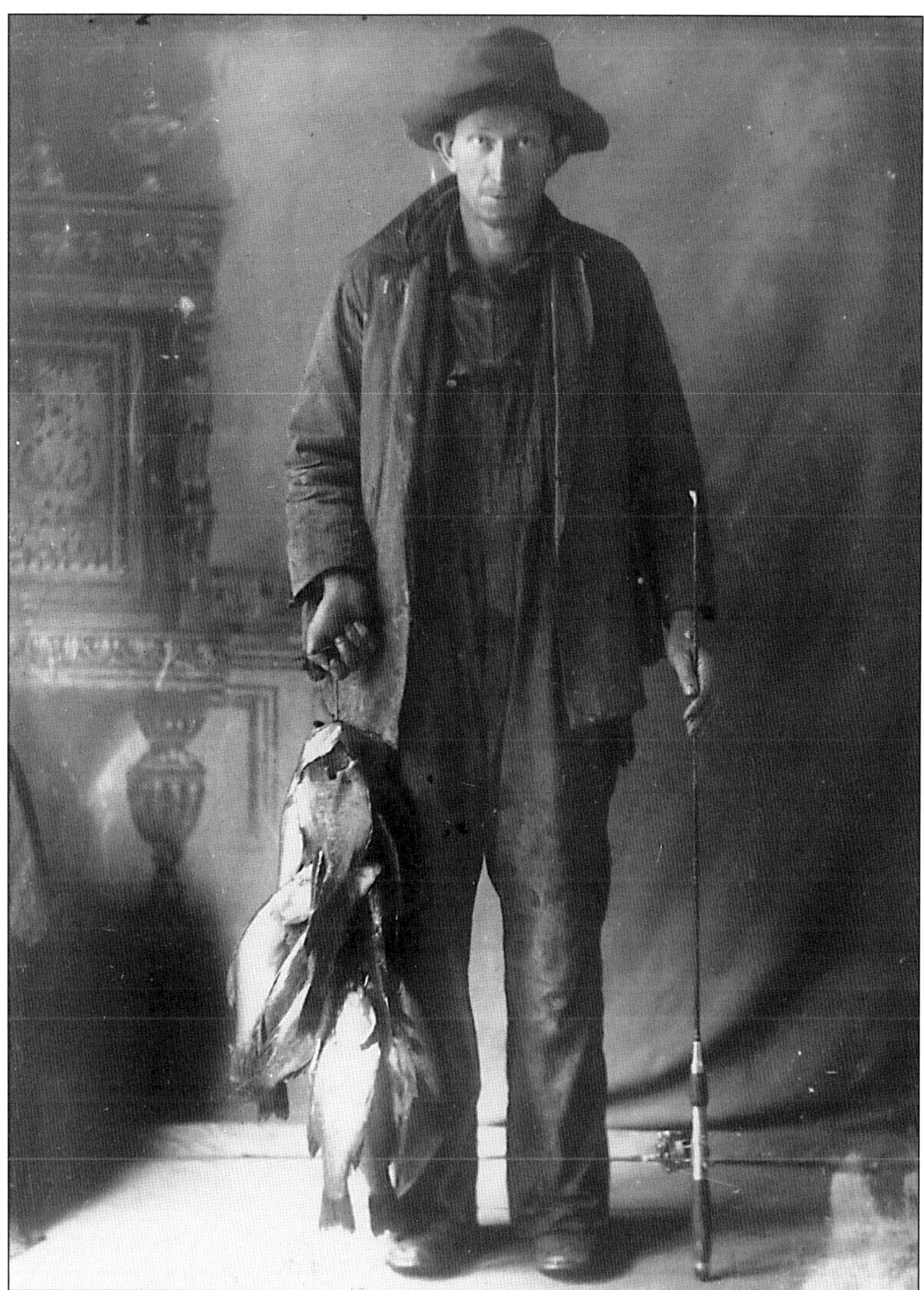

This gentleman posed for Walter Hunnicutt while holding his impressive catch. The studio photograph, with its elaborate Victorian backdrop, provides an unusual context in which to display one's fish. Hunnicutt, a Tallulah Falls native, was born in 1869. His early interests included making willow furniture, operating a drugstore, and publishing the town's first newspaper, *The Tallulah Falls Spray*. As a photographer, Hunnicutt captured hundreds of images of scenery, hotels, and the people of Tallulah Falls, providing a lasting legacy of a unique time and place. (Courtesy of Jorene Lavender.)

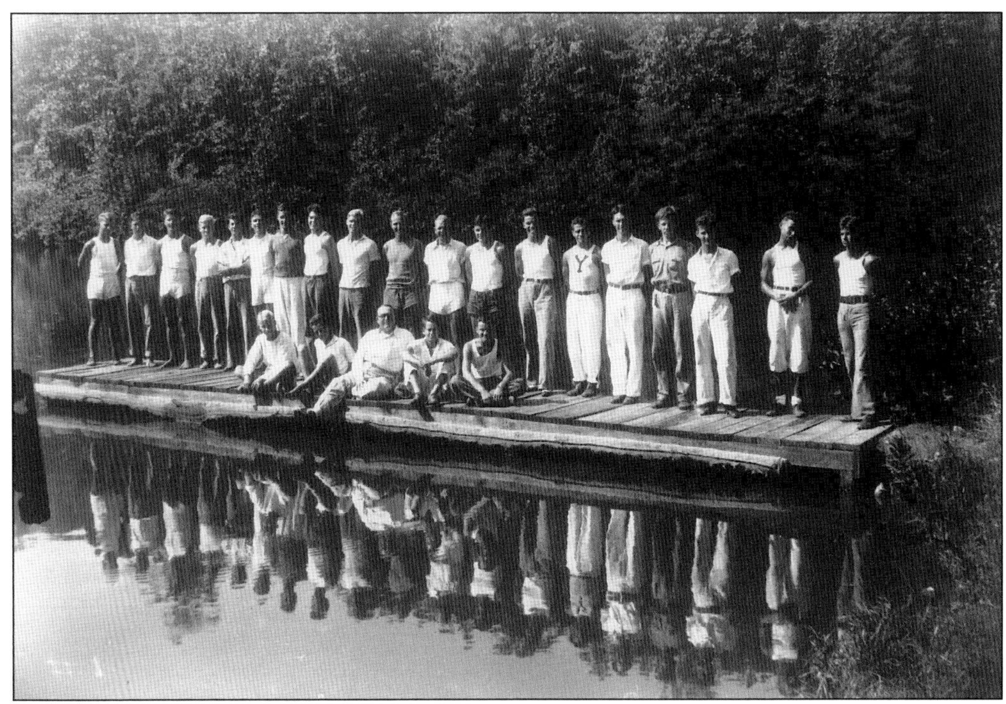

This photograph of the counselors and staff at the Athens Y-Camp near Tallulah Falls Lake dates from c. 1925. The lakes provided recreation for many of the mountain camps, including Riverside, Laurel Falls, Pinnacle, Roper, Marist, Rabun, and Dixie. In advertisements for the Dixie Camps for Boys and Girls, the camps assured parents that its separate facilities were located 12 miles apart. (Photograph by Walter Hunnicutt, courtesy of Jorene Lavender.)

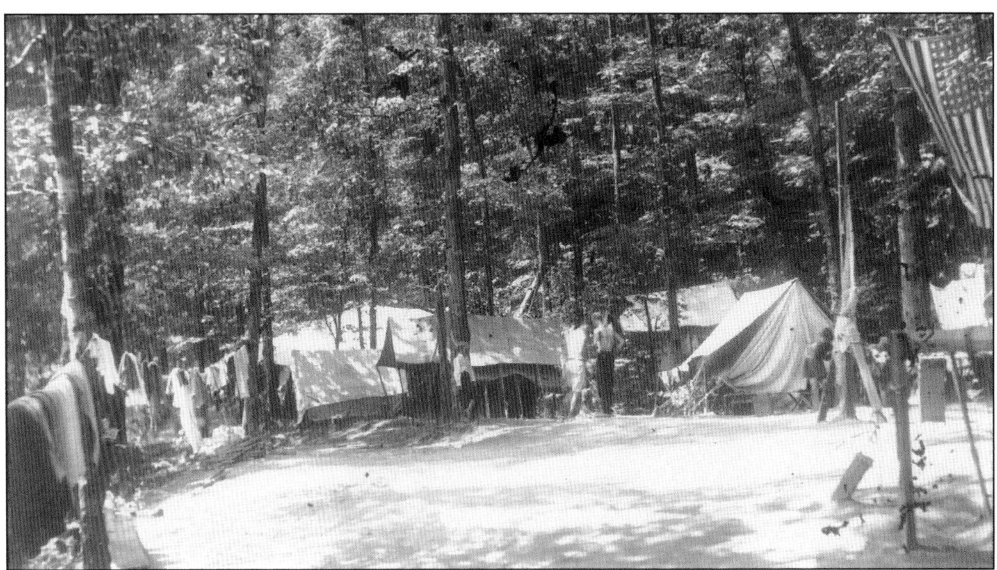

Tent camping was a popular pastime in the early part of the 20th century, as it still is today. (Photograph by Walter Hunnicutt, courtesy of Jorene Lavender.)

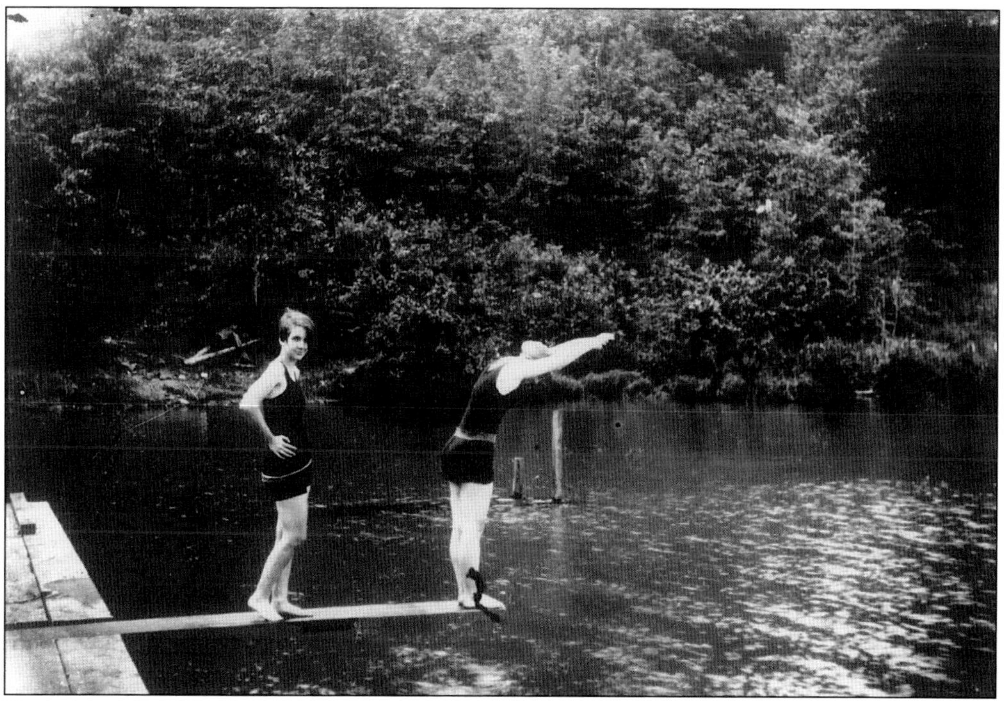

These beauties sport the latest in bathing attire of the 1920s. (Photograph by Walter Hunnicutt, courtesy of Jorene Lavender.)

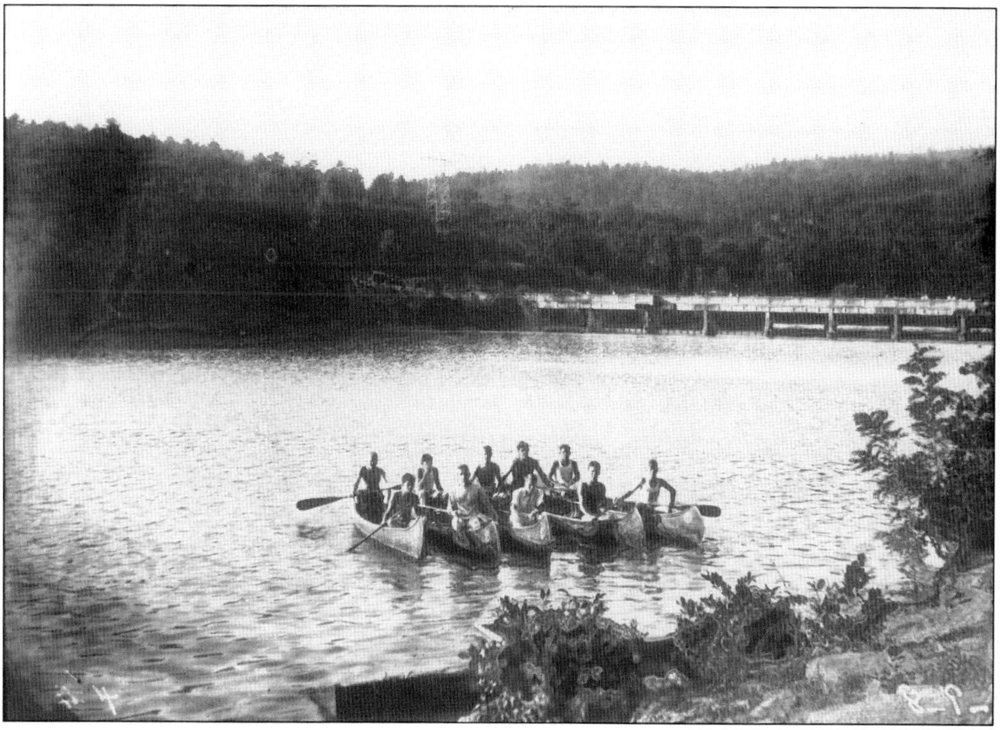

Canoeists from a local boys camp enjoyed a day of boating near Tallulah dam. (Photograph by Walter Hunnicutt, courtesy of Jorene Lavender.)

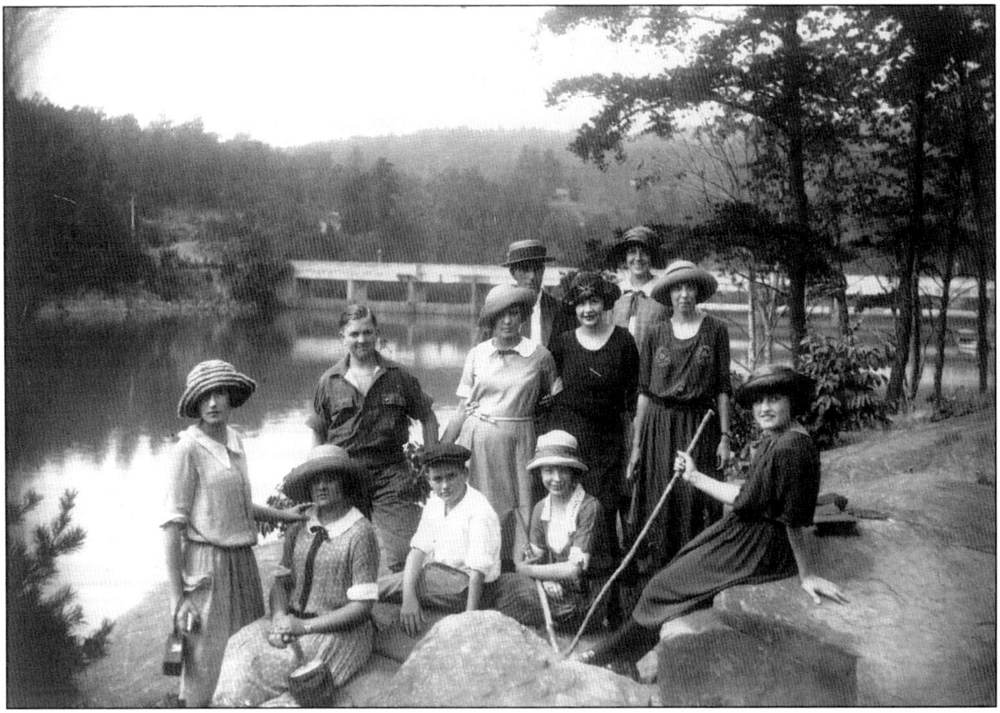

Hiking was a popular diversion, whether along the shore of the lake, in the gorge, or along a mountain trail. (Photograph by Walter Hunnicutt, courtesy of Jorene Lavender.)

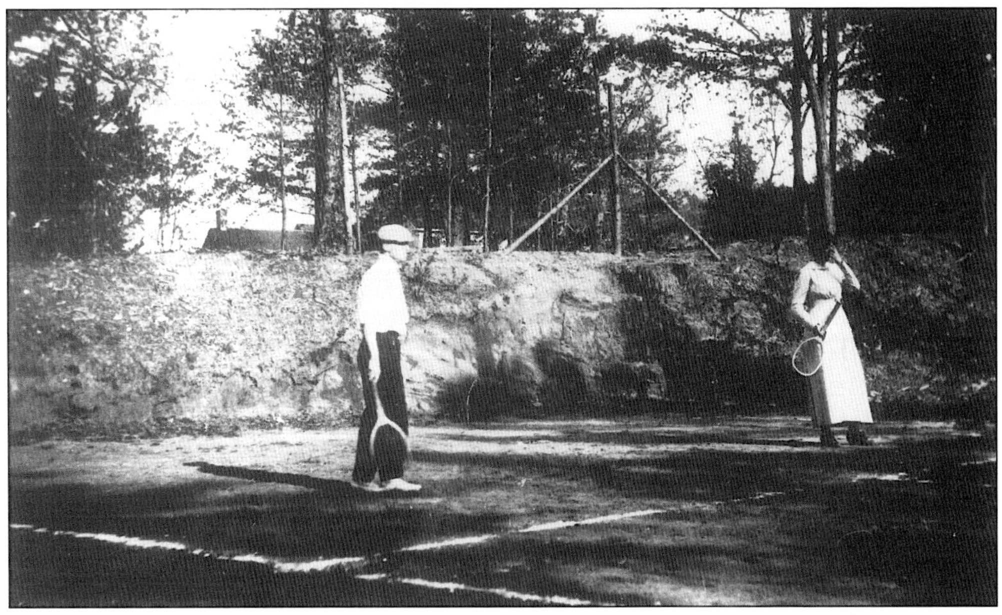

Tennis, popular on grass courts of the day, must have been difficult for women in their long skirts. This photograph of power company personnel was taken c. 1912. (Courtesy of Georgia Power Land Department Photo Archives.)

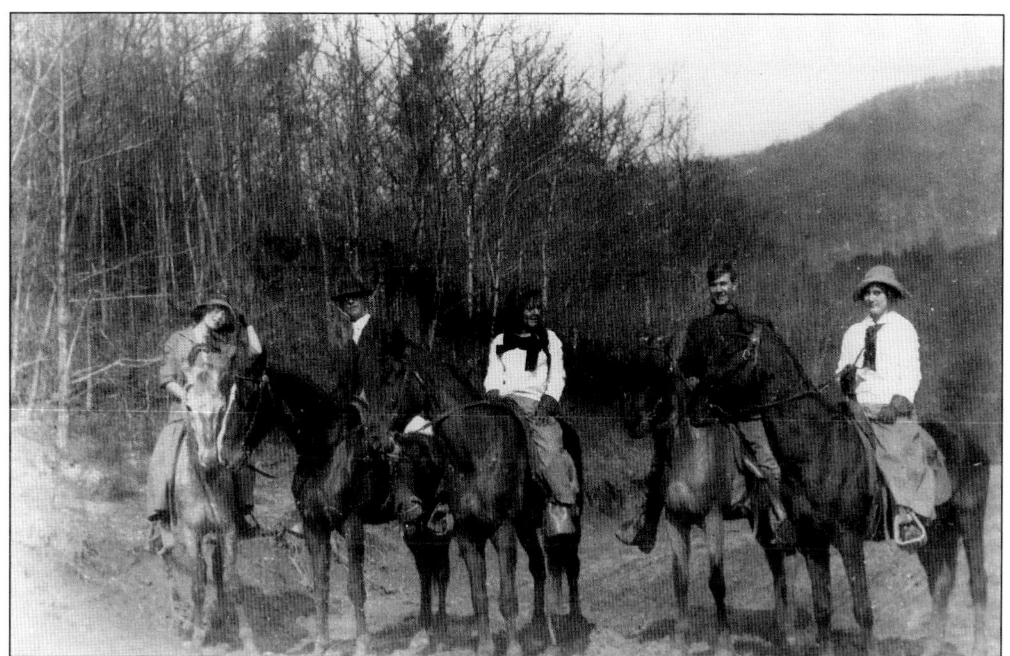

Horseback riding along trails in the nearby mountains was a pleasant pastime, as well as the main mode of transportation. Pictured riding are two construction engineers and friends. One of the engineers reported that when riding at night one could hear the sound of wildcats jumping from tree to tree. (Courtesy of Georgia Power Land Department Photo Archives.)

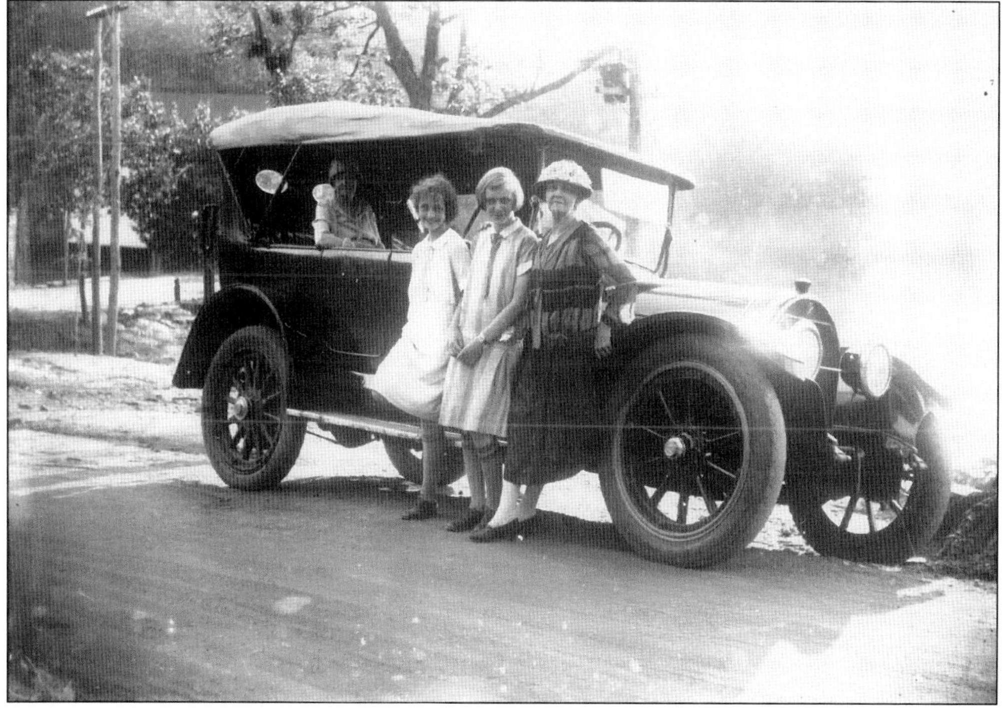

Motoring along the improved highways of the 1920s provided a new form of recreation for vacationers to Tallulah Falls. (Photograph by Walter Hunnicutt, courtesy of Jorene Lavender.)

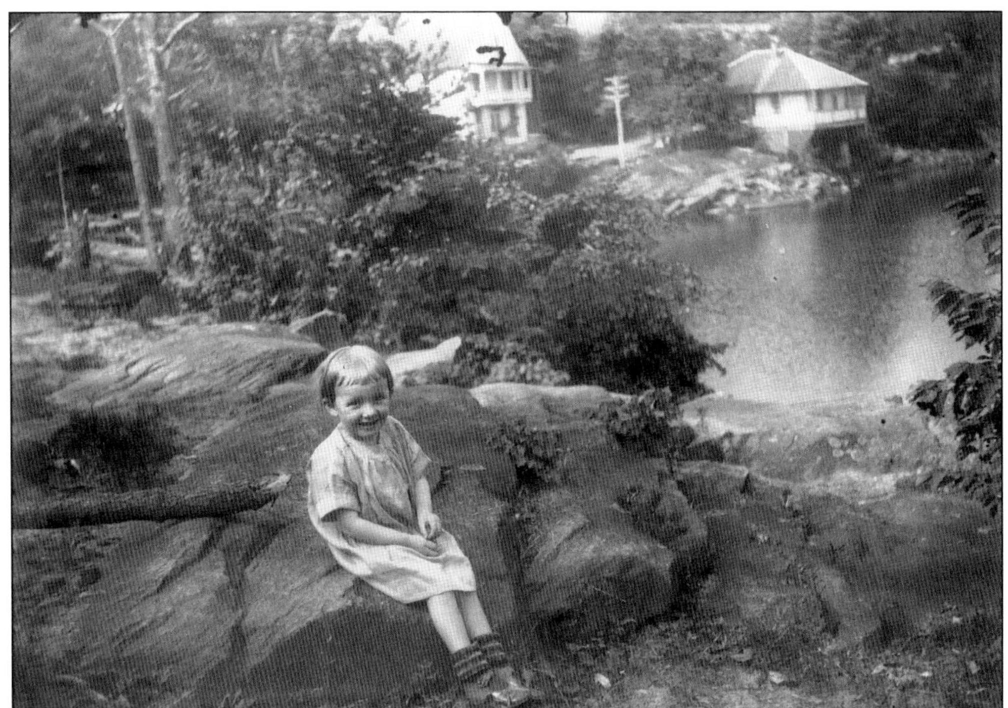

The images by Walter Hunnicutt, so beautifully preserved, were made by a dry-plate glass negative process. This photographic process was popular from about 1880 to 1920 and produced high-quality images. The jail/city hall is the building to the right on Tallulah Falls Lake. (Photograph by Walter Hunnicutt, courtesy of Jorene Lavender.)

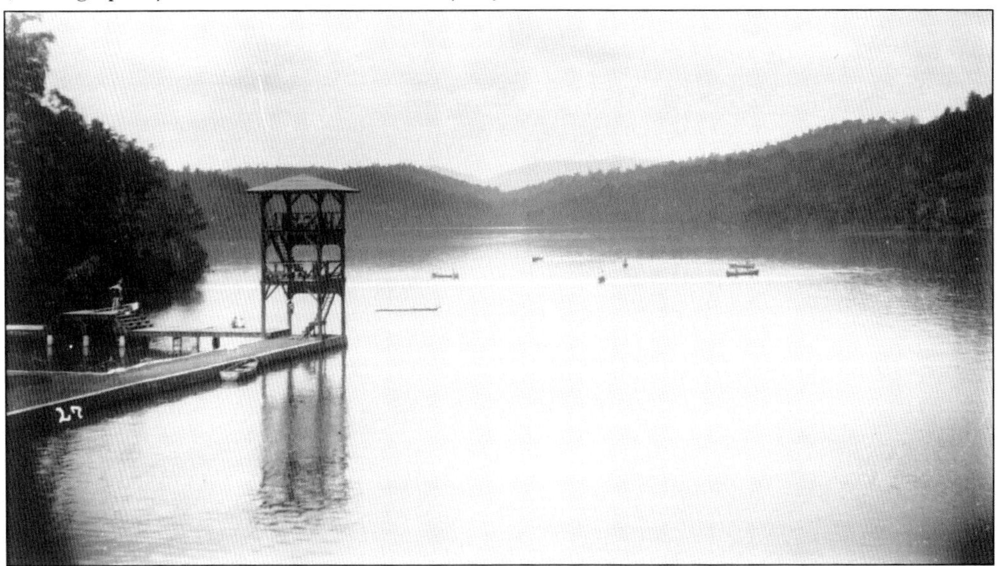

Sunset along the lake, a popular swimming and boating spot during the 1920s, is captured in a serene moment. The gorge, along with the abundant forests and streams containing lavish flora and fauna, continues to draw people to Tallulah Falls and the surrounding mountains and lakes of northeast Georgia. It has been described as one of the most beautiful spots on earth. (Photograph by Walter Hunnicutt, courtesy of Jorene Lavender.)

INDEX